COMING OUT

Also by Glen O'Brien
Praying from the Margins:
Gospel Reflections of a Gay Man

coming out

Irish Gay Experiences

Edited by Glen O'Brien

CURRACH
PRESS

First published in 2003 by
CURRACH PRESS
55A Spruce Avenue, Stillorgan Industrial Park, Blackrock, Co Dublin

www.currach.ie

Cover by Anú Design
Origination by Currach Press
Printed in Ireland by ColourBooks Ltd, Dublin

ISBN 1-85607-904-X

Acknowledgements

The author and publisher gratefully acknowledge the permission of the following to reproduce material in their copyright: *Gay Community News* for 'Galway Wedding' by Rachel Armstrong, and *Woman's Way* for 'We're Gay But Still Mums'. Thanks also to *Gay Community News* for the listing of support groups.

Every effort has been made to trace copyright holders. If we have inadvertently used copyright material without permission we apologise and will put it right in future editions.

CONTENTS

PART ONE

(Where a name is in italics, it indicates a pseudonym)

PART TWO

INDEX

foreword

I T WAS 1998 in Sydney, Australia. The entire city was getting ready for the Gay and Lesbian Mardi Gras. There were going to be parades and parties and poetry readings. The big parade, which more than a million people would see, is the largest dollar earner for Australian tourism, with many men and women flying in from the west coast of the United States, and from Europe, to take part in the proceedings. It is where love stories begin. The dressing up is beyond belief.

Everybody in the city has their own story about the best float in the parade they've ever seen. A friend describes a float the previous year with twenty gay men dressed up as the Australian politician Clover Moore, complete with her customary make-up and big hair. Everyone laughed and applauded as their float passed; some of the imitations were pure perfection. 'And then, can you imagine,' my friend said, 'the next float actually had Clover Moore herself. It was really her, waving and joining in the joke. People couldn't believe their eyes. It was all so good-humoured. Next year maybe we'll have John Howard.'

This year, however, there was controversy. The gay and lesbian police were going to march in their uniforms as usual, dressed proudly as themselves. But some people thought that they should not be paid for this, that it should be done in their own time. I followed the arguments as they unfolded on radio and television and in the newspapers. It was all about money, public spending. Since there were cutbacks in other areas, people asked, why should taxpayers' money be spent on this? No one once mentioned that the gay and lesbian police should stay at home, however, or not display themselves so openly in their uniforms. No one once said that they should be ashamed of themselves or be transferred to some remote outback. Sydney seemed at that time, unless you were a public servant looking for a raise in salary, a most liberal and wonderful place.

It was not always thus. 1998 was the twenty-first anniversary of the gay and lesbian parade and a useful time to remember what happened in Sydney when a few brave men and women took to the streets to celebrate their sexuality for the first time in 1977. They were not only arrested and held overnight in prison cells, but they had their names published in the newspapers and some of them lost their jobs. The authorities, in their efforts to stamp out sexual freedom, thus managed instead to create a very angry and determined group of lesbian and gay activists who worked each year to make the parade bigger and better and louder and more fun.

Slowly, gradually, but certainly, then, the annual parade became part of the civic life of Sydney and then its main carnival. Parents who lived in the suburbs brought their children into the centre to see it. Families who did not have a gay son or daughter, aunt or uncle, I was assured in the heady days and the slightly drunken nights before the parade began, longed for one; mothers dragged their sons and daughters by the scruff of the neck out of the closet and onto the floats. Or so it was said.

Over one decade urban Australia became liberal and easy-going about homosexuality. The change was more sudden and far-reaching than the change in Ireland, which was more subtle. But it was only when you spoke to people away from the heady hedonism and hilarity of the Mardi Gras that you realised that while every country fought prejudice and changed laws under different pressures and for different reasons, what happened to all of us as gay men and women has been similar. What happened to us when we were alone and vulnerable — the fears and the uncertainties — remained the same the world over.

This book is a testament then to the lives of gay women and men in Ireland over the past few decades. It is a testament, some of the time, that contains fear and pain, lives maimed, decisions postponed, secrecy and shame. But it is also a testament to those organisations and individuals who offered help with such selfless ease and care when help was desperately needed by gay people and by those close to us. These powerful and moving stories are useful to us now, not only as history — what the search for love and sexual self-realisation was like in a dark time — but part of what is happening all around us still, as, in the silence of the self, and in the society we have built, young people come to terms with who they really are and who they might become.

Just as Irish identity or Jewish identity would be impossible to imagine without a sense of history, however gnarled and disputed that history might be, so too our past is important. The thin faint line that connects us with those of earlier generations, who lived happily despite everything or suffered in silence for the sin of being themselves, is a line we need to trace with greater definition on our road to liberty. It is essential for us to say what we are. Most people can define themselves without a thought. It is easy to say 'I am Irish' or 'I am a civil servant' or 'I am a politician' or 'I am a member of the Gárda Síochána'. In the future, following the example of the men and women who tell their stories in this book, it will, we hope, be just as easy to say: 'I am gay' and 'I am lesbian' and then, without difficulty, join the parade in Ireland and live and love in greater freedom.

Colm Tóibín
Dublin
July 2003

introduction

'P EOPLE ARE LIKE stained glass windows. They sparkle and shine when the sun is out, but when the darkness sets in, their true beauty is revealed only if there is light within'. (Elizabeth Kubler-Ross) These stories are concerned with the 'light within' and the journeys involved in trying to recognise 'true beauty' and, of course, the 'darkness' and the costs involved, sometimes quite horrific.

Some of the contributors to this book are personal friends of mine and I have been humbled by the openness with which they have shared their very intimate stories of growing up and 'coming out'. Many of the stories paint moments of intense intimacy, moments of fear and trepidation, of joy and sadness, moments of liberation and moments of existential heartbreak and devastation. It has taken many months and much determination to collect these stories. There were times when I was ready to abandon the project and then another story arrived! Each story had to be told and this is what kept me going. My friends have been very encouraging at those times and I am grateful for their love and support. I would like to thank a good friend for typing up the handwritten manuscripts, done in loving memory of a dear uncle.

Each story has precious and sacred cameos that I have been privileged to have placed initially in my care and then to open them up to the general reader. I can only recommend that the care and the honesty, the love, thoughtfulness and the heartbreak which went into their composition be matched by respectful, open and thoughtful reading so as not to miss some of the depth that can lie sometimes between the lines. I am most grateful to all the contributors for their stories.

The range of stories is by no means exhaustive nor are the individual stories representative of everyone in that particular situation. Many gay people create a very strong shield around their personal lives and perhaps because of this I have failed to obtain a number of stories from bisexual and transgendered people. Other accounts missing are those concerned with dying and death, by suicide or from AIDS.

The stories are the responsibility of each contributor and their approaches and opinions are not necessarily endorsed by the editor, the publisher, the other contributors, the Irish Hospice Foundation or The Irish Queer Archive.

Colm Tóibín has been very supportive and affirming with regard to this collection and I am delighted that he has written a foreword that challenges us to move forward to the time when we can all together live and love in greater freedom. Here in Ireland we have progressed officially in creating a climate for that opportunity to live and love in greater freedom and I am very grateful to Niall Crowley, CEO of the Equality Authority for his contribution. A lack of freedom can still prevent us being who we are and who God intended us to be. The sacred scriptures are often used to perpetuate homophobia, sometimes virulently, and I am grateful to Sean Freyne for his contribution on this issue. An Garda Síochána has acknowledged its responsibility in respect of our community as much as in respect of other communities in society and have appointed liaison officers for the gay community. The pioneering and brave work in this area has been forged by Finbarr Murphy and I am very pleased to have his essay in part two. One of the few churches I am aware of that are happy to celebrate same-sex unions is the Unitarian Church and I welcome the essay from Chris Hudson.

Bernard Lynch in his thought-provoking essay in part two states that 'It is far better to be hated for who we are than loved for who we are not'. It is up to each of us, whatever our sexual orientation, to address this issue in the best way we can. While we are endlessly submitted to heterosexuality 'in your face' today, many straight people will say that homosexuality is fine provided it's not 'in your face'. Such a stance makes me stop and wonder, and I hope that these stories will address that issue, among others.

Recently I spoke to a woman who is researching for a doctorate, about the lack of gay role models for gay people growing up and forming relationships. Imagine my surprise when she said, 'What about Micheál Mac Liammóir and Hilton Edwards?' When I got married, my role models were my parents, my wife's parents, my older siblings, my grandparents, my aunts and uncles, all of whom I knew, loved, admired and respected. There were also family friends and neighbours, people I knew from voluntary groups, societies, sports clubs, my school, my parish, people in public office. Where are all these role models for young, and not so young, gay people? They are there, but invisible by and large. Gay people constitute around ten per cent of the population and that means more than one hundred thousand in Dublin alone! They and their partners are all around you, your family, your next door neighbour, your doctor, soldier, teacher, shopkeeper, farmer, garda, plumber, nurse, priest; they are to be found in voluntary groups, charitable organisations, GAA clubs, golf clubs; they attend christenings, weddings, funerals, office parties, football matches, concerts, films, churches; they are in your living rooms every evening on television and radio and in your newspapers, again largely invisible. I hope this book will bring them a little more into visibility.

Frank Lloyd Wright, speaking on architecture, stated that 'When we perceive a thing to be beautiful, it is because we instinctively recognise its rightness.' Do we, gay people, see ourselves and our sexual orientation as 'beautiful…because we instinctively recognise its rightness'? I, for one, do. If I don't, how can I help both my gay and straight friends and colleagues and society to recognise its 'rightness'? In many of these stories there is the journey, sometimes over half a lifetime, to come to perceive ourselves to be 'beautiful' and to allow ourselves trust our instincts as to our 'rightness'. Unless you are gay you don't experience the awful weight of history, both secular and religious, both past and present, that works to convince us that in the very depths of our being there dwells no 'rightness'. Sadly, many of the stories in this book witness to this fact and its awful consequences. Society has to accompany us on our journey. Laws, reports, recommendations, etc., are signposts for that journey, but ultimately it is a journey of the individual person, the head and the heart and the soul, which must challenge our internalised homophobia and allow all of us to recognise our 'light within', with which we are all endowed.

Borrowing on a concept from Edward Said, gay people must willingly and eagerly venture out into the world, and encounter challenges and menaces, in order finally, authentically, to return home. Is this the answer to being hated for what you are rather than loved for what you are not? It is a challenge to all of us, gay or straight, to strive to live authentically and I hope this collection of life stories may shine a little light on what that involves for us in the gay community so that we may 'return home', witnessing to our 'rightness' and standing tall in the wider community.

In my own striving to live authentically over the last eight years, I have been accompanied by the courage, creativity and graciousness of those nearest and dearest to me. This book is a grateful testimony.

Glen O'Brien
Dublin
October 2003

PART ONE

complete reversal

Iain Gill

BORN IN DARNDALE, on the northside of Dublin, raised in Coolock from a family grown out of Sheriff Street working class stock — not the ideal environment for someone to 'come out' in. Seventeen years later the location for this much-anticipated episode in my life was not much better — Santa Ponsa, Spanish cabaret show, drag queens screaming the lyrics of 'Barcelona' in the background, the audience, my mother, father and my little sister!

Being gay in school was difficult for me, yet, in saying that, I was never bullied to the same extent as others around me. My brother – and I was never proud of this – was actually the school bully. I also played on the school football team, which allowed me an opportunity to belong to the rigid stereotype of the male adolescent. I often pondered the thought that black children or students with disabilities who got bullied could go home to their parents and tell them why they had been bullied. They wouldn't suffer racial or disablist abuse at home, they would be reassured, supported, and comforted. For gay and lesbian children this isn't possible. I felt this could have helped so many other gay people, including myself.

I had girlfriends and hung out with the lads, in fact I was perfectly happy to live that life as long as I wasn't 'outed'. However, looking back retrospectively I get angry. I was denied my gay adolescence, I was made conform to societal requirements to keep parents, teachers, and especially the Church content. We're all valuable human beings. Developing self-esteem is very important for young people. It's hard for gay and lesbian youth to feel good about ourselves because all around us are people who believe that we're immoral, perverted, or destined to live very unhappy lives. The result is isolation, fear and depression. Something is rotten in a society that prioritises the rhetoric of a decaying religious institution with all its shady history over the needs and wants of our LGB youth.

The drag queens had just wrapped up their dreadful performance, my father headed straight to the bar, walking not unlike John Wayne, my mother knew there was something on my mind, although she had no idea how the next four minutes would impact on all our lives. She asked 'Is that a hickey on your neck from that scrubber?' I calmly answered 'Yes.' She wasn't impressed, but I got the feeling that she would quickly learn to regret expressing certain disappointment at that particular heterosexual moment. My father returned and proudly declared, 'Son, there's your pint.' I still don't know why, but I proudly replied, 'I don't want your pint…I'm gay.' It was almost like slow motion — the pint slammed to the ground, he fled and paced the bar, Mam kicked me in the shins, screamed 'disgusting' and ran quickly out of the show. Before my thirteen-year-old sister had the chance to follow on her heels, she kissed me on the cheek. To this day I swear she knew what was discussed that night in Majorca, although she doesn't recollect.

Unfortunately the results of my seemingly honest actions were to have quite damaging consequences on my personal, psychological and educational development for at least the next three years until I was well into my university years. On returning home my parents basically raided my room, found magazines, nothing sordid — *Gay Times* and *GCN* — also personal pen-pal letters and my diary. They called me into the sitting room and emptied what they had found on the floor in front of me. It was the most humiliating experience of my life — they went through every detail of my diary, which was so shattering. They told me that I would die of AIDS, 'Gay people are all paedophiles', 'No one will employ you', 'You are sick'. Naturally enough I was seventeen, didn't know anyone gay, wasn't sure what I was. I felt I was an embarrassment and something pretty awful.

My willingness to work on behalf of lesbian, gay and bisexual students at a national student level arises out of personal experiences from resolving issues affecting LGB students as Trinity College LGB Rights Officer. Through duties such as co-organising Trinity's annual 'Rainbow

Week' and holding 'coming out' workshops for students, I became a vocal and active representative of LGB issues on the Students' Union Executive and Welfare Committees.

I became involved in student politics and gay politics in particular. At about the age of twenty-one, as a member of Trinity's LGB Society, I attended Pink Training, the Union of Students in Ireland's annual weekend training course for LGB students. I recall about forty people in a room telling their coming out stories, in what were very difficult circumstances. It was the most emotional experience of my life. I had come out once before and had avoided it since I was doing my Leaving Cert. I decided then and there that I wanted to become more active in addressing the problems students face as part of university and college life. While my coming out experience in college was positive, the family were still in the dark, the word 'gay' hadn't been mentioned for over three years However, my role as Trinity's LGB Rights Officer helped my parents become more comfortable with my sexuality and I would have to describe their change in attitude as a complete reversal.

It was after Pink Training in Belfast that I felt strong enough to confront not only my sexuality but my parents. My mum found my LGB Rights Officer name card and came up to my room and asked 'What's the LGB?' I remember her face — it was angry, reminded me of that Spanish club when I first came out. I told her, 'It's the Ladies and Gents Basketball'! She stopped for a moment — I was hopeful she had bought it. She then screamed, 'You're too small to play basketball. Now you tell me now, are you lesbian, gay and bisexual?' 'Not this again,' I said. 'I'm one of them.' 'Which one?' she asked. I said, 'I'm gay.' And she said, 'Well, just as long as you're not bisexual,' and walked out. It was comical yet distressing. She cried continuously for months and so too did my dad — although I never saw him I could see it in his eyes. Now, about a year and a half later, as I look back on it, Mam is still coming to terms, but still she's absolutely brilliant. They still find it hard but are coping really well. I suppose the pain of the experience, the rejection, the confusion, the loneliness all added to my passion in taking the job as National LGB Rights Officer, adding to my expertise in understanding the difficulties facing gay and lesbian people.

Because I have come from a situation that was so bad in comparison to where I am now, I could give support and personal reassurance to people that they can get through their difficulties too.

I felt, although not at the time, my proudest moment was organising USI's LGB event Pink Training 2002, though the same event that helped me so much in my life direction was the same event that almost gave me a nervous breakdown — what pressure, but it was well worth it. Now, I should explain that despite its name it is not a recruitment ground for a lesbian, gay, bisexual army; this training event for LGB students includes workshops, modules, etc., which aid and assist networking and socialising, creating a safe space for LGB students to be more comfortable within themselves. The event itself was amazing: 170 delegates attended and it turned out to be the biggest ever training event in the history of USI since its inception in 1959. It was attended by LGB societies across the country, both north and south, and also by individual LGB students. When I think of those names that have been involved through the years in the National Union — Pat Rabitte TD, Joe Duffy, Eamon Gilmore TD — it makes me proud that I played my part in putting the LGB campaign up there in the history books of the National Campaign.

I dearly hope when I read this in the years to come that some brave student who at the moment may be living the misery of being in the closet with their entire future ahead of them, will have bettered this record. I hope my story can give hope to those who feel there is none.

Words of advice to young people
Your parents will have their own 'coming out' to face. They will have to decide whom, if anybody, they are going to tell that they are the parents of a lesbian daughter or whatever. They fear that they will lose prestige in the eyes of their friends, neighbours and work colleagues. They may be afraid that their position in the community will be undermined if it is thought by their friends that they have a gay child. However insulted we may be by such a concept, we have to acknowledge that these are real fears for some people, and we have to allow them the time, sometimes years, to sort them out. Parents can't be expected to accept such a fundamental change in their child overnight. They have to reassess a whole swathe of expectations and hopes for the future. They have to deal with a lot of fear and misunderstanding. They need to be educated themselves about

homosexuality, and what it means for them and you in the years to come. That's a tall order for anyone.

Don't be too impatient and don't be too hard on them. We have to let them experience their feelings. Although we may consider them to be an over-reaction, they are, nonetheless, very real for the people experiencing them. You can allow this adjustment time without having to compromise your own needs. I have never been so happy in my life as I am now. I'm confident in the direction of my career; my parents and myself have never been so close. People can change, people do change, but it takes time, and although things are getting better we have to be a patient people.

i, deaf, lesbian

Sarah

IFE'S GOING TO be really hard for you, now that you're gay as well as deaf.' That was my mother's response at my coming out.

Now, that is certainly not true. I'm happy being deaf and gay, as they are my identities. If these identities were taken away from me, life would definitely be a lot harder, as I wouldn't know who I am. Being deaf all my life has formed my personality, so I would be a very different person today if I did not have the experience of being born deaf. The same applies to my sexuality. I think that being deaf makes me a better person, not a disadvantage. Well, most of the time! Yes, life can be hard for a deaf person, but the difficulties come from people's attitudes, not from being deaf itself. Being deaf can be good — people tell me all the time that I'm lucky I can't hear people talking rubbish!

But I personally don't think that being gay makes life harder. People ask me which do I identify myself first as being — gay or deaf. I'd say I identify myself as me first, then deaf and lastly gay. I am me first of all. Secondly, I identify with being deaf. It is a big feature of me, as I adapt my life around being deaf, e.g. lip-reading, subtitles on tv, absorbing all information visually as I cannot depend on my ears to give me information. Lastly I am gay, as I don't believe that your sexuality really defines who you are.

I was born deaf; the doctors unable to diagnose the cause. It might have come from genes, as a distant cousin is deaf. I was put in a local school for deaf people in the country until post primary when I went to boarding school in Dublin. My parents had asked me, curiously at about fifteen, if I would have liked to go to a local 'hearing' school where my sisters and brothers went. I replied no, simply because I was happy amongst my deaf peers. Statistics show that the majority of deaf people who went to mainstream schools have lower self-esteem and confidence, so I am grateful to have gone to a 'deaf' school. I had speech therapy (which I hated!), so I can talk very well — the majority of people do understand me, only a few do not. I lip-read very well; it is improving all the time. I can communicate with a couple of people at the same time, but I am lost in a big crowd of people, as I don't have multi-vision! I also have trouble with people who mumble or speak too fast.

Sign language comes naturally from a very young age. My family knows finger spelling, nothing more. My parents actually learned sign language when I was young, but they never practised it so they'd forgotten it! They wanted me to improve speech; it was much encouraged in the house, so sign language was never used. I do sometimes wish my family learned sign language, although most of the time it doesn't bother me. We communicate no problem, but about my sexuality — that's altogether a different story with my parents.

My sisters and brothers had accepted my sexuality readily; they made no fuss about my revelation at twenty. I was trying to find the 'right' moment to tell my parents. It was my brother who ended up telling my parents one night when he came home drunk! My mother was disappointed, as she believed that my gay friends were a 'bad influence', and that I was choosing to have a hard life being deaf and gay. For years she refused to talk about it, now she only politely inquires about my love life with a lot of tension in the air. It had hurt a lot, now I'm used to it. My father was brilliant talking about it on the first day, he had asked me, 'Are you happy?' When I said I was, he was fine about it. We don't talk about it anymore as he is reserved, my siblings and I don't really talk to him about our personal lives in any case.

I had hearing friends when I was young who accepted my deafness without any difficulty. I suspect it's due to the fact that kids are into activities — they are not really verbal. When I started boarding school, I lost them as I had gained new friends. Kids around the town did mock me when they heard my speech (it was so bad back then); they laughed, made faces and noises. I was hurt but grew immune to it. Eventually I'd scoff at them and use sign language with my sisters or friends and glance/laugh at them, letting them know that we were mocking them too, but they would never understand what we were saying! People tend to stare when I use sign language with friends, but they look away immediately when they realise that I've noticed them doing so. Only kids do not look away, as they gape in fascination. They ask their parents all sorts of questions; the parents just slap them and scold them for staring or asking improper questions. I always find it amusing as they are only expressing their thoughts, which are also the thoughts of adults who are too polite to stare or inquire.

My deafness is only visible when I use sign language or when I talk. If you saw me passing by in the street, you'd think I was just a 'normal' person. It's the same thing for gay people, when you see them on the street you'd never suspect — it's only when you get to be acquainted with them or when they express their sexuality that you would know. People should realise that we all, whether deaf, gay, blind, etc., have the same desires and fears, and most importantly we are all human, we are not to be feared. I am so used to expecting a variety of reactions when a new person I meet realises that I'm deaf. Most are fine, and don't ever mention it, but some go: 'Oh...I'm really sorry for bothering you,' and walk off, or act awkward throughout the conversation, wishing they could escape. These are only examples from a wide range of reactions.

When I meet a new person, I never tell the person straight out that I'm deaf; I only tell them if we have a problem communicating. That's why I never make a big issue about my sexuality. In the same way, when people say 'Do you have a boyfriend?' I say casually, 'Oh, you mean girlfriend...' I believe that if they act negatively, it's their problem, not mine. You get what you see and deal with it whatever way you like. An ex-girlfriend admitted a couple of weeks after meeting me that when she first approached me, she panicked and became nervous when she grasped that I was deaf. Her first instinct was to try to leave, and then she thought, no, give her a chance. Five minutes into the conversation with me, she was glad she didn't leave.

I grew up in a cushioned life, my life revolved around the family and boarding school. The 'outside' world was too alien for me, I never thought much about it. Hearing kids would only mock and adults would patronise me. That's why, partially, the realisation of my sexuality hit me hard. At twelve, friends would talk about boys obsessively; I did not think they were that important! I did like girls, but kept my desires to myself; I didn't think it was something essential to ponder on. I had told my best friend at thirteen, but she swatted it away saying it was probably a phase. I hoped passionately that she was correct. One day the girls were talking about seeing a film where two lesbians had kissed. It hit me, there is a word after all for what I am — a lesbian. They found all those gays and lesbians revolting and disgusting, so I didn't want to reveal my realisation — I went along with their opinions. It was the first time I could define what I was. So that is what I was — a lesbian. I panicked inside; as I knew no gay people, remember my world revolved around school and family. I was not really involved with nor did I give much thought to the outside world. I was careful not to act strange around girls, there was no way I would turn out to be gay. I wanted to be just like them. I tried to pretend to be interested in guys, but gave up quickly because I couldn't bear to be fake. Instead I pretended to be shy about boys.

Gradually I told my close group of friends one by one, and they accepted me readily as they subconsciously knew anyway. They didn't make a big deal about it. I was surprised how easy it was to come out at school. A friend let it slip to the school's biggest gossip. Of course the gossiper did the newscaster's job by telling everyone. I was terrified as a couple of lesbians a few years above me were bullied. The reactions at school were only curious questions but no one was malicious. My group of friends were only interested to know information about a different world from theirs. Only one popular question I absolutely refused to answer was: 'Who did you fancy at school and who do you fancy now?'! Only one girl was too uneasy to ask questions; she just listened to the conversations with friends on homosexuality. I had, with the help of friends, drawn her out. Her only question was: 'Did you not snog any guys? That's why you think you're gay.' I had snogged a good few guys, and I told her that, so we laughed at that. At that moment, I knew I had nothing to worry about, my friends saw no difference in me, and they even laughed at the foolishness of the uneasy friend! I was a bit mean to her, I suppose, she reacted violently whenever I flirted with her for fun. I was no different with other friends, they just laughed and never took me seriously. But not Claire! She took it personally, complaining to other friends that I was flirting with her. They just rolled their eyes and told her that I was only provoking her because I loved her funny reactions! Even today, she still believes that I secretly fancied her at school! My coming out was relatively easy I think, compared to most people.

Looking back, they probably accepted me for two main reasons. The deaf community is a minority, not unlike the gay community. The deaf understand better than some people what it is like to be in the minority in general society. So my schoolmates probably accepted me easily because they understood what it was like to be different. Gay hearing people have taken a strong interest in the deaf community, and accepted us a lot more easily than straight hearing people for the same reason. It was always really obvious to me as they are so relaxed around us. The deaf community is very close-knit — picture an old-fashioned tiny village where everyone absolutely loves to gossip about everyone's goings on around the village. The deaf community is exactly like that. So I'm sure that a lot of those in the deaf community know about my sexuality. It doesn't bother me but you have to be careful what you say, as it goes all around! That frustrates me, as I hate pathetic gossip and rumours. It annoys me when deaf people say to me, 'I heard that so-and-so is gay. Is that true?' I just tell them, 'Why don't you ask him/her? Are you afraid to?' and change the subject. But there are great things about the deaf community — the closeness, the strong bond of the sharing of the deaf culture and, I know it sounds corny, but the feeling of family is found there. You gain some great strong lifelong friendships. Whenever I need a break from the claustrophobia of the deaf community, I go to the hearing community. Whenever I need a break from the hard work of lip-reading, and missing out in conversations, the deaf community is always there. The same applies when I need a break from the gay scene; I go to my straight friends. Although most of my friends are deaf, I have more straight than gay friends. I am lucky that I can communicate between two worlds. I have a friend who is deaf; he was brought up in a hearing world. He never learned sign language. It is only recently that he took part in the deaf world and is learning sign language. He finds it frustrating that he cannot get all the information in the hearing conversations, as he also finds it hard to understand the deaf conversations too. He feels stuck in the middle. So he is learning sign language now, as he wants to be able to fit in fully somewhere.

A close friend, who I had just discovered was gay, introduced me to the gay scene when I was eighteen. He brought me to a Greenbow (the deaf gay and lesbian society) meeting at the Out on the Liffey pub. Greenbow was set up in 1996, and was mainly a social society. It was that day which introduced me to the gay scene; where I formed new friendships. But I was still in school at the time, so I was very shy to the 'outside' world. It was only when I started college that I became more confident and extroverted in meeting new people.

I was so nervous starting college. The only people I knew outside school and home were those who had mocked me. I had anticipated people in college mocking me on the first day too. But they made me feel so welcome that I fitted in no problem. Of course there were bad days when everyone ignored me or didn't make an effort in communicating. But that's life. People sometimes do tend to give me basic information on conversations if I miss out or say, 'Oh it was nothing important'. It's frustrating sometimes. Deaf people will always have to face these situations constantly. It took me a while to tell them about my sexuality, as I wanted to test the waters on their attitude to my deafness. They found it unimportant, to my relief. I became so much more confident and outgoing since starting college, as I met new people every day and am in general society. I am very different today to what I was in school. I am not really shy in the gay scene anymore, meeting girls and new people. I have always preferred having hearing girlfriends, as there are a lot more choices of girls out there! And also because I need my own space from the close-knit deaf community.

In the past gay people were considered sick and perverted. Homosexuality was not encouraged — it had to be hidden. They had to abide by the norms of proper society by getting married to the opposite sex, etc. Deaf people were considered unintelligent and mentally retarded. Sign language was forbidden, as it was a sign of madness. They had to learn how to talk, talk, and talk with their hands tied back. And be given menial jobs or kept at home. They all had to love and sign behind closed doors.

Today a lot of gay people are free to be themselves — there has been a lot of change in attitudes towards homosexuality. But there is still some way to go in terms of encouraging those who haven't come out of the closet, education of homosexuality awareness, job protection, marriage, and legal rights. Deaf people are free to sign away, express themselves fully with each other and with hearing people who know sign language. A lot of improvements have been made in deaf awareness and acceptance of the deaf culture, education and job achievements. But there is still work to be done: sign language has yet to be recognised as a legal language, we need to work towards getting people to meet us some of the way by learning sign language, we need to increase the number of interpreters, and we need to have greater choices in our careers, amongst other things. These are things that would improve my life so that I can be what I am and fulfil my abilities and dreams. It is not like what my mother said, life is not hard for me because of what I 'choose' to be, it's society's attitudes on deafness and homosexuality that are a problem, and these are steadily changing for the better.

father and son I

Jim Egan

M Y NAME IS Jim and I have a gay son. His name is Graham. He is twenty-nine years of age now and he came out when he was seventeen years old. I have another son, Leeson, who is thirty-three years old. I have been a widower for the last twenty-eight years and both of my sons lost their mother at a very early age, and as a result we have become a very close family.

When Graham was seventeen, he sat his Leaving Certificate. Before Christmas of that year we noticed that he was moody and quiet in himself and had started to miss classes. He was suffering from depression and anxiety. The following spring he went into hospital for approximately two months. While there, we found out about him being gay. It was a long process and both he and his doctor had all sorts of doubts, but gradually he began to accept himself and his sexuality.

Being gay in Ireland was not easy at that time, but today it is becoming more acceptable. When I first learned of Graham being gay I felt a mixture of emotions. What is it like to be told your son or daughter is gay? In my case, total shock and fear of the unknown. Thousands of thoughts race through your mind and you don't have any answers: Is he going to have a very lonely life? Will he always be by himself? How is he going to cope/to live? Where did I go wrong? Who can I talk to? How are we going to keep it a secret? I went around asking myself all these questions in my mind for about two to three weeks. In the end, out of desperation, I went to my local GP, who knew our family very well. He did not know much about gay people except to say that the majority of 'them' were very kind and gentle! He suggested that I get in touch with the Gay Switchboard.

Eventually I rang the Gay Switchboard and spoke to a gay man. After talking to him I knew that there were two ways I could go. I could forget that this had ever happened, walk away from it, and let Graham get on with his life as best he could; or I could go out and get more information. I decided on the latter approach, and I am very glad I chose that path. Gradually a whole new world and culture began to open up. I read books on gay issues, watched tv programmes and generally got involved in gay affairs. I learned that statistics showed that 8 per cent of the population is gay. This made me think about many of the situations where in the past I had likely encountered several gay people before without ever realising it. For example, in the workplace or at social gatherings such as weddings, where the typical Irish wedding of 100 people contained an average of 8 to 12 gay men and women among the guests. By developing this new level of awareness I began to slowly let go of many of my initial fears surrounding my son's sexuality.

Graham at this stage was slowly beginning to socialise in the gay community. He began by attending 'Icebreakers' and later became a regular member of the youth group. He was meeting other gay men and women and feeling comfortable in their company. I decided to go the whole way and told him if he wanted to invite any of his friends home that they would be very welcome.

In my experience, accepting that your son or daughter is gay is not easy. However, as parents we cannot form or mould our children strictly from our model of the world, and we must learn to accept them as God gives them to us. It takes time for parents to come out too! We also need time to gradually accept our sons and daughters as gay. All sorts of problems arise. For instance, in a family a mother will often say, 'Well I knew he was gay, but I still love my son,' but the father may have problems accepting this. Do you call your family together and tell them? Other members of the family may have problems accepting this. What do you do? How will they react and are you ready for the consequences? What do you do about the neighbours? (These are often people that we as parents come into contact with regularly and sometimes rely on to help out with our family.) What about the gay person in question — suppose he or she does not want anyone to know in the neighbourhood? (You have to respect their wishes at all times.) What about work?

Although the decriminalisation of sexual acts between gay men was passed into law ten years ago, there is a lot of prejudice still around. I was speaking to a well-known gay man in the media and he said that he is one of the 'lucky ones'. But in a typical workplace environment, if you put your head above your desk and make people aware of your sexual orientation, you will soon find out who your friends are.

For the past twelve years I have been involved in the running of a small group of parents of gay and lesbian children who support one another. Parents may feel they would like to talk to someone who has 'been there before'. They contact us through the Gay Switchboard. From meeting and talking to parents you realise how hard it is. For some it is easier than for others. One father told me the thought of his son kissing and holding hands with another man was extremely distressing. On the other hand, some parents decide right from the start that the only thing that counts is their son's or daughter's happiness, so they accept them. Some frequently asked questions from parent ringing for advice are: 'Accepting your son or daughter is gay is one thing, but what does a parent do when their child starts a relationship?'; 'Do you accept their partner or turn a blind eye?'; 'Do you allow him/her to take home their 'friend'?' I sometimes argue that if your son who is not gay has a girlfriend, naturally he wants to talk about her. You will also want to know who she is; who her family is; what she does, etc. Why deny the same interest in your gay son or daughter's life? After all, they want and expect the same rules that we apply to their siblings. They have the same feelings and the same hopes for a long-term relationship. They may be 'in love' and we aren't even aware of this important part of their life.

My son, Graham, like many gay people, knew that he was gay before telling anyone. Others may have carried this secret around with them for years. It takes courage to come out, and for some it may take years to come out in many small stages. What do gay people want from their parents and friends? I think that the most important thing for parents, if at all possible, is to accept their children totally as normal ordinary human beings, and they will have no problems.

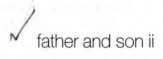

father and son ii

Graham Egan

I HAVE KNOWN that I am gay from a very young age. I have memories of being attracted to boys since I was about eight years of age. However, it was not until my early teenage years when these feelings became much stronger. One day in the school playground some of the kids were taunting a fellow classmates of mine as being gay and calling him a 'queer'. I painfully realised this description was also true for me. Finally, I had a label that named the thoughts and feelings I had been experiencing for years! In one way this was a relief, as I had always known that I was different from my friends, and on the other hand, I was aware of the shame that having such feelings evoked in my classmates. So, I vowed never to tell anyone my secret, not even my best friend, who rather ironically was also similarly struggling with his own sexuality and did not feel comfortable disclosing his 'secret' of being gay until many years after leaving school. Overall, my secondary school years were very unhappy as a result, and I became very withdrawn from my friends. I reasoned that if I isolated myself from the rest of the world while in school, then nobody would discover my shameful secret. Sadly, back in the early 1980s, there was little or no positive discussion or role models in the media to offset the negativity being circulated both in and out of school.

Finally, in 1990, during my Leaving Certificate year, I confided in my best friend. His inability to cope with his own battle in coming to terms with being gay caused him to end the friendship, which in turn left me feeling very alone, angry and rejected. Eventually, my dad noticed I had become distant and withdrawn and brought me to our local GP.

Although he was a nice man and easy to talk to, I still couldn't bring myself to admit what the real problem was. So as a result of not talking, he concluded that I was suffering from depression and referred me to a psychiatrist in St Patrick's Hospital. In the meantime, my schoolmates had somehow guessed that I was gay and began bullying me each day, making my life a misery. At Christmas that year I took an overdose and was subsequently admitted to St Pat's for six weeks. Whilst this was a very low moment in my life, some good did come out of it. Firstly, I told my family about my secret, and secondly, I met a young gay man while in hospital who was suffering from depression but who was completely comfortable with his sexuality. I suppose he became my first ever positive role model for being gay. He inspired me so much to accept myself as I was and helped me to regain the confidence that had been lost through the years of bullying in school. I suppose I was very lucky to have met him at that time as the doctors were hopeless in their dealing with my problems and had prescribed anti-depressant medication and had stated that it was 'just a phase' that I was going through.

My dad was also a fantastic support to me when I came out at seventeen in the hospital. I had not felt very close to him while growing up, as my mum had died when I was an infant and there was only my older brother and Dad at home. Mostly the elderly neighbours who lived next door had reared me. When I came home from hospital, I decided not to return to school and instead got a part-time job working in a shop and then later that September began my final year of school in a new area. During that summer, my dad and myself became much closer and he encouraged me to join the Dublin gay youth group. I never really looked back from that moment on, and not long afterwards I met my first boyfriend, Donal, and had a relationship that lasted for the next eleven years!

Now, I am twenty-nine years old, and am happy to be gay. It's no longer a big issue to be gay today, and it's certainly not something that I feel ashamed about. I would describe myself as a very happy-go-lucky kind of person. I enjoy life very much and have a varied mixture of straight and gay friends who socialise together most weekends.

Over the last twelve years I have been out to all my friends and family and also most of my work colleagues and have never personally encountered any hostility. I am aware that I have been fortunate in my experiences of coming out and that not everybody's sexuality is accepted so freely and completely, in particular by one's own family, as mine. I don't think it's ever the fault of parents if their child is gay. I think that a parent with a gay child needs to ask themselves, 'Do I want my child to be in my life?' And if the answer is yes, to then treat them with respect, and allow them to make their decisions to choose what makes them personally happy. It is such a pity for a parent to lose the relationship with their child because the child if gay. Life is too short for that.

fragments of a fairy

Maurice

T HE MEMORIES THAT follow are biographical fragments of my becoming the sexual person I am today. I write them in the present tense using some of the words for sex that I had available to me at the time because the memories are present to me, graphical and real. I write of them not because they are universal — they are totally particular — but because in them perhaps you will find cause to pause and reflect on what it has been like for you.

This is but one line of narrative that makes up me; there are others, whether of place, or work, or friendship or... There are also others in this narrative and one should not assume to know much of their narrative or judge them in any way from the brief allusion to their entwinement in this single thread of mine.

Finally, I write anonymously. Not because I am not out. I am and have been in successive and widening circles for many years. I do so simply because for those who know me there will be no mystery as to my identity whilst for those of you who do not know me, anonymity allows me to open a door for you into intimate space within me without losing my privacy.

Birth into Difference
The sunlight shines a shaft of brilliance across the hallway. Tiny specks of dust thrown up by the feet of us rushing children swirl in its path. At the other side of the hallway a boy stands in the light, he stands a distance away from me that is large because I am small. He is older, maybe eight, his blond curls glow in the sunlight and he smiles. In my heart a hunger is

opened, it flowers in unworded need and desire. I step inwardly into the space of being different. His nickname is Eggy; I am four.

Ireland is a cloudy country and not filled with blonds. So the sheer brilliance of sunlit curls was light in my darkness. Somewhere in the shadows I learnt that sex was bad. I don't know where or when or even precisely from whom. Perhaps it was in the bath when holding my wee wee place nervously because I was third to be washed and the water had become chill, hearing my mother say, 'Don't do that, it's dirty.' Is it strange to learn something so massive from such details? Culture is an air we breathe, a smell that surrounds us that is only apparent when we step outside. The bath was just one artefact of the culture that I bathed in.

Back then, amidst bungalows, Hillmans and Zephyr Fords, Avon ladies, Procea Bread, holidays in Rush and on the farm, PYE tv, a simple personal battle was already being waged. I was uneasy, un-belonging, needy for affection, wanting to know, in a home with close siblings competing. I looked, but the 'nuclear' family has its fallout. Daddy working so hard in the office, carrying home his stress and frustration, hidden behind *The Irish Times*. Mammy working so hard at home and her tired smiles and light hugs shared between four.

I stopped eating. Reactive waste. The doctor said force-feed him or he will die. Would that be bad to die? I wondered. Nose held, wooden spoon raised, open your mouth to breathe, food goes in, spit it out and you will have to lick it up. A strange way to gain an adventurous palate! It is odd how even today I want to finish every meal I buy in a restaurant, eating the last crumbs that fill me to discomfort. I am a good boy who cleans his plate. But I am a boy with a secret knowledge of rebellion. The ordinary is never what it seems. Its placid face conceals muscles ready to tighten into emotion.

Friends of Mammy and Daddy are in the sitting room. Down the hall I am smothered in the midst of cotton and crimpoline. The scent of perfume and Mammy mingles, false pearls, earrings and rich lush lipstick — Avon's best. I dress up in her clothes; it is fun and more. It is in touch with some desire, a queer joy without queer irony. Hand on the door I swan forth into the sitting room. Heads turn and there are smiles and a fraction of silence. Mammy says 'That's lovely, now be a good boy and dress in your own clothes.' I do.

Being a Nigger on the Inside in a Racist Society

The Church is a counter-sexual space. Warm wooden roofing, an upturned boat floating on the celestial skies pushed forward by the waft of wax and wick burning, ironed linen, polished brass, artifice and praise. I was carried away in that craft... if truth be told.

God is good, sex is bad; two insights towering in my heart. I whiten a Sacred Heart image with the polish for my runners. It is a plush white cushion in the shape of a heart surrounded by lace with Jesus there centred, bleeding and praying, suffering and joyful — glowing. I keep it under my mattress; it is a comfort of holiness, a celestial teddy bear.

I lie awake tense, on that mattress, wanting the pleasure of rubbing my willie to relax me into sleep, sleep I need to escape the surfeit of tension in the day, tension of difference, of family conflict at the table. I plunge into that pleasure often; I am so bad. Maybe the white plush cushion will soften my fall. At nine I want to give up rubbing my willie, still thinking of Eggy. I keep records but give up and give in.

I began my adolescence with a shock in a wood. I cycled my bike maybe hoping to see an attractive man. In a clearing far from the sight of anyone I began to wank. My prick got hard, wow amazing, the first time. I came quickly, shot some semen, wow again, amazing, the first time. As I cycled home I began to panic, my prick was still hard. Would it stay like that and brand me, like Cain, an outcast for my crime? I rushed in past everyone in the kitchen and then into the dining room. A few minutes later my penis was restored and my panic subsided.

Sex education was breathless and late. Not a word but a small book given to study. It told me what I already knew, sex as I experienced it was bad, but it told me more — it was very bad, worthy of and leading towards damnation. I read that I should pray to the Virgin Mary if I was aroused. I tried initially, full of the hope of healing, of harmony. Sorry Virgin Mary but it did not work. Was I too far gone already?

When did I know I was gay? Since Eggy? If one can know something with no words for it, perhaps then I knew. I knew like a baby 'knows' cold or hunger by crying without words. I cried inside without words, because the words I knew meant I had to be something different.

You are a queer! My friend J turns around once and turns me forever. It started then for two years. I am fourteen. Every day a torture, deadners in my arm, compasses stuck into me, ink poured on my copybook, threats to write on the board that I am gay. Exposed as a gay boy in a world of boys. Would it be bad to die? I wonder.

I am mute about the bullying because it is true. I know that I am gay because of the rush of pleasure I get when I see the centrefold of Playgirl magazine lying beneath a desk in school. I check to see if anyone is around and once certain the coast is clear gather up the picture of a most handsome naked man half sitting on a fence drying himself with a towel after a shower. I bathe in male beauty but I cannot dry off my shame.

Sport brings a kind of salvation. Camus wrote that swimming is sacramental. It is my sacrament. An escape from tension at table to go training, a place where my body feels good, gliding through the water, touched, embraced, fluid. 'Odd' people open a way forward for me. A wonderfully camp drama teacher at school teaches me in one hour that my body is good, so open am I, an insight grasped and never lost, yet feelings take years to catch up with it. Swim coaches, two men, one very tall, the other small, both gentle, encourage me, care for me, give me responsibility, allow me to flourish.

Even odder, I am naked, undressed, sitting in women's tights being measured for the school show. The teacher asks me do I masturbate. I nod and blush. It is normal, still bad, but normal, maybe therefore not so damning? I confess my sins and he gives me absolution. He is a priest, charismatic, witty and a bully. I leave flooded with relief — the unspoken has been spoken of. I am not so totally alone. It is only a few years later that I notice the danger, the boundary that he had crossed with me. Trust is so easy to betray, boundaries so important to protect with the vulnerable. In retrospect I am grateful that I was a late developer, gangly and skinny.

Finding One Kind of Love

I am seventeen and summer holidays are over. I come back to school and the bullying is over. Perhaps it is that we no longer have that teacher who measured me, and who also bullied us twice a day every day of the week for the previous two years. Perhaps, in consequence, there is no need for the bullying to be transferred within the class. Who knows?

I fall in love; it is the first time. Two years we are friends discovering much, discussing, helping each other. We share secrets that bind us — bind us still. One day Andrew says to me he is thinking of joining religious life. Schoolboys still thought like that then. He had been captivated by something of the vision of service that some of the younger religious in our school had communicated. In an instant, like the flick of a switch, I decide I am going to do that too, to be with him. The vision of faith that would really matter and bring about a more just world is new breath for the sails of that upturned boat that will carry us both along. So romantic!

It fragmented. That summer after sixth year he went away on holidays and changed his mind. He was not going to join religious life. I was devastated. I had been accepted, had stunned my not especially religious family with the news of my imminent departure to start my training. Now I was to join alone. I didn't change my mind. Why?

I walk along the strand in Portmarnock, look out to sea in the moonlight and decide to go ahead anyway. The only possible way for me to love deeply and fully is asexually. Andrew is straight. My love for him is impossible unless it is not sexual. We are still the closest of friends.

Today it seems strange that I should think the possibilities for love were so restricted for me. Yet then and for many years I had nightmares about my 'criminal' orientation. Me being arrested for having gay sex, me in a garda station being laughed at, the forced and shamed coming out. David Norris' victory in achieving the decriminalisation of homosexuality only happened in my late twenties.

One-Dimensional Man

A pattern had been set. I had found a way of resolving my contradiction. I fall in love again, and again, and again; always with straight guys. Rather remarkable, don't you think, to fall only for the straight guys in a religious order! It makes me believe in the power of the unconscious, because I surely needed to keep those relationships asexual in order not to collapse the only way of love that seemed possible, that seemed safe, into dark shame. Yet I also believe in the power of consciousness, because with Andrew and with each of the others, a friendship of lasting value remains. I am successful in religious life; unfortunately neither gangly nor awkward at the work or the life. So no one has asked too many searching questions.

Underneath however, buried in my fantasy life, concentrated and displaced onto the straight guys I have fallen for, was the burning desire to love and truly be loved by another man. I am open with my spiritual guides and superiors about my feelings. They surprise me by their understanding. For years I am encouraged to bear my interior struggles with masturbation, etc., manfully. Celibacy is difficult, it is a struggle; masturbation and fantasy are part of it. I should open up to God about it. Yet hidden in their kindness there is a curious conservatism. It is okay to struggle just as long as you do nothing with anyone else! Yet we learn from experience, so how was I to learn? So easy to get trapped in fantasy where all is promised and nothing delivered!

Every time I do a retreat it is like a game of table tennis. God is on one side, sex on the other. Back and forth, day after day, I play. No one wins. I am stuck and it begins to corrode something in me, freeze something in me. I laugh less from my heart; I open myself through words but less through feelings; I tire myself out in working, in loving the only way I think I can, while running from the shame of my covert auto-erotic sexual life.

It is hard to convey the dilemma. The truth is that I do love in religious life. To hold someone whose husband has just died and in her own words protect her from despair; to provide a context for forgiveness and healing in listening over time to those who have been wounded, almost mortally but not quite; to speak words that make sense and deepen sense at those moments of transition, birth, marriage, death. These are things that are so intensely valuable.

And yet, to be in those spaces, I have to truly be me. Can I be? I am stuck between a rock and a hard place.

Old Patterns Unfraying

In the late 1980s I am away studying. I am sitting watching tv in an attic in a large, beautiful European city. It is late and everyone except Karl has gone to bed. We are sitting beside each other. Our hands touch and remain like that, touching, an electric shock of desire passing from one to the other, consuming, so we barely notice the programme on tv. I am in love again and this time perhaps not with a straight guy. What to do? My spiritual guide suggests that I should tell him how I feel about him. I am terrified and I cannot do it. Even as I write, my shame at my lack of courage then is still sharp. It was a beginning though, a loose thread in the centre of the tight-woven pattern of me in religious life.

A year later I am on my way to a meeting of my contemporaries in the order. On a bus, my head leaning against a steamed-up window, my heart begins to thump. A decision has happened in me. I am going to come out to the group. It includes one of the guys I first fell for early on in my training. I do. They take time to get used to it but are good about it.

It is the beginning of the 1990s. Then I meet Colm. Something deep and emotional grows between us. We lunch together, go on cycling holidays all over Europe together. It even changes my relationship with God. God holds me. One day walking around a field, my heart bursting, I tell Colm that I am gay and that I love him. I have ripped through the old pattern. What I was afraid to say to Karl has now been said — ecstasy and expectation. He says he does not really understand. I am the first gay guy he has ever met in this way. He loves me, yes, with that unbreakable love of a blood brother — the brother he never had. He is not gay.

I drink deeply of the insight that I cannot assume that my feelings are the same as any other person's; it is a valuable lesson but one that does not satisfy the heart's hunger. It is a lesson for the long term of relating, not for falling in love or the first embrace.

There I am on the step of something new. I stumble. Yes, our love continues and changes. It is still love, still different from both sides. But I stumble because so much hope is there in that moment and, though not dashed, it is dissipated. I leave Ireland again for a grey, uphill couple of years in a cloudy, flat European country and return to the old patterns of one-dimensional living and closeted acting out.

But with those words to Colm, I had made a far more radical step than I thought. I had stepped out of fantasy and into reality. Even if that step had been made tentatively in love, it was also made, that selfsame step, in sex… I began to have sex with men.

Re-weave

At first there was a lot of shame, but that changed over time. Casual encounters, some fringed on something more, but telling guys I am in religious life frightens them off, especially if they are in the closet and afraid of scandal. It is 1996. I learn something from the sex, basic things, like the feeling that my body is attractive, a feeling to knit to that thread of insight from school drama. I learn that there is something to be learnt about sex, that I can be a good sexual partner. Or maybe they were just saying? Casualness doesn't allow for verification!

Somewhere in the midst of this I forget my feelings of shame about sex. Sharing pleasure with men in different sorts of contexts means that they stand on the same ground as me, I am no longer alone, abnormal, distorted, perverted; I am just like them. Somewhere in the midst of it too I discover other things about sex. Casualness is sometimes lack of care for myself. It doesn't matter because I don't matter. The payoff is to unite in pleasure standing on the same ground of simulated intimacy. I can forget the lack of relationship and cover my loneliness in the chase, the approach to forbidden pleasure.

Of course I feel intensely the contradiction in my living — in one context appearing to others as if I am a celibate priest, in others having casual sex. It seems hypocritical. Yet I refused to teach the Catholic Church's line on sexuality and for a long time have lobbied for acceptance of the goodness of homosexuality. I even was excluded for consideration for a job because of my stance. It still seems hypocritical. Yet in Hopkins's words:

> Each mortal thing does one thing and the same:
> Deals out that being indoors each one dwells;
> Selves — goes itself; myself it speaks and spells,
> Crying 'What I do is me: for that I came.'
> How am I to be and not go myself?

A woman friend of mine to whom I've come out invites me to go to the George pub. I go and for a time it becomes a space of liberation. Then one night a few years ago she leaves with my jacket. I am wandering around looking for her. Upstairs I catch a beautiful guy's eye. I stand by the side wall. He smiles, I smile. Nothing happens. I go for another tour, vaguely hoping to find my jacket. But I gravitate upstairs and wait again. We look into each other's eyes across the space. There is something there. Nothing happens. I take one last tour around but do not find my jacket. I am downstairs and just going to leave. He appears, we kiss. I can't remember what we said but he scribbled his mobile number on a beer mat. I have it still. Is there any need to say it? The long search of my heart for that sunbeam of love has found a deep echo. David is my partner and I love him, yes, and am loved by him. To be sure there are stories to tell. But they are ours.

As I write I have left religious life. It has been a terrible choice to make. I have been very open from the beginning with very many people within the religious order and outside about what I was doing and about David. Ultimately, however, in the words of Robert Frost, you cannot travel two roads and be one traveller. You have to be able to walk out your front door as yourself and not be bound to put on another inconsistent persona. It is as simple as that. In the end I found that living a double life was both damaging me and beginning to harm the person I love.

Religious life leaves me as I leave it with memories of some of the most valuable things I will ever do in my life. The group I belonged to were accepting of gayness and wise in many ways. Perhaps had they been harsher I would have left much sooner. What a waste it is that the Catholic Church's twin deep historically intertwined neuroses about sex and power should mean that I, like many before me, gay and straight, face such a wasteful and horrible choice. Do what you love and give up being loved by another, or find love with another and give up doing what you love. Yet I live in history, and a sense of history helps to understand. It is not all about me! I can wish myself into a parallel universe where all this would be resolved. However, I am not about to return from reality into fantasy!

On retreat before making my decision to leave I broke down reading Niall Williams's novel *Four Letters of Love* and wept for hours. What got to me was the healing of the paralysed brother of the main character. I have been so deeply paralysed. Yet God has been whispering, subversively, beyond Church neurosis, in my feelings, impulses, even in my compulsiveness: 'Take up your mat and walk!'

Sand

I am tempted to give some concluding reflections and since, like Oscar, I can resist everything except... I am going to do just that! Throughout this often painful process, I now know in heart and head that sex is basically (though not always actually) good and that sex, at least for me, is best when it expresses love. I know that God does not let us bypass life or sex. We are meant to be ourselves as we are given to be. It is often difficult to find the courage to do just that. At many points I was immersed in one or other of the fragments I have written of. Where I am now seemed an impossibility, light years away from my shadows. We can all move forward. These conclusions I hold like a fistful of sand, knowing that grains seep out even as I speak, even as my hands continue to be filled.

a woman dispossessed

J. C. Feierhardts

ONIGHT I AM a woman dispossessed. Because once, I hoarded a wealth of self-loathing, cultivated it until it flourished, and allowed it to spread through me like a cancer. I could not see the positive things in my life; I could only focus on the negative, or what I perceived to be negative. Being gay was just another one of those things that I hated about myself, just another aspect of what a sham I really was. I could never quite come to grips with it, but these feelings were there for as long as I can remember.

At seven years of age, compulsively watching *The Wonder Years* on tv with my family, I wondered how come the other girls at school would always harp on about Kevin, when Winnie was the one that made me feel all funny, a bit gooey, and make my little heart thump like a rabbit's foot? Sharing this feeling with the other girls only brought rejection and loneliness. I was called a queer before I discovered what the word meant. Sometimes I heard about alien concepts like gay 'pride' that simultaneously amazed and horrified me. How could someone be proud of being gay? Wasn't that illegal? Wouldn't they disgrace their families? I mean, a girl liking a girl…eugh…that just isn't natural, I'd think to myself at the back of maths class.

I wanted to fit in, but my emotions just wouldn't let me. I suppose I always felt different, a little left out. Individuality was discouraged at all costs in the Catholic schools I attended, sex was something that happened on *Dallas*, the part I would always be sent to my room for. Being with boys, even talking to them, was frowned upon. This made the girls in my class very disgruntled, but as far as I was concerned, the further I got from them the better.

As the years went on, I seemed to be able to repress these 'urges', as I called them, more and more. While all the other girls in my secondary school were beginning to 'notice' teenage boys, I would whole-heartedly agree that, yes, they were indeed there. And add that they were lovely, that I wanted one... the phrase 'I need a man' came into my vocabulary, I found it a great icebreaker, a reaffirmation to myself and others in my peer group that I was perfectly normal. I didn't feel normal when I thought about women, so I tried to give them as little thought as possible. I threw myself into my studies and social network for years, and gave myself thoroughly to the various areas of my life, like the preparation of my art college portfolio or copying homework I hadn't done for class, and of course my social life, which had become so precious to me.

Alcohol was a serious stress-buster, as was the odd spliff on a weekend. They heightened my perception of the world around me, gave me confidence that I knew I didn't have, turned me into someone else for a night. I felt like I could be myself, without being myself. 'One can smile and smile and be a villain,' said Hamlet of Claudius in the Shakespearian play I studied for English in my final year in school. With alcohol, I could smile and smile and be as gay as I wanted to be, and no one would ever have to know. So it was Ethyl Alcohol who was my first lesbian lover. She gave me everything I needed, and I was always on top. When I was with her I was anyone I felt like being. Although by then I had acknowledged my feelings for women, there was still not one person in six billion that I felt I could tell. I didn't have time to dwell on it though, far too busy for that. The Leaving Cert came and went. I was accepted for art college, and during the summer before, I began work as a domestic in the local psychiatric hospital. I can only say that my experience of working on the wards instilled a great fear in me that one day I'd have one of those mid-life crises, go 'nuts', and be incarcerated. Schizophrenia was an illness that particularly frightened me, not because the patients were frightening, but because they were so debilitated by that awful disease. There seemed to be nothing I could do for them apart from giving them their meals. I wasn't a doctor or nurse, I was only there to clean the huge long Victorian corridors every morning and make their tea, giving them the best I could.

At seven each evening, I'd lock the ward door and head to the pub to forget about things, to unwind, to meet people. There I'd stay until three or so, still sweaty after a hard day mopping floors, trying to forget. Forget everything. It worked so well, sometimes I'd even forget I had to work the next day.

In the beginning, college was a waking dream for me. Among creative people like myself, I could finally come clean, take the risk of coming out, and undoubtedly be accepted. No problem. Except for the problem of knowing when to tell my newfound friends. It sure was a conundrum, that all these great new people were getting to know me under what I termed as being false pretences. I was still that little sham underneath it all, I thought. I'm a fucking fake and I know it, but no one else does. I was stubbornly determined to keep it that way, but kept my eye on the various women that the college had to offer. By then, I had given up talking about men, I had stopped pretending that it was something that appealed to me. I just got on with my work all week, doing as many all-nighters as my body could bear, until Thursday night when I'd go on the cider with my friends, usually ending up in drunkenness and vomiting. I was having fun, and I didn't want it to stop.

The posters on the student noticeboard would say that one in ten people were gay, but I didn't believe them. That would mean that there were other gay people right here in the building, and I couldn't find any. I inspected people as they walked past for signs of gaiety, but none prevailed. Apart from those guys in Fashion, that is. Fair play to them, I reckoned, I couldn't do it. Their courage always amazed me, because my life was governed by fear. Fear of failure, and fear of rejection. The fear of failure almost swallowed me whole, when in that first term I worked myself down into a nervous breakdown. There were times that I felt as though my world was caving in on me, but I kept working, now at a slower pace to combat the stress that I was under. The only time I relaxed was when I had a joint between my teeth, and that developed into habitual use throughout the last term of first year and into my second one. But I had hope. My counsellor in college knew that I was gay, that was somebody at least. Two in six billion, just her and me against all the straight ones. I even told her that I got off on thinking about them, and she had just laughed at me when I went puce with shame. In second year,

I didn't see her anymore. I was busy climbing the social ladder among my fellow artists, and throwing myself into the work. A joint helped me to draw, to transcend my own being, and to give me inspiration. I still hadn't told anybody else about my sexuality, it was none of their goddamn business anyway. I was too absorbed in confronting a six foot canvas to confront myself.

Second year was the year I had begun to take ecstasy. After my first, everything else came second. I recall the feeling of unity, togetherness and love that those pills gave me. 'Is this what love feels like? I hope so, I've never quite felt like this and I never will again… I'm never comin' down now, never comin' down no more no more no more…' I rambled off into reams of shite while some girl from Painting massaged my back and shoulders, and we watched the stars together until the rhythm of the music began to move through us both. I loved everybody, but I didn't feel like I needed anyone. I was just myself, no one else. After all, ecstasy helped me to be honest with myself and others, I was just letting them know how I really felt. I wasn't horny, I just wanted to dance like a lunatic until dawn. I saw many a dawn through the bleary eyes of a drug-induced insomniac, smoking dope until I started to see vivid colourful images racing inside my head every time I closed my eyes, sometimes when I opened them. As the insomnia worsened, the images changed shape, blackened, and moved like shadows. They shivered, and when they did it would traverse my whole body. In my mind's eye, sometimes I could see myself like those shadows, changing colour and shape, becoming engulfed in the universe within myself until I was miniscule, then morphing again, exploding into Bridget Riley patterns, blossoming, withering, decaying as the sun came up… like a vampire. 'Vampyros Lesbos'…is that me? Is that who I am? The thoughts came too quickly for anything singular but that one stayed and nagged me incessantly. A whole chorus of voices started up in my head, debating the issue as though I weren't there. Then a roomful of people inside me introduced themselves and asked my opinion. Even my inner child was in on it, she started talking about Winnie, and they all called her a queer. I was desperate for sleep, and I got it — the night afterwards. I was inconsolable for days, even weeks. Those people at the party weren't my real friends at all. They had been discussing me behind my back, I suppose I heard them and it hadn't registered at the time, I had been so off my face.

It was around that time I noticed I was a little bit down, and I wasn't thinking straight. My head was in the clouds, but as long as I had the card of valium I was prescribed for this 'mild depression', it was fine. More parties came and went, I attended less and less. College enveloped me again, my work was back on track, so to speak. It was at the end of my second year that my head took off into inner space. A new batch of LSD had arrived from somewhere, and since the reviews were good, I decided to indulge myself. I did this several times over the course of a fortnight while I waited for my end-of-year results. But the day the results arrived, and my work was rated highly, I was still trying to come down from the night before. I spoke to my tutor, off my face, thanking him for his guidance. All that came from his mouth were trumpet sounds, alternated by flocks of seagulls, lesbian seagulls that hurled abuse at me from ethereal skies, daring me to own up to him about what a fake I was. I turned and ran outside where all the crows were gathered, and it felt like my feet weren't touching the ground. I was levitating, I believed, but part of me also said that this is not real and… neither am I.

I never finished third year that next year. I did enrol, but without any academic success or achievement. Trying to write an art history essay was a battle between me and the pen, attempting to grasp it in my shaking hand and watching my detached body scrawl across the vertical of the page. It was as though someone else had my body and I sat watching, totally helpless inside myself. I became disillusioned with art, and began to focus on two things, writing and alcohol. These were the only two things that gave me any solace, being painfully aware that drugs, and art, had backed me into a corner, that I had lost my mind. They were to blame. There I stayed for a year or so, until one night those awful voices in my head became so loud, the terrifying images so real to me, that I buckled under the pressure. I recall some of that night, my housemate's friend sitting on my hands to stop me from tearing my hair out in clumps, staring in the mirror and seeing my mother's face gazing back, crying, screaming in torment. I was what those hospital nurses would have regarded as being 'a danger to myself and others'. They'd lock me up. The men in white coats would dope me up and I'd never get out, being institutionalised and walking around those corridors like a beached whale on crack, grounded there forever and gasping for a breath of sanity, serenity, a little inner peace, and all I would get in return was another fucking pill. Pills got me into this mess, and they'd keep me there, sedated and unhappy, for the rest of my days.

For the next three months, I lay in my parents' back garden, sunning myself back to an acceptable level of misery. I imagined that there were shiny centipedes crawling all over my limp body at times, but the dope my psychiatrist had given to me, the happy pills, were working quite well, so nothing seemed to matter that much. I felt better, I could speak without drooling and made sense most of the time, although slightly off-beat, odd, and fairly eccentric. Starting work again was trying, but the beers afterwards were well-deserved and numerous. I worked all day to drink all night. It wasn't long before I had left. My head would race all day and all night, fear and anxiety engulfed me, but I found that three pints turned into a ritualistic piss-up, and it had all faded away. Repressed. I knew it had to come out sooner or later, but I preferred the latter. Time enough for all that shite. And they said there were no solutions in alcohol? I had found mine, that solution was in the bottom of every pint, every shot glass. The hangovers lasted longer and longer, alcohol poisoning was frequent, as were blackouts, aggression and a desire for the end. Every time I lifted that glass, I'd wake up someplace different, with only a vague recollection of the oblivion that I had sought upon ordering that first drink. I couldn't stop doing it, I knew I needed help. I surrendered to the repeated pleas of my mother, and decided to go into treatment for what she called 'my problem'. Not hers. Mine. I felt like the whole world had beaten me to a pulp, leaving me bruised and broken. 'I have four words for you,' a friend had said, 'get your shit together!'

Treatment was the last place I wanted to be. But it was there that, after all the faults I found with the place, I began to rebuild my shell of a life. I admitted, forcibly at first, that I was powerless over those substances that I had abused, and that my life to date was a wreck. It had been my doing, my counsellor added. I didn't like her for that, but I had to take it on the chin. 'Time to grow up, I suppose,' I groaned. Before that four months or so, all coming out had meant to me was a drunken slur uttered in oblivion. I would sit in group therapy, secretly cringing at all the times I had made a pass at some poor unsuspecting woman, whoever happened to be sitting next to me when I was drinking that 'liquid gold' in the pub on any number of nights, probably more times than I could remember. I kept those times to myself, the humiliation was already too much in that first thirty-day programme. We were the ones being programmed, I reckoned, we weren't just following one. But some of the words they said began to filter through the haze of alcohol. During secondary treatment, I went to live in a halfway house for women, where I could at last be free to uncross the wires in my aching brain. It had been four years since I took that acid. Intermittently, between those fleeting moments of peace that I began to see, my thoughts would swim about, become entangled, and then fluid once more. I was getting better, I knew that much. I'd almost become myself again, and was able to be myself with people without scaring them away with my self-directed aggression or scathing cynicism. I felt that I could accept my place in the world among other people again. It was there that I could tell some of these new friends of mine, all addicts, recovering from one substance or another, who I really was and what drove me. 'My sexuality is something that I get out of bed for in the morning,' I explained. 'If you don't get out there then how will you ever meet the person of your dreams? So I think I'll just go and do it.' I didn't always find acceptance from them, but it doesn't really seem to matter anymore. I accept myself and others as we are, without hiding myself away in a bottle. I know I don't have to spend the rest of my time dreaming my life away on a barstool. For today, I have a choice.

(At the time of writing, I am in my final year in college, hoping to receive my degree in five more months. Here's to Bill and Bob for that!)

i never knew i was gay

Colm O'Gorman

I NEVER KNEW I was gay. I never actually managed to work it out and by the time I realised it, or felt able to identify as gay, I had been on the scene in Dublin for a year or so. I did know that I was someone who had sex with men, but that was about it — sex — something sordid, dirty, wrong, sinful and, at its core, evil. I used to think it was a bad habit, something I would grow out of and become once again good and true and above all normal. For me, sexuality, being gay, was all mixed up with the experience of rape, of childhood abuse. Love had nothing at all to do with it.

To say that there were no 'positive role models' of gay men available to me as a child is an understatement. I was born in 1966 and for the first eleven years of my life I lived on a farm in a small village in Co. Wexford. Gay men didn't exist; the concept of gay men didn't exist. I never even heard the word 'queer' — nothing, no clichés, and no stereotypes good or bad, nothing. The only experience I had of sexuality was of being sexually abused as a child, first at five, then again at nine and most significantly at fourteen for some two and a half years by Seán Fortune.

Like many people who have been abused, one of the impacts on me was identification with the abuse. I had no words to describe what happened to me, no language with which to name it and no context within which I could try to understand what had been done to me. I knew what had happened was bad, that it was wrong, but I also knew that grown-ups didn't do bad things. I knew it was me; I felt bad, I felt to blame and I knew it was all my fault. I knew that grown-ups were good and that they only hurt you when you were bad. I must have been very,

very bad. And so it began, so began my compulsive, hate-filled relationship with sex and sexuality: a relationship in which love had no place, in which respect and tenderness were alien, in which my only purpose was to be an object for the pleasure of another. All this happened in a world that existed in parallel with the other world in which everyone else was good and normal, where my deviancy was hidden and had to be denied. A world in which the truth of what I had done, what I was, would disgrace and shame me and my family, would break my parents' hearts, would kill them.

I remember the first time I met two men who were in a relationship. It was in the Viking pub on Dame Street, we were talking when one referred to himself as married to the other, as in love. I was shocked, I couldn't understand what that meant, couldn't make any sense of the whole idea of love having anything to do with being gay. It is horrifying to me now to remember how lost I was to my own heart, to my enormous capacity and tendency to love.

If life has thrown challenges at me, and it undoubtedly has, they have all had to do with love, with staying true to my heart's instinctive loving. I love, it's what I do. I believe it's what we all as human beings do if given half a chance and if we can get beyond the fear and hurt that denies us access to our true loving nature, if we can feel able to sit in our hearts and live in love. I know that this has been my greatest challenge: to live in love. It was the reason why I was so devastated by the whole experience of abuse. I discovered that not everyone lived in love, that some people lived or were stuck in a place in which power and control, intimidation and humiliation were used to fulfil their needs, to live with their fears and hurts. I was devastated, I left my heart — or rather I hid it. I learnt to please others to hide what now seemed to be true, my badness. I lived in terror of being found out for what I was, for the foulness that I now believed myself to be.

When I was eleven my family moved to Wexford town. Things changed and I began to feel better about myself. I began to become excited about life and about being in the world again and I wanted to be part of it all. I became active in the Catholic Church, in folk groups and youth groups and as I moved into puberty I began to feel much better about who I was.

It was doubly devastating then to be abused at fourteen. It was a time when I was now sexually responsive and, like most fourteen-year-olds, highly confused and uncertain about what to do with all of this sexual energy. I know that my heart was crushed once again. Any chance of discovering what sexuality was all about, even in the Ireland of the early 1980s, vanished. I was now undoubtedly the problem — my body, my sexuality, was betraying me. I was part of something sick and wrong and evil. I was sick.

Escaping Wexford and finding the Dublin gay scene was a new beginning. I will never forget the first time I walked into the Hirschfeld Centre and stood in a corner thinking 'My God, all these people are like me.' I didn't understand what 'like me' meant but I began to think that I just might finally be able to begin to find out.

I'm thirty-seven now. It's twenty years since that first nervous step into the NGF. A lot has changed; a lot has changed for me and for us all. For a start I am no longer a criminal because I'm gay, which is all a bit of a relief. I live in love, I live in the truth of love, I am in love, have been for four years this August. My love is a case study in why Friday the thirteenth isn't an unlucky day. Let me explain:

In 1999 I was living in London. I had moved there in 1986 and had settled, never to return to Ireland, or so I thought. I had been in one long-term relationship that had lasted ten years, a relationship that I really needed to be in — well, one that met my need to be in a relationship more than it met me, if you know what I mean. My partner was a good man but we were both troubled souls who had been hurt in the same way and who were looking for a sanctuary to hide in from life. We found it in each other; if we want to get into 'therapyspeak' (not always a good idea), we would call it a co-dependent relationship. Our issues, or 'crap' as I used to call it, fitted together. We could act it all out without ever having to face it or name it in any way; you may well know what I mean! In 1995 I reported my abuse and like the 'good' boy that I was decided to go into therapy because that is what one was meant to do, and I was determined to do this right. So off I went, to do it right. I had no idea what kind of trouble I was getting into. Over the next three years I had to face my own guilt and shame, the memory of what had been done to me and the consequences of it all. I had to face my own fear of my sexuality, how I still really believed myself to be bad, how as a gay man I was less than others: my own inner homophobe, and a rampant hateful little sod he was too. The upshot was that in 1999, the same year as Seán Fortune's trial and suicide and the same year as I founded the charity 'One in Four' in the UK, I knew it was time to get out of my relationship. I knew that I wasn't being true to my own heart, that staying wouldn't respect either myself or my partner. I left; after much agonising I left our home and for the first time in eleven years decided to be single, to discover who I was and to get out there in the world as myself. I did not want to be in a relationship, didn't want to get involved in anything serious. I realised I had never dated, never just went out with someone for an evening, or several evenings, never been romanced as an adult and I wanted to try it. So I did, and it was good. Nothing serious, a few dinner dates, well okay, thirteen dinner dates, that were fun but that was it, and that was all I wanted it to be. No sex, no pressure and no desire for anything else — perfect.

Then on Friday, 13 August 1999, I had a blind date. A blind date that went against all my rules — yes, I had rules! They were: no men under thirty, because the chances were men under thirty would have issues! No one from a 'difficult' background — who needs the hassle — and I would probably end up jumping straight into another cosy co-dependency. Finally, if he wasn't Irish that might be interesting. I'd better explain that one quickly before I lose a lot of friends: it's not that I had any issue with Irish men... I just thought it might be interesting to see someone from another culture, okay? Anyway, rules like those, as I discovered, only exist so that life can make a mockery of them.

So back to Friday the thirteenth. Here I was heading out on a blind date to meet someone called Paul. Paul was twenty-five, from Northern Ireland and as such broke the rules, but two friends really liked him so off I went. I arranged to meet Paul in The Yard in London's Soho for a drink, quite late on a Friday evening. I had only been to The Yard once before, so it took me forever to find it. I arrived at 10.45p.m., convinced he would be gone, and that a beer alone was going to be the end result of my poor map reading. I went in anyway and headed upstairs to the upper bar where Paul said he would be. I had no idea what to expect or what he looked like, only that he was wearing cream combats and a white T-shirt.

Now, I don't know about you but my experience of gay men and the scene circa 1999 was that cream combats and white T-shirts were not all that unusual! I walked into the bar, looked around, couldn't see him. I got a beer and walked out onto the balcony of the bar. As I walked out I saw a man leaning over the balcony looking downstairs. I knew it was him. The bizarre part is that I started to panic; it all felt very odd. I walked over and said his name and he turned around. I remember feeling shocked as I looked into his eyes. All that I could think was 'Oh God, now I'm in trouble!' I was in a state and unable to understand what was happening to me. All I knew was that life would never be the same again. I was terrified; I knew that he was someone special. I also knew that I was really, really in trouble. Now most people seem to think I have a bit to say. I have been called articulate, I have also been called a big mouth, and perhaps they are the same thing. The thing is though when I met Paul that particular curse or quality (depending on your view) abandoned me. I was speechless, I mean it, speechless! I couldn't put a sentence together that didn't sound like total gibberish! I couldn't speak, couldn't think and had alarm bells ringing in my head. Get the drift? The evening went from terrifying to embarrassing as I spilt coffee over poor Paul twice and lost the plot. How he didn't run away screaming I don't know!

As luck would have it, he actually felt the same way. We were doomed. My new life of bachelorhood was at a rapid and frankly unexpected end. I was, however, certainly not in mourning. By the way, remember the rules? Well they were pretty much smashed. Paul was actually twenty-three, ten years younger than I was, and he did indeed come from a less than fully functional background. He was and is, however, incredible, clear, honest, open-hearted, loving, full of integrity and with a truly beautiful heart. He is also rather gorgeous but let's not give him too big a head!

Paul made me love. He opened my heart to love and to him. It was ready to open; if it wasn't, if I wasn't ready and able to love myself and another I would simply have run. My heart was ripe and hungry for love in all its glory, all of its spiritual, sensual and, yes, sexual glory! That was the panic, the terror. I took one look into his eyes and my heart knew it was in trouble. My heart, my spirit — that to know this man would be to love him. Really love him, with all that I am, my heart, my spirit, my body. I had always felt unable to be really free sexually. I always needed to be in control, to stay aware of where I was and what was happening. I always felt that abuse had robbed me of real sexual freedom, where I could let go and explore my sexuality. I was too scared. My heart, so much wiser than my head and so much more connected with my body, knew with Paul that I would have to love freely, without fear and without all those restrictions, in a way that I had never loved before and in a way that I was born to love… and I was terrified, and lost! Lost because I knew I had no choice, I knew I would and I did. I do.

If this all sounds a little too 'Hansel & Hansel', a bit Prince Charming… then let me put the record straight. Loving Paul means that he drives me to distraction, he drives me crazy. Loving him has been the most challenging thing I have ever done because he makes me be real, warts and all. I am capable of hating him (in a moment) as passionately as I love him. No one, and I mean no one, can get to me the way he does and that can be terrifying and very, very difficult. All the shit that I have pulled in relationships before doesn't work, it can't, our relationship has to be about respect and truth, in as far as we are capable of identifying that in the moment. That means that we have challenged each other in ways that I never would have believed possible and in ways that have dragged my murky, fear-driven issues screaming into the light. The same goes for him, and I can promise you he hates and values it in equal measure.

It's been four years now and we are blessed. It amazes me that through my sexuality I was robbed of my confidence in my own heart, and yet, it was through my sexuality in all its raw, sensual truth that I again found the depth of my heart. My love for Paul and his love for me has allowed me to embrace my sexuality, and by that I don't really mean my homosexuality but my sexuality, which as I have learned in the past four years, is all about love. It is a celebration of all that I am, all that I can be, the best of me. He is the best of me, and I believe I am the best of him. In the end it is real, alive, mutual love; love with passion and desire and with tenderness and respect that has helped to heal my lost and wounded heart. I am all that I can be now that I am able to feel this love. My love for him has unleashed in me my love, my heart full of optimism, belief in truth and goodness and my love for myself and others. Not bad for Friday the thirteenth, don't let anyone ever tell you it's unlucky!

mary and joe

Mary

I WAS MARRIED TO my husband for twenty-three years. We were relatively happy, with the usual ups and downs of every other normal marriage. We had our first and only child that year who has grown up to be a happy, contented and well-adjusted young man. We had a relaxed, easy-going marriage, good friendship and trust. Over the course of time, however, I did feel constant change, like the lack of affection at times. My husband would distance himself from me and this would be obvious at times. Mainly when there were no arguments or confrontations. I tried to tell myself things were normal, but situations with him staying out or sleeping on the far side of the bed with no conversation or explanation made me feel that there was more wrong with my marriage. I could carry on as normal or confront these issues or questions, which made little sense at the time.

We went out socially on a regular basis together. I decided on a particular night that I was going to confront him on my insecurities in the hope of some reassurance and understanding. Little did I know that it was at this moment that my life would change forever. To my absolute astonishment he revealed he had been leading a double life as a homosexual, for what I now believe the duration of our marriage. Naturally I felt betrayed. Where did I go from this point? How should we tell our son? I had many questions that I feel are still unanswered today. The words of reassurance of love that he felt for me couldn't compensate for the huge loss I felt.

This was the beginning of a rollercoaster of emotions, anger, fear and loss that brought me now to the road of recovery. With nowhere else to go, in my despair I went to my family doctor. He was very understanding of my situation. However, there was nothing he could do for me. I left him with the number of the Gay Helpline. There was no number for me to contact with my problem. I was alone. Surely not, there had to be more out there like me. One day by chance, I came across an article about a woman who discovered her husband was gay and decided to share her story. I knew then I was not alone and I was very relieved. I rang the number printed below and it turned out many more rang that day. The response was so big that a support group formed. Meeting other people in the same situation has been tremendous and has been a great help in getting my life back.

My husband and I continued to live together for a year and talked continuously about our situation. What would be best for both of us? Our marriage was over but ironically our friendship seemed to grow — maybe due to the fact that we isolated the problem between us. We also had our son to consider and how the revelation was going to affect him and how we could approach the issue as sensitively as possible. We discussed our assets and divided them amicably.

Two years on I am now at the stage where I forgive my husband and wish him well. Through meeting the support group it has helped me become positive about my abilities and has given me the strength to build a new life for myself.

silent screams

Francis (son of Mary and Joe)

THIS IS MY story of being an only child of a gay parent. I don't know where to start or what to say, as I've never really shared this with anyone, so we could be here for a while.

When I was younger my relationship with my dad wasn't great, in fact at the best of times I hated him. If he walked into the sitting room I could only sit there for five to ten minutes, as I couldn't stand him. I always remember asking him, on more than one occasion, could we go out on a Sunday afternoon. We'd never or hardly ever go, because his excuse was, 'I'm tired and I want to read my Sunday papers.' This was not always his excuse but for some reason it sticks in my head. And when it came to money, if I borrowed anything he'd never forget it and I would always have to pay it back, whether it was 50p or £5. Which looking back on it now wasn't a bad thing because I respect money and I always make sure I have enough and never like to borrow. As my mum always said, 'Money borrowed is twice spent' and this is true, so in that way I don't fault him for being like that. It's a pity he didn't take his own advice as, nowadays, for someone who seemed to be good with money and had their own business he owes a lot of money, in fact he is very bad with money and I don't think he'll ever learn unless it hits him very hard.

I find it hard at times having this bottled up inside me because I've no brothers or sisters to whom I could turn and talk to. I wish I had. There are times when I'm out and having a laugh with my friends, David and Eamonn (these are the only two I've told), and we would be laughing and joking and then maybe we might go dancing; these are the times I think about 'it' and I begin to get really angry. I just switch on about it. I feel at times I want to fight someone, or just scream at the top of my voice and just smash up the kitchen or sitting room. I never do anything like that because I always think, what is the point? And where will it get me? Nowhere! I've had some harsh words with my dad because he was 'out' for three months and I only saw his place twice. He never told me for the other three months (September to December) that he was living with someone, never invited me up for a cup of tea or anything. I don't want to know, that's his business. I've told him he's made his bed, now he has to lie in it! I know I don't need to know all the details but all I wanted was for him to be a bit honest and he wasn't. His whole life was just one big fucking lie. I hate lies! I don't lie, as I don't see the reason to do so, as you always, always get found out!!

I'll never forget the night he told me he was moving out. It was the night before Ireland played the Cameroon in the World Cup. We were all in the kitchen and we had had a few drinks. Mum went to bed and then he just said to me 'I've something to tell you,' and he said that he was moving out to a flat and that I'd have to help my ma a bit more with the house. That was no problem, as my mate David always says, 'You only have one mum,' and he's right. But I remember some time back, before Dad told me he was moving out, that I was looking for a sports bag and I came across gay magazines. I was shocked. I didn't know what to do. I told my girlfriend at the time and she just told me that I couldn't say a thing and I didn't. I just had to get on with it. I wanted to say something about it to my uncle Peter, but I was afraid of the way he would react (he's Mum's brother). Instead I said it to my dad's brother and he just said the same as my girlfriend. But getting back to the night he said he was moving out, I can honestly say that when he said 'I've something to tell you,' I had it in my head that he was going to tell me 'I'm gay,' but he didn't. He said he was moving out because of problems with his business. He came back after Christmas because 'his relationship' was over and he had nowhere else to go. I felt sorry for him at this time, his whole life in just four black sacks in the hallway. But after a few weeks I felt he was taking liberties again because his dinners were being made for him, his washing was being done. He was going out all the time and shoving everything back in our faces.

We went to a Dubs game in Parnell Park. Four of us went. Afterwards we went to a pub for a while. Dad's friend had said to him that he knew that Dad was gay and that it wouldn't change his attitude towards him. At about 9 o'clock Dad said he was going home. He never did come home that night; he came in the next morning at about 8.30a.m. He sat at the table saying to me that he was up early, as we had people coming early that day to view our house as it was up for sale. I had only found out from my mum that he had only come in that morning after she told him to go and live with his own father.

You see, I couldn't stick the lies any more and it came to a decision that either he or I move out. But I didn't want to rock the boat as I only had six weeks left in Ireland, as I was going to Australia. So, I said what was the point, didn't say a lot and just bottled it up. Then he went and Mum and I felt a lot better. It's sad to say but it's true. He would cry poverty but at the same time he was staying in bed and not getting up 'til 12.30p.m. and he didn't go to work. I couldn't stand looking at this either.

Now a few more people know about him and he has lost good friends and he is burning bridges very rapidly; he only has himself to blame, nobody else.

I thought about going to a counsellor, but didn't. I don't know whether they are more harm than good. I've a good family and that helps a lot. People to whom I can talk and not get the piss taken out of me. I have mixed feelings about all of this. I get angry very easily, maybe too easily. It's getting to the stage now that I don't even want to talk about him or what's happening with our house, as it seems to put pressure on me and it doesn't seem to bother him. I don't know how he sleeps at night worrying where the next few pounds will come from. Maybe he'll borrow it! Anyway, he's not my problem. I have my own life to live. Going to Australia couldn't have come at a better time or at a worse time. I don't know what the future has in store for me but I'll soldier on because all that's happened will make me a better and stronger person. As I always say to myself and I honestly believe in this — you only get something out of life if you put something into it.

dublin in the rare auld times!

Edward Roberts

T HIS IS THE story of somebody in his late fifties, now looking back on the last thirty-plus years of how the gay scene has changed, like everything else in our city, but also all over the world, as far as I know.

I, like most people I presume, growing up, knew nothing about homosexuality. It was a taboo subject, it wasn't spoken about. Your friends, pals whom you hung around with — they didn't seem to discuss it. So, therefore, a lot of us lived in ignorance in those days of what it was about. And on my part I took it as normal to be fond of my male friends. It worked out that I was in my mid-twenties before the penny dropped, when all my friends were going off with girls, getting engaged and then getting married. And I was the one that was left on the shelf then.

So one evening in the very early 1970s, I saw an article in one of the evening newspapers stating that there was a group for, as far as I remember, homosexuals with a religious outlook, and it was run by the Legion of Mary. So duly, on a cold, dark November evening, I rang up one of the people in charge of the meeting, who was called Joe — he was running the group, and I met him down where they had their headquarters in those days, right beside what's now the new apartments of the Richmond Hospital. The Legion had a little place there for all sorts of down-and-outs and dropouts — I think it's still there. So I was introduced to Joe.

In retrospect, that was the best thing that happened to me because it introduced me to a whole group of new people who were homosexual or gay, and gave me, as well as a lot of other people who were there, a great feeling of camaraderie. It also helped to dispel that guilt feeling in those days that you were the only person who was gay, there was nobody else in the world like you. So after going to the meetings for a while, you built up a confidence, in meeting all the different types of people — from just the ordinary 'Joe Soaps' like myself, to very well educated people from all walks of life, people who had been married, and who had separated, young people and elderly people, the whole gamut was there. And then it in turn led on to my finding out about a group who were called the Irish Gay Rights Movement. Before it started, there was a seminar in Trinity College, and one of the speakers at that time was a woman from England who was giving a talk on how parents should deal with their gay offspring.

And when the seminar was over, on that Sunday night, there was a get-together where Trinity College had premises facing Westland Row Station and it was the first gay disco I attended, as it was for some of the others also. It was comprised of just a record-player and a few speakers in a large room. That was my first time to see a whole group of males all dancing together. It was an unusual feeling at the beginning, it was just out of the ordinary where you normally went to the dance hall and you had a mixture of both sexes, but this it was just the one sex.

Later on, the Irish Gay Rights Movement was formed and they got a place in Leeson Street, where every Saturday afternoon from two 'til five or six o'clock, they held a get-together. On one Sunday in each month, a cheese and wine reception was held. It was a fine building, with two large rooms, one of them was kept afterwards for a phone service which was started, called Tel-A-Friend, TAF, which another member and myself got involved in. In the beginning it operated on Saturday afternoons, and eventually it was extended over the whole week from evening time for many years. It has now changed its name, it's part of the Gay Switchboard, as far as I know. But in those days it was the only contact for people who were gay and isolated and who were, as they say, alienated from the mainstream. People from the country, especially, found it a great source of comfort — a lifeline, in a way. And we used to invite people, if they wished to drop in to us, and also we would go out and meet people, get to know them, inform them what the Irish Gay Rights Movement was about. And if they had the confidence, if they wished, they could come back to the premises with us. Many a time we went out and met nobody, we also went out and did meet people for the first time, and a lot of people have the old Irish Gay Rights Movement to thank for putting them on the first step of becoming integrated into the gay community.

As for most of us, being gay in those days was a very lonely experience. There weren't many opportunities to meet gay people, unless you knew of the one bar — two bars, actually, in Dublin at that time, Bartley Dunne's and Rice's. Bartley Dunne's and Rice's have long gone. Rice's was on the corner of Stephen's Green, where the shopping centre is now. Bartley Dunne's was just off George's Street. They were the two pubs and if you hadn't met gay people, you wouldn't have known about these pubs; there was no advertising in those days, and it was all through word-of-mouth. And then there was the sadder side, where people used toilets to meet people. Often times these were people who didn't have any way of contacting other people, especially professional people such as doctors or solicitors or businessmen who wished to be anonymous, and couldn't afford to be seen in the pubs. A lot of them would drive along to these urinals, and pick up rent boys. In those days it was a lot safer, in many ways. Firstly, regarding being mugged or seriously attacked, and secondly age wasn't a problem in those days, so therefore people felt it was a safe way to make contact with people.

The IGRM got off the ground to the extent that it had its own discotheque, it had a huge building in Parnell Square, which had pool tables, a library, a room for meeting people, a phone service and various other facilities, which was a marvellous way for people to meet. The building was used most of the week, it had discos in the basement at the weekends. And also the women used to meet there occasionally as well. The whole group gelled together well in those days.

Eventually the IGRM fragmented, the Parnell Square premises closed down, and one section moved to Lott's Lane with its own disco — but the premises were not as nice as Parnell Square. The other place that opened up was the Hirschfeld Centre, which was run by David Norris. When the premises in Parnell Square went, the phone service moved over to the Hirschfeld Centre. Now the Hirschfeld Centre was housed in a reasonably good building and had plenty of space. It was located near the Central Bank. They also had their own discos and once a month in one of the rooms upstairs they also had a film show, often, though not always, with a gay theme or aspect. Eventually, the Hirschfeld Centre also closed down.

Meanwhile, on the Legion of Mary side, things had gone from strength to strength. It had started with Joe in Marlborough Street, in the CIÉ Hall, in a little room that held about twelve people, and it would be full. And then it moved over to their premises in Baggot Street, which was an old building with spacious rooms, and eventually to Marianella where it's now been operating from for many a year. And the numbers attending are quite steady and it's really thanks to all the hard work that volunteers have put into it. When Joe withdrew from it a number of years back, he handed it over to dedicated people who had their own views on running it and they started their own committees and it flourished from there. At the present moment, the Irish Gay Rights Movement has faded into history. There are many other small groups, fragmented, but the Marianella group, which started out from the Legion, has gone on and on. It looks like it will go on for quite a few more years. Many, many people have passed through it, and they have gained a lot of insight into the whole subject of homosexuality, coming to terms with it. The religious aspect was covered by many a speaker and priest who came and spoke about the way that the Church and outside people view gay people.

And with the group strengthening, it has also given them more impetus to move on, and as the laws have been changed, gay people are now feeling stronger, more inclined to be able to stand up and proclaim their sexuality without fear of being attacked, isolated or alienated from the rest of society. We have come a long way since the 1970s.

The next thing on the agenda will be legalisation of same sex property rights and things like that. It will make life much easier for gay people who are in a relationship so that they don't feel isolated, especially when their partner dies and usually the family steps in and take over. So we have another few years to go but we hope that that handicap will be removed and eventually gay people will be integrated into the rest of society and we can move on together to a brighter and better future.

a rambling garden

John Curtis

E HUGGED ME. It was a bit boring, standing there in the dark hall. Then his hands slid down my back, and for the first time I began to feel turned on. That's how it started. I liked it, and I liked him. I liked him very much indeed, and we were special friends for twenty years, and I miss him very much.

Was I underage? I don't think so. I was old enough to be married! But there was no age of consent then for 'the likes of us'. It was all illegal, and it was all forbidden. I can hardly think of anything that was fun that wasn't forbidden. Is that an exaggeration? I don't think so. In 1950's Ireland people lived a strict and frugal life. Enjoyment was 'tempting providence'. The 1960s, in my experience, were exactly the same.

He was so much older than I was that he found it easier than I did to value friendship more than sex. As well as that, it made him totally depressed. He would regret bitterly that it had ever happened. I went on, and found my way into those places in Dublin where men had a lot of fun without much fuss, and seldom any bother.

He lived in an old house with a rambling garden. I loved my time there. It's all gone now. But then there were lawns and trees, flowers and shrubs, roses, lilac and laburnum in profusion. It was Eden for me. I loved the quiet spacious house and spent many, many happy hours there doing all the things that need to be done in neglected old houses and gardens. It was a very safe place, away from the world in which I didn't fit.

Was that the first time? I remember, further back, finding a pleasant sensation spiralling round previously unnoticed body parts. Nobody told me what was going on. My parents and my brothers, like everyone else, were silent rather than talk about rude things. Somehow I was one to whom people never did say rude things, all the more so when I was — even as a teenager — in line for the priesthood. My mother left women's magazines about the house, which were full of information. There was no television. My big brother hid his girlie magazines where younger siblings alive with curiosity eventually found them. But I remember no hint of anything to do with feeling or coping, except practical matters. My father taught us scientific names instead of childish ones for parts of the body. Another of my brothers warned me to change my clothes without too much modesty — I was always covering myself with something — both at home and at school. I never saw another boy naked. We put our sports clothes on over our underclothes, and the showers were not used.

Maria Edgeworth wrote *Castle Rackrent*, a school textbook that became a favourite story. I love nostalgia about old houses and the people that lived in them. She described an old lady who threw a shawl over the mirror while bathing. I began to wonder if I was doing the right thing by covering the bathroom mirror with a towel. I also began to wonder if I should try to fantasise about girls as well as boys. I could put them in the picture, but never in the limelight. I soon realised that I looked at boys the way boys looked at girls. When it came time to be interviewed, to see if I was fit to be a priest, I pretended. Years later, when I tried to talk to one of the staff, he was very upset. He said he was disappointed in me. And because I wasn't sorry for what I was doing, I was refused absolution, or any further counsel.

The boys I was friends with were studious, and we spent our lives in uniform. We never thought about clothes. I remember feeling that it would only be a waste of money to wear fashionable clothes, because I was earmarked for black. Some gay men have great flair for fashion. It was something I never learnt! I could cope with no clothes at all, in the sauna, or plain clothes, in dark places, but never with the bright lights or the disco. I don't think it was a feeling of guilt. It was just that I wasn't very confident. I still admire hugely the men who exude confidence — singers, dancers, Pride marchers, Mardi Gras performers — men who've got it and flaunt it. I never had the nerve, but I love to look at those who do!

There was a kind of camaraderie in the places where we met, which made it possible to cope with the demands of much older men, but I always preferred my own age. I was never athletic but admired athletes hopelessly. I never met any (that I knew of!). Still, as a student I had the leisure to spend hours in search of anonymous silent sex. I couldn't be sociable. I had no vocabulary. I still find that I want to talk and that I still don't know how. At that time, to meet someone who knew me was a strange and difficult experience. The religious man that they recognised and the gay man that they discovered me to be were irreconcilable, I assumed, so I was either a monster or a fraud. It was almost unknown for me to have sex with someone whose name I knew, and equally rare to have sex with the same person twice. This hard attitude was reinforced as time went on. Once, a man took me home to his flat, high over a city street. I took an immediate liking to him, and wondered if I might find a new friend. That little daydream didn't last long. His first and last words were 'I won't know you,' and as often as we have met since, his glazed expression has never been animated by the least trace of recognition.

I don't think my early experience was the same as victims of abuse, of whom so much is known now, but so little then. I feel my old friend and I were victims of a system and a society that made old men lonely and kept young men ignorant and unable to cope with their own needs, never mind anyone else's. I think I suffered more through fear of what family members and other people would think, rather than in the arms of a very dear, kind friend whose love for me was unconditional.

I never experienced unconditional love from anyone else, but I knew that in theory at least, the love of God was like that. So, from that old man I learnt that it's possible for gay men to share a little of God's love with one another. And my brother, who gave me advice so long ago, has set me a good example — he has been living with his boyfriend for years! He has explained to me the new laws in Ireland that take gay relationships seriously, giving gay people security in their homes. I hope for a future in which there may be new laws in the Church, which might give me security with Carl.

I met Carl many years ago, but then he and I were tied up in relationships that were difficult, in a world where it was forbidden to be gay. I met him at a time when I felt that I would never be able to have a steady home life, and when I thought God wanted me to be a monk. I wanted to live a life in which no one could blame me for anything, so I became good at doing nothing. I found it hard to care about other people and difficult to keep in touch with them, even with good friends.

I couldn't imagine, then, that the life I enjoy with him now might be either desirable or possible.

Now we have met again. We live together in a little house in Dublin, in a world quite unlike the one we grew up in. I think we have found the freedom that you get when you take responsibility for yourself, and the happiness that comes from being able to make a commitment in love to that one special person you want to be with, for the rest of your life.

I still find it difficult to integrate a sexual relationship with my religious faith. When the two were kept apart, there was no conflict. So now, rather late in life, I have to try to make sense of the responsibilities I have taken on, as well as the freedom I now claim. I can begin by saying that the Lord himself spoke very severely against the remarriage of divorced people, and said nothing about homosexuality — in the Gospel. If our culture can cope with divorced and remarried people (the reason why a King lost his crown, in living memory), then our culture should be able to cope with gay relationships. I can go on, and say to myself, that 'where charity and love are, there is God'. I remember expressions such as 'what does the Lord require of you, but to do justice, and to love kindness, and to walk humbly with your God?' I remember 'religion that is pure and undefiled before God and the Father is this, to visit orphans and widows in their affliction, and to keep oneself unstained from the world'.

I'm still trying to cope with the obvious conflict between a conventional idea of 'unstained' and the life I live now. I don't think ideals should be thrown away. But the ideal is love, love in the sense of charity, charity in the sense of love, which makes a sacrifice. So the more I grow in love with my partner, and make the changes in my own outlook that a relationship demands, the more I feel I grow in love and in the knowledge of the love of God. And I have learnt this, not from all the many, many books I have read in the past, but from a very, very fine man in the present. I am blessed to be with him.

God's love shines out like the light of the Sun, but no one is forced to love God in return. The nature of God is the nature of love, and you can't make someone love you. You can't really pretend, for long, to be in love with someone if you're not. So I have found an alternative to the sterility I thought I faced, and I find the warmth of that love upon my face instead. It comes to me from a human person. God showed his love for us long before, in the human person of Jesus of Nazareth. In the mundane and homely domesticity that we have, I find something special and unexpected. In normality, I think that I see theology in action, and I believe that I have an experience of God, in the ordinary life that we lead. Is it too much too hope that God will bless us both? Will restore Eden, and recreate that rambling garden for me, after all this time? I will take care not to lose it again.

how shall we sing the lord's song in a strange land?

Carl McManus

I LIKE DOING JIGSAW puzzles. This has been a favourite hobby throughout my life. There is one jigsaw puzzle, though, that has taken me more than thirty years to solve. Only in very recent times did I even realise just how many pieces there were — all of them there from the time I was a young man. This jigsaw, however, isn't the usual kind. The pieces represent dozens of individual incidents and signals that, if they were all put together, would have left me in no doubt about my sexuality. I couldn't, or wouldn't, put them together. I don't think it was denial so much as rejection: I did not want to be gay! After all, the rulebook said it was a sin. My homophobia was comprehensive.

The rulebook also said 'self-abuse' was a sin. And, God love me, it was there. I remember in my late teens screwing up my courage to go and talk to a priest, and the furthest we were able to get was to talk very reluctantly about my problems with masturbation. I remember going to confession twice and three times a week to purge my never-ending guilt. Only when I met my counselling priest (a guest at a Reach meeting) 'half a lifetime' later was I able to forgive the earlier priest for not being able to read my mind. By then I was married, and I had already come out — painfully — to my wife Mary.

The impetus for my coming out to Mary was my need to stop living a lie, simply that. I was attempting to hold on to my marriage and at the same time trying to find ways of giving expression to who and what I was. Ideally, this expression needed to be wholesome — or at least had to appear to be wholesome. I got involved in Tel-a-Friend, the Gay

Switchboard at the time. And I wrote for *Out* magazine, a forerunner to *GCN* and *GI*. A priest in confession, as penance (truly!), got me to make contact with Reach, the gay Christian group. An important part of my personal motivation is believing in what I am doing: it was abundantly present in all these outlets. Through all these wholesome outlets, and also through many less wholesome (and some very wonderful) ones, I grew.

Let me sing!

If I like doing jigsaws, then I love to sing. I would like to compliment my wife here for nurturing in me a great love of music; little did we know that it would contribute so significantly to the ultimate destiny of our relationship. I remember as a young man being at a party and being asked to sing; people did that kind of thing at parties in the olden days. (I neither feel nor look as old as I obviously must be!) Just as my reticence was about to leave me, the cajoling stopped. I was so bitterly disappointed that I promised myself that night that whenever I was asked to sing again I would immediately agree. And, if I wanted to sing at parties, then I should also be prepared to sing in church. It must have been at the transition time when Catholic churches still had functioning organs and organists, but very reluctant congregations. The initial embarrassment of being one of the few singing in the church soon faded.

My joy of singing in church came into its own in Reach, Dublin's gay Christian group. With Mary's help, I prepared a huge hymnal, part of which is still used in the group. Through Reach came a spiritual journey that I am still making today. I remember those early days and the sheer joy of my involvement with it. As much as I put into it, I got so much more out of it: it gave great meaning to my very confused existence.

The earliest part of my spiritual journey is best summed up in the dawning that Jesus loves me. In time this developed into the understanding that not only does Jesus love me, but also He loves me as I am. In more recent times this has taken the further quantum leap to Jesus not only loving me as I am, but also as He wants me to be — as He made me. Leave the religion out of it, though, and what is left? I like myself, as I am, as I want to be — me. Each of these self-affirming progressions has been a tremendous revelation to me.

Unchristian Churches

Through my spiritual journey also came the slow dawning that the rulebook simply didn't fit the reality of my life and ultimately, indeed, that the rulebook was wrong! I could no longer accept the dogma that a thousand one-night stands was more forgivable than a loving 'intrinsically disordered' relationship unless it was celibate. I truly believe that the Catholic Church's official teaching is profoundly unchristian. It is downright cruel to unwitting straight spouses! Unfortunately, the Catholic Church is in very good company with most of the main Christian denominations. I disdain the eleventh commandment — don't get caught — attitude to gay clergy. I also believe that Catholicism in particular, and Christianity in general, pays a very high price for the way it treats its gay sons and lesbian daughters — so too our whole society.

Yes, there has been great pain for me, my wife — hugely for Mary — and our children, Janet and David, in the various steps of this great journey. Indeed, our pain is not yet done. There were many crises — some supported by various kinds and qualities of outside intervention — interspersed with sometimes long periods of calm. The initial presenting problem was that I was gay; then it was that I was married; then it wasn't that I was either married or gay, but that I was both; then it was that I wanted to be both.

Like in so many other challenges in our marriage and family — no matter what intervention we managed to harness to help us — we became our own experts. In my attempts to understand our situation and how others have coped with it, I spared no effort to get my hands on the small amount of literature there was on the subject. I still do, though now it is far more readily available.

To my amazement, having thought such a thing was impossible for someone in my position, at one point a special friend came into my life, which continued for over a year. He and I are still good friends. When Mary found out about it — just before it came to its natural end — it was the cause of more pain and heartache for her. It was a very slow dawning for me that having the liberty to have a special friend — another man with whom I could be intimate in all the ways we needed to be with one another on at least some kind of an ongoing basis — was the essence of my desire for fulfilment as a gay man. If our marriage could have tolerated such a special friend, it is quite likely our journey together would not have taken the course it finally did.

Is It Possible to Be Happily Gay and Happily Married?

I remember being asked to contribute to another book, to be called *Out for Ourselves*, which wanted to tell the stories of Irish gays and lesbians. I entitled my contribution 'Is It Possible to Be Happily Gay and Happily Married?' My answer was far from conclusive. It was rejected, as it offended the sensibilities of some of those involved in editing the book. *Out* magazine published the article instead.

Another time, Mary and I were asked to talk about our situation at a Catholic Marriage Advisory Council (now ACCORD) workshop for counsellors in the west of Ireland. Having told my story, I summed up our marriage as likely being one of the best second-rate relationships in the country.

I took grave offence at the result of the first divorce referendum: annulment — denying our marriage ever existed and thus our love for one another — was the only full remedy to be afforded by our society if our marriage failed.

I remember making contact with a now defunct group in England called SIGMA, a support group for the straight spouses of gay husbands and lesbian wives. We attended a couple of their workshops in London where we met other Irish couples in similar situations to ourselves. I would have liked for a similar group to come together in Dublin, but sadly this was not to be. I was the one anxious for my wife to build a support network, as I had been building mine; but Mary is such a private person, the idea of being very personal with a friend or stranger about many things — never mind something like this — is totally alien to her nature. For a short time, in the early stages of it, I belonged to a local married gay men's support group. In my hunger to learn as much as I could about my situation — along with my determination to leave no stone unturned in my quest for information — I became aware of support groups in North America and the UK for people in my kind of situation and those affected by it. This was in the days before the Internet as we now know it. There were no other support groups at the time in Ireland — and fairly few since. I had absolutely no intention of leaving my marriage then.

Turning Point

For several years Mary and I attended the AIDS Memorial Service in St Patrick's Cathedral in Dublin. At this service, in 1998, for the first time I heard Glória sing. Glória is a gay and lesbian choir, the only one based in Ireland currently. I was spellbound. That night I told Mary I would love to sing with them. Matter of factly, she simply said that, of course, it was impossible. All summer long the notion kept coming back to me. Despite Mary's huge reservations, I joined Glória — on the premise that I would not sing with them in non-gay public events. Unbeknownst to me at the time, this was a turning point in our relationship. I remember singing to a rapturous audience with Glória and the Pink Singers in the architecturally and acoustically beautiful Duke's Hall in the Royal Academy of Music in London. It was one of the most thrilling experiences of my life. At home, the fact that I was away — never mind that I was singing, let alone that I was with my GLBT choir — was being hidden from family, acquaintances and friends.

I don't know that I ever reached the stage of intending to leave my marriage until, through joint counselling with Mary, I came to the conclusion that there was no other satisfactory way forward. To my honest surprise, the decision to separate became mine and mine alone. We looked at every conceivable (and inconceivable) option from living a celibate relationship together, to an open relationship, to going back to the stolen time and lies that had already put us into such a terrible rut, to separation. The single precondition on which I entered counselling was that the stolen time and lies coping strategy just had to stop. None of the other options, except the extremely daunting prospect of separation, were remotely viable. It saddens me deeply to acknowledge that, if Janet and David were not there, Mary has told me that suicide would have been a very real option for her.

Maybe it is little wonder I hold the beliefs I now do: they are informed by my lived experience.

When I can afford it, I like to take a flutter with shares on the stock exchange. The current rollercoaster of share price volatility is nothing compared with the emotional rollercoaster of separation. It has validly been described as bereavement without a corpse. My strongest emotion immediately following our separation was one of incredible relief. In time this was replaced by a feeling of phenomenal loneliness. This, in turn, was followed by waves of sadness — which, at times, continue to this day. Sometimes, the most ordinary things become charged with huge emotion. My work suffered: this continued for quite a long time and only recently has it at last taken a turn for the better.

Very shortly after our separation I met Robby, a man little more than half my age, very handsome, very charming, very cavalier. I was chuffed that one so delightful and exotic might be remotely interested in me. I saw what he was doing quite clearly: he took advantage of me, and I let him. He borrowed money from me that I did not have to spare at the time; I saw very clearly the risks involved. A man of great promise(s), the magnificent Mr Robby fulfilled that promise!

Through all the trauma leading up to and following our separation, I was kept afloat by the prospect of Glória's participation in GALA Choruses Festival 2000 in San Jose, California. As the time approached, my enthusiasm was almost down to nil: after all the preparations and fundraising, I could not have cared less whether I went or not. I went. I loved every minute of it! Almost 150 choirs participated, involving more than 5,000 singers. Choral singing in a GLBT milieu — my essence and my life's joy — I was in my element.

When I least expected it, almost immediately upon my return from America, I met John. He is someone I had known slightly for very many years and had fancied from afar. I bumped into him one night in Lynch's, a short-lived men-only hostelry in Dublin. In our banter, and truly without expectation, I happened to mention my fancying him since first we met so long before. We have been more or less together ever since. Our relationship is more than congenial but fraught, yet fulfilling. Like possibly all relationships, ours has the seeds of its own destruction and, hopefully, the seeds of its continued success: we choose to stay together, I believe, simply because we want to stay together. Despite our difficulties, and maybe even sometimes because of them, in very many ways we are very good for one another. While John, I expect, would be daunted by the prospect of meeting Janet and David — never mind Mary — to my chagrin, there seems to be little likelihood of that anywhere in the immediate future.

Whatever else can be said of my life's journey, it certainly has not been boring. 'Some people learn from their experiences, others never recover' was a favourite motto I had stuck on my wall in work during the darkest days of my traumatic transition. It is possibly still a bit soon to assess which way it has worked for me.

Grant Me the Serenity...

I have tried to paint a positive, though honest, picture of what it is that has brought me thus far. And what of my hopes for the future? Through the people and things I care about comes my happiness. There is still a long distance to go: for Mary, that beyond her pain comes peace and new fulfilment; for Janet and David, that they rediscover the meaning in their relationship with me; for John, that he finds his own contentment in the world just as it is; for our relationship, that it continues and blossoms; for me in my work, that I rediscover the soul satisfaction I have been fortunate enough to have had in the past; for the GLBT community, that some day it no longer needs to fight for its rights, and until that day we will continue to sing our songs in this strange land; for the Church, that through liberation theology it finds a way out of its mistaken righteousness; for society at large, that it soon realises that being yourself is much more valuable and worthwhile than damaging yourself (and others) trying to be someone you are not. The jigsaw of my identity may be complete; the jigsaw of my life still unfolds. God, grant me the serenity to accept the things I cannot change!

I Wouldn't Be Where I Am Today...

My life's journey began with an overwhelming desire to belong, to fit in, to comply — to be accepted. I am now exiled from the life I worked so hard to build on such flimsy foundations, while acceptance comes from within. It would be easy to simply and deeply resent the negative consequences of my journey, or to spend my life in abject remorse for the great hurt I've caused people I love. I cannot do this!

My extraordinary journey also has had its many rewards, of course, and the whole of my experience — good and not so good — marks my formation and transformation as a worthy member of human society. I honestly feel this. Even without my particular lived experience, it is probable that I would anyway be in the process of developing a personal moral code, one divergent from those imposed on me by Church, state and society — and with which, for too long, I tried to comply. It is likely, though, that I would not otherwise be remotely as advanced in that process as I now am. Through it all, I have become aware of who I am, not just in terms of my sexuality, but also in so many different ways. I know what makes me tick.

Throughout my life, I have been fortunate to feel there was purpose and meaning to it — something that is important to me. Even at its darkest, I knew that purpose wasn't just to be a thorn in Mary's side. Albeit still fraught in several dimensions, there is new purpose and meaning to the life I now live. For this I am truly blessed.

'Blessed are those who are persecuted for righteousness' sake, for theirs is the kingdom of heaven'. (Matthew 5:10)

enjoying retirement

Beth and Sara

Beth's Story

I DIDN'T COME TO the realise my sexual orientation until I was about fifty. (I am now in my early sixties). My mother died when I was ten which made me quite insecure. I threw myself into sport to the exclusion of academic strivings, and my other interests were pop music and dancing. Because of this I found myself drawn into a 'normal' environment, resulting in heterosexual relationships, a few becoming quite serious. During these years having dreams and fantasies of women never occurred to me as being strange or unusual. On reflection I really must have been very naïve.

However, for many years throughout the '70s there was one particular woman whom I dreamt of most of the time. She worked in the same building as myself and we became good friends, but she never guessed how I felt about her. We even went together on several holidays, which were wonderful but hugely difficult for me. She did eventually marry and I was involved in her preparations for the wedding – I was pretty cut-up following it but eventually managed to put it behind me.

In the late '70s another friend confided to me that she was a lesbian and this was my first experience of knowing a gay person. She emigrated to Australia mainly because of its gay-friendliness, as opposed to the rampant homophobia in Ireland at that time.

Following my father's death in the mid '80s I realised how lonely I was and felt a longing for a loving relationship and to share my life and home with someone. Around this time there was much media discussion of lesbians and gays and I could identify with what I was hearing. Then in

1990 my Australian friend was home on holiday and I told her how I was feeling. She said she had guessed that I might be lesbian all along and was sorry we hadn't discussed the possability years ago. I told her I was glad she hadn't as I had been too immature then and definitely not ready for a relationship. She did, however, introduce me to a lesbian friend of hers in Dublin and I arranged to meet her. Predicabily I fell for her but this was not reciprocated, which left me feeling very flat.

I did eventually emerge from the doldrums and began to do some research, finding the Gay and Lesbian Helpline in the phonebook. It was sometime before I plucked up the courage to make contact and like many others I'm sure, put the phone down on a few occasions. I told the volunteer that being actively involved in my church I would like to meet with like-minded 'non-scene' women. I was eventually put in contact with the Julian Fellowship, a gay women's group with a Christian or spiritual ethos. The members were relatively mature in years and not 'out', as most worked in sensitive professions. I attended the monthly meetings which were very affirming and encouraging.

The group introduced me to various aspects of gay life, including the *Gay Community News*, which I eagerly scanned for the personal adverts. I eventually dared to put in my own ad. Hoping I had portrayed myself honestly and sincerely. I had now reached the grand old age of 53! I placed the ad in the July '92 edition and waited hopefully.

It wasn't until early September that I finally received a reply. It was from Sara and I was astounded that she had revealed her full name, address and telephone number. I telephoned her IMMEDIATELY, we talked for ages and arranged to meet.

From the start I felt completely comfortable with her. It felt as if we had always known each other. In the early days we travelled to each others homes in our free time, (both of us were working then) and every holiday was spent together. We gradually became more confident attending gay functions, like the annual Gay and Lesbian film festival and the Reach Carol Service. Although we are still amazed that we dare to attend such functions we are constantly struck and a little bit envious of the confidence and self-assurance of the younger gays.

Now that we are both retired, we live in Dublin most of the time, regularly travelling to Sara's home in Northern Ireland to visit the mutual friends we have there, but who still think we are 'just good friends', with the exception of Sara's one confidante. It has ceased to be important to us that we're not shouting from the rooftops. We feel at our stage in life that discretion is the better part of valour.

Sara's Story

I suppose I've always known that I am gay, without being able to articulate it. There were the usual crushes on teachers or older women (always older), some very intense and I had no desire to have a boyfriend. I can't say I felt any guilt about my penchant for women, but I wouldn't have dreamt of admitting it to anyone.

I went to an all-girls convent school in Northern Ireland and thoroughly enjoyed my education, acquiring a love of poetry and music which sustained me during a somewhat lonely adolescence. I am an only child of very loving parents but I refuse to believe I was 'spoilt' despite assertions of privilege by some schoolmates! My father was unemployed mainly due to a progressive illness of my mother and we survived on the 'dole' for many years, quite adequately thanks to my mother's domestic prowess and good management. However, I know they made great sacrifices to give me a secondary education and I am deeply grateful for that. Both my parents are now dead, my mother when I was 21, my father four years ago.

I chose nursing as a career and following training in Belfast worked without a break for thirty-five years until taking early retirement five years ago. It wasn't all plain sailing – I had a few episodes of depression which thankfully responded each time to medication, but which were due in no small measure to the insecurity and loneliness of being a closet lesbian. I had a few very close friends – and strangely was never attracted to any of them – the 'older woman' thing persisting for many years. I still have these friends but have come out to only one who was and remains extremely positive and supportive.

During the '70s I did go through a period of pretending I was 'normal' and put myself through a series of heterosexual relationships, none of them giving me any satisfaction, physically or spiritually!

Throughout my forties I threw myself into my work and decided to abandon hope of ever finding a soul mate – or a body mate! Then in 1992 on an organised group holiday I fell hopelessly in love with yet another older woman. Realising that this would lead nowhere, as she was obviously straight, I was driven to take action. I contacted the Belfast Lesbian Line and amongst other things learned of the existence of the *Gay Community News*. I travelled to Belfast and with what I thought was the utmost temerity went into a gay bookshop, bought several books – some of them rubbish – and acquired a copy of the *GCN*. Once home I devoured the classified ads., and amazingly found one that struck a chord. Something about it stirred me to throw caution to the wind and I replied giving my full name, address and telephone number.

To condense a long story I eventually got a phone call from Beth and arranged to meet. Beth's first reaction was astonishment at my recklessness in revealing my full identity (she had used a box number of course). Wasn't I lucky that she turned out to be the most honest and trustworthy person I had ever met. We talked for hours – it was a lovely September Sunday – and she missed an important pre-arranged function that evening to stay with me. I flew home on gossamer wings feeling I was embarking on the rest of my life. And so it has proved. Ten years on we remain together, still seeing new facets of each other, enriching each other's lives, enjoying our retirement and having great fun. This is so important – we laugh a lot, sometimes to the point of collapse. The Julian Fellowship features largely in our lives now and many of our social activities revolve around it, although we have by no means abandoned our very good straight friends who may or may not guess the true nature of our relationship. Who cares, anyway?

I think the fact that we are both mature enhances our relationship, so I don't regret the years of loneliness and longing. I can't imagine life without Beth and often recall the line of Edmun Blunden's poem 'Almswomen' about two dear friends who 'pray that both be summoned in the selfsame day'.

Would that be TOO much to hope for?

life begins

David Caron

THREE YEARS AGO, on the cusp of forty, I finally 'came out'. Looking back, I marvel at why it took me so long. Undoubtedly, my Catholic upbringing and beliefs were a very significant factor. Approaching forty I felt, perhaps, that I had left it too late. Would it be worthwhile coming out? What benefits might I accrue? Would I be rejected by people I loved as a result? But my life had become so lonely, unfulfilled and miserable that I decided on balance it had to be worth the gamble.

So how to come out to friends and family? In some instances I met people in person; in other cases I phoned them. Many of my oldest and closest friends were living abroad and so to them and others at home I decided to write a letter. This turned out to be the easiest thing I have ever done. I thought I would be struggling at my computer, cutting and pasting, rewriting again and again. I sat down and a page and a half later I was finished. I varied the letter slightly from person to person but basically the content was the same.

My intention in writing my letter was simply to notify friends that I was now 'out' as a gay man; it never crossed my mind that I might receive replies. But I did, and they were wonderfully reaffirming. I no longer have a copy of the letter I sent but I kept all the replies I received. Here are extracts from three of them: the first two are from American friends whom I have known for fifteen years; the third from an Irish friend, now living abroad, whom I've known since I was four.

David,

I am both honoured and humbled that you've chosen to share with me the personal struggle that you have been going through. I know I speak for all of the people who know and love you on both sides of the Atlantic when I say that you deserve to be happy and fulfilled, and I strongly suspect that God feels the same way too.

I've had other friends who recognised themselves gay as adults (although none were as close to me as you). No one ever discussed it with me, or announced it to me in any way. I imagine they just assumed I would learn when the general word got out. And I did…I guess all that I can offer you is unconditional love and support.

I'm sorry to hear that the last ten years were so lonely for you. And I'm delighted that now things are brightening up. Thanks again for sharing what you've been going through, and I hope and pray that the most difficult part is behind you and the future will continue to be sunny.

Love always,
John

****

Dear David,

I am glad you felt comfortable — hmmm, doubt this was a comfy communiqué — to tell me what has been going on in your life. As for your being gay, my first Sheryl-like-off-the-cuff comment is 'Yeah? OK — so what? Where are you staying in April? How long are you over for? You want a dinner party at our place like last time?'

But I know that this has been a long, uneasy path for you — and you have the utmost respect for your hard work and honesty in personal reflection and growth. I too believe our sexuality is something we are born with, like eye colour, and the only trouble is when we deny our true selves. It seems to me that you are doing all the right things to make this transition/acceptance of yourself. I'm happy you are taking such good care of yourself.

I'm resisting making a comment on the narrow-mindedness of the Catholic Church — it's not easy.

This letter writing is sounding so clinical — it would be a whole lot easier for me if I could give you a big hug now! I feel this all sounds like a wretched new age Hallmark card.

Looking forward to seeing you in April, dear friend.

Love, Sheryl

****

Dear David,

Got your great letter. The first thing to say is that I should have sent you the same letter — and I'm sure that doesn't surprise you. I did my journey about ten years ago so it is very remiss of me not to have talked to you about it.

It struck me when we had coffee last month that you were very much at peace with the world and your place in it — I even commented on it when I met my mother a few hours later and she asked how you were. Don't know if your letter is the entire reason for your state of mind, but I suspect it does have a lot to do with it. I know I felt like a weight had literally been taken off my shoulders.

Was I surprised by your letter? Yes, actually I was. The thought that you might be gay had crossed my mind some years ago on more than one occasion, but as time went by I decided that it wasn't the case.

I am very glad that you have found a group [Reach] that you can relate to on your own terms. I have always known how important your faith is to you and am always saddened when I hear of gay men and woman who are wrenched in two trying to reconcile their religious beliefs with who they are.

I have a lot of very good gay friends out here, though as a rule I prefer mixed company. I have no real interest in show tunes, ice skating (yes, those clichés are all true) and — above all — no interest in the gym. And my apartment continues to look like it is inhabited by a slovenly, squash-playing, divorced accountant from Pittsburgh who knows that a few books on the shelves will impress the ladies.

Your letter was wonderful and I am very flattered that you chose to include me in your circle. No matter what they tell you, there is no set of rules for coming out and no two cases are the same. Only you can set the pace.

Be happy — it's your life.

All the best,
Anthony

****

So how has my life changed in the past three years since I officially came out? I count myself extremely fortunate that almost immediately I was introduced to the fabulous world of gay hill-walking. Sounds like an exotic pastime? Simply a bunch of gay men (and a small number of lesbians) who meet up twice a month and take to the hills. In the 'Out and About' group, I discovered a large bunch (roughly 20 to 40 on any given walk) of surprisingly ordinary yet remarkably interesting individuals of various ages and from all walks of life. I had never been hill-walking beforehand but took to it immediately. As well as the exercise dimension, it is distinctly sociable: the activity lends itself to drifting in and out of conversations. I also liked the democratic nature of the group; anyone can turn up on a walk and is made welcome so there is always a mix of regulars (which I would now count myself as) and newcomers. Sometimes we all follow the same route; more often than not we split in two — a faster and slower walk, so different levels of fitness are accommodated. Afterwards we all adjourn to a country pub, sometimes going for a pizza in town afterwards.

I now find that my social life largely revolves around my 'Out and About' friends. I feel my coming out experience would have been very different and probably less positive if I had not encountered this group. Even at the best of times I was never a pub and club person and dreaded the idea of having to walk into a gay bar and start up conversations with strangers. Launching oneself on the gay scene (however you define it) is never easy. Although only 'out' a relatively short time, it is easy to forget what a momentous step it was for me to take. And as I said at the start of this article, I still marvel that it took me so long.

And am I happier and more fulfilled? Undoubtedly so. For me, I feel life did indeed begin at forty.

coming to terms with being gay

Rossa O'Donovan

WHEN I WAS in secondary school, I had a girlfriend for about a year. As the relationship went on, we wanted to explore sex so one day we had penetrative sex. I thought it was good but felt there was something missing — or was this what all the lads got so excited about? Based on my first experiences, I felt it was totally overrated and that there must be more to it than this.

I gradually found myself looking at men more and more — admiring their bodies and physiques. I would walk down the street and men would catch my attention when I felt that I should be looking at the women instead. I still found women aesthetically attractive but realised I wasn't the typical lad drooling over 'women's tits' and other parts. I began to realise that I was sexually interested in men, and for me that was a big dilemma. I kept feeling that this was not normal: I wanted to marry a lovely young girl, have three beautiful children, have a mortgage and a good job and in some naïve way live happily ever after. But this was just not happening for me. At the age of eighteen my relationship with that girl ended.

I had a male friend from primary school who occasionally stayed in my house. From the age of about fifteen we had relatively innocent encounters — more fumbling around than full sex — which I enjoyed very much. Afterwards I would feel very guilty and hope not to have any more sexual encounters with him or with other men. But they kept happening. It may seem strange that, despite these same sex experiences, I still would not call myself gay or even bisexual. But even by their late teens, many young Irish men still have no concept of the different forms of sexuality. And of course the instinct of self-denial is overwhelming in the circumstances.

So I very slowly began to accept that things might not reach my ideal state of marriage, babies and a house. But I was very afraid that liking other men would not be accepted in a society where you are taught that the only valid relationship is a monogamous, heterosexual, procreative one.

Both my parents worked in television and thus knew a lot of gay men who became friends of theirs — so I knew that my parents would be open and would accept people of a different persuasion. At the time I did not know which of my parents' friends were gay, but as I got older they told me. I was quite surprised about some of them.

As time went on I was becoming very unhappy within myself. By this time I knew that I was gay and felt I had to do something about it — which I was dreading — but I hoped there would be a huge relief if I told someone. I have always had a good relationship with my mum and dad, so the obvious place to start was with them. But I felt I had to come out to myself so as to feel comfortable in telling them. I also felt that once I told them, there was no going back into the closet. The act of telling them confirmed my sexuality. I had to pluck up the courage to tell them. I had been seeing a guy for a brief period, so that made it a bit easier.

I was in the kitchen where most of my chats with my parents take place. I told my mum on her own — it just came out. I said to her, 'I think I might be gay'. I told her I was sort of seeing a man. Her first response was to ask if I was being careful. Then she said, 'You are my son, and no matter what, I will still love you.' I felt a big weight lifting off my shoulders and began to feel I could start to live my gay life. Shortly afterwards I came out to my sister, whose reaction was, 'I knew that already.' When I asked how she knew she said she just 'knew' but that it did not change anything between us.

I knew at the start that it was going to be difficult for me, because as life went on I would have to tell people eventually that I was gay. Mum also advised me to contact a helpline she knew about called the Gay Switchboard, to see if they could give me any advice. Dad came into the kitchen, and I told him too. I had been dreading that more because I expected he would find it much harder to accept that I was gay and that he wouldn't be having any grandchildren from the male side of the family.

On the same evening I found the courage to ring the Switchboard. I was very nervous about telling some stranger that I might be gay. I spoke to them; they asked me a few questions; they told me about the various social groups that they run or liaise with. They mentioned in particular a group called Icebreakers, which tries to help people on their first venture onto the gay scene.

I remember clearly the night I went to the Icebreakers meeting. I was extremely anxious because again it involved facing up to the reality of my being gay but more so because it was the first gay event I had ever attended. Looking back on it, it was great. I met other gay people and after the meeting went to a gay pub. We all got on very well, exchanged phone numbers and met up over the subsequent weekends. It was there that I met my first serious partner. The relationship lasted seven years with a couple of breaks.

This first relationship fulfilled many of my hopes about living long-term with a partner. I always had hopes of waking up in bed beside my partner and the idea of us getting our own apartment. He moved from a rural part of Ireland, and I moved out from my family home, which was a very exciting and bold step for me. I very much enjoyed living with my partner in our new rented apartment. For the first few years we did everything together. We both had the same ideas about life: he was a friend as well as my partner. But sadly the relationship ended for many reasons — one being that we no longer wanted the same things in life. It took me the best part of two years to get over the break-up, and it knocked my confidence. But ultimately the split was good for me: it got me out meeting other people again.

I am now content with my sexuality and would even be reluctant to change it, if given the choice. The only real gap in my life is that I will not have any children — but as well as two lovely nieces I have a wonderful godson who is the nearest I will ever have to my own son. I have had ten years of being out to friends and family. Whether gay or straight, you have many ups and downs in love. Monogamy is very important to me, but as I get older, looking at gay men and at the gay scene, I find this increasingly unrealistic. I know few gay friends who are in long-term, fully monogamous relationships.

Many people, including psychoanalysts, have tried to explain why gay relationships are relatively short-lived and why the level of promiscuity is higher than among straight men. Clearly, the reasons include the lack of the traditional family model — stay-at-home wife, children, resultant reduced socialising, the possibility of a Church- or state-recognised union, respect for Church teachings, etc. Also, gay men since childhood are generally used to hiding their sexuality and being secretive about their sexual encounters — so even when they are completely 'out', they are still in the habit of being furtive. And the feeling of guilt and low sexual self-esteem induced by societal disapproval may reduce the relative stigma of 'cheating'. In my opinion, another factor could be simply the fact that gay relationships are male-male and are unconstrained by the higher expectation or instinct for monogamy that females may possess.

I still live in hope that I will meet my ideal partner who will have the same values as myself, including monogamy. I believe that, as gay couples integrate more into society and become more socially integrated with straight couples, the values of the groups will converge. This needs to be supported by true social and legislative equality for gay relationships, including weddings or blessings, inheritance and financial rights and so on.

out of the cold i have called my son

Fr Brian

'**S**O THAT'S WHY you treated all my girl friends as if they were your sisters!' That was the immediate response of one of my sisters when I told her I was gay. Her comment brought me back to my puzzlement as a young boy. The girls in my street seemed to really enjoy what seemed to me to be rough treatment by the boys. I recognised that there was some energy between the boys and the girls that was lacking in me. And as I moved into adolescence I was confused at how excited many of my peers would get if they got a glimpse of a scantily clad woman. And then with some women I sensed that they were looking for some response from me, which I just did not seem to possess. It wasn't until my twenties and especially my thirties that I really was ready to accept what the difference was about, but the wondering had begun in a little boy of five or six!

In secondary school during my first year I fell in love with Joe, a second year student. I was conscious of the fact that he was a bit of a bully and I was confused as to why I still enjoyed being with him. He never bullied me. We conspired to be in one another's company and he taught me how to write on parchment in an Italic style. We never spoke of our attraction nor did we ever touch. Going home after the first term, one of his classmates said he had a message for me from Joe. He told me that Joe wanted to kiss me. In my family we all kissed one another regularly so kissing wasn't unusual for me. But Joe wasn't family and so I asked his classmate: 'Why does he want to kiss me?' This was met with awkward silence and a red face! I really did not get it! However, during the holidays

I must have been talking about Joe non-stop because I got a little speech from my older brother about boarding schools and boys being cut off from the company of girls. Joe was expelled at the end of the second term.

Thirty years later I hoped he'd turn up at a reunion. I now understood the attraction and was interested to meet him and see what he was like. He didn't turn up. But one of his classmates brought old photographs. One of them was of Joe. I didn't recognise him and asked who he was. Looking back over those thirty years I could well imagine how I fell for him. I would have been thirteen and he would have been a year older. No doubt he stole my young heart as I did his! I regret that I was so unaware and afraid of the nature of our attraction.

It was to take me many years before I was able to say with deep peace and acceptance that I am a gay man. I was very frozen around sexuality. It was not even part of my awareness of self. Sexuality was bad, dirty and dangerous. It was best to stay completely clear of it. The less sexual you were, the holier you could be and the less danger you were in of going to hell. And all of that without much of a sense whatsoever concretely of what sex was really about at all! To admit that I was a sexual being took many years. I was already ordained some years. I had an intellectual knowledge obviously before that, but now sexuality entered into my sense of self, into my sense of identity. And after that struggle it took some more years of fear, anxiety, confusion, prayer, soul searching, spiritual direction, therapy, and experimentation before I could say with the deepest of conviction and peace that I am gay.

Looking back over the seminary years I believe now that I was living out of a very false self. This was not all due to being gay. I just did not have the inner freedom — or outer freedom either — to be myself. I was just a very good, super-responsible, pious, friendly student. I mixed but never got that close to anyone. I kept the rules but realised that I did so more because I would be too uncomfortable to break them. Even then I realised that it wasn't virtue that drove me. I recognised that while others might have considered me to be very good, I knew that fear of disapproval played a major part in my being 'good'. I seemed to be liked by my family, neighbours, classmates and my fellow students and the staff in the seminary. I never understood why. It always came as a bit of a surprise. I never had any intimate friendship with any of the seminarians, either emotionally or sexually, but was becoming aware of a great rush of energy and enjoyment in the presence of certain individuals. I was still not able to admit that I had a crush on some of them. I was afraid to fully let myself know. But a friendly touch, a smile, a word of friendship from one of these students would nourish me for months and even years! The enjoyment, however, would always be conflicted. I would be suspicious that there might be something sinful about it, something wrong. I was becoming aware that there probably was some sexual component to such attraction and I had not figured out then that this is the way God made us!

I attempted to talk about my attractions, my awareness of sexuality, and my questions about celibacy with different priests during my seminary years. They were all good men but rather unhelpful. I wasn't able to be very frank, because I was only beginning to thaw out, and they did not seem very comfortable talking about relationships, intimacy and sexuality. None of them seemed at all able to hear my tentative questions about the possibility of being gay. About two years after ordination, while on retreat, I talked to one of the priests in a retreat house. It took a great deal of effort and even courage to tell him that more and more I was wondering was I gay, although the word I would have used then was the more clinical and cold word 'homosexual'. He listened carefully and without any evidence of judgement or rejection. That was important for me, as the dawning reality was very frightening for me. However, he told me that he knew almost nothing about homosexuality. And while that was a disappointment, over time I came to appreciate his honesty. Since then I've heard many people speak of homosexuality, including psychologists and Church people, who thought they knew what they were talking about and did not!

And then the Lord sent someone my way. They say that when the student is ready, the teacher will arrive! I was taking a week's holiday and met another priest on holiday. He asked me to go to a film with him. I was not that keen as I was tired but he seemed lonely so I agreed. On the way to the film he invited me to visit him in his nearby parish the following week. I accepted the invitation.

On the way into the film I noticed something in the way Tom looked at me and in the way he spoke to me. I couldn't quite understand it but I felt a mixture of joy and caution and fear all at once. I became so hyper alert that I could hardly follow the film. I was so conscious of this man sitting beside me. I noticed his every move, glance and word. I just had this sense that I had never sat beside someone in this way before in my life. Something came alive within me and at the same time I wanted to run away. At one stage he touched my hand. I both wanted his touch and wanted to push him away. I was very confused. A deep part of me could understand the attraction between us but another part of me wanted to deny everything. After the film neither of us spoke about the energy between us. Inside I was torn. I wanted to run. I wanted to say that I had changed my mind and would not visit him in his parish. I was literally shaking inside with anxiety and confusion and the newness of this experience. Another part of me did not want him to feel rejected, especially if he was gay because I had read that gay men experienced a lot of rejection in their lives. I was not aware of how deeply curious I really was. I saw him as different to me. It would take me years to realise that unconsciously I was identifying with him and was both attracted and repulsed by him.

We agreed to meet a few days later and have lunch and a swim before driving to his parish. I was again anxious and curious. Again there was this tension or energy at lunch. When I looked into his warm brown eyes, I felt a surge of energy and peace throughout my body. But it was all so strange and I felt so out of my depth. What is happening, I wondered? The swim was easier. The sea has always been a joy for me. And even when we played and touched, for me that was not unusual or charged, so I could relax more. I probably didn't let myself know at the time but my eyes were feasting on how great Tom looked. He had a naturally defined body and was comfortable in himself.

We travelled on to Tom's parish and stopped off at a school to celebrate mass. As we did so I was impressed with Tom's friendly way with the students. I liked the way he prayed. It was real, down to earth and honest. And at the same time I prayed for guidance. I prayed in my confusion: 'God, what are you doing in my life? Why is this happening? You know I am yours 100 per cent, so why are you allowing this?' I was annoyed at God for not protecting me, thinking God was a God of control and safety rather than a God of life. At the same time I prayed not to hurt or reject Tom and his liking for me. I asked God to guide me. I wasn't free enough to recognise even 5 per cent of my liking for Tom.

After Mass we cooked supper together. Tom was friendly and funny. I could only half enjoy, however, because I was so aware of being in new emotional territory. I was fairly sure Tom was attracted to me and did not know what I felt or what to do. I did not know whether to, or how to, talk about this directly with Tom. But Tom did speak before we went to sleep. Very directly he told me that he liked me, that he was attracted to me from the first time he set eyes on me, that he couldn't get me out of his mind, and that he wanted to be my friend. Much of what Tom said I probably longed to hear, but it was too much for me and I could only respond in a very heady sort of way. Then Tom asked me could he hug me before we went to our beds. I agreed. But the hug was different from anything I'd experienced before. It was like arriving home after a long, long journey. It was like being flooded with energy or excitement. It was like being called out of a tomb and, like Lazarus, being unbound. Most of this, however, I could only acknowledge years later. At the time it was all rather a shock to my system. It was an experience of pleasure and joy and acceptance and even love that I would bury for many years to come. Buried but never fully forgotten.

Tom ended the long hug with a kiss. The kiss was so explosive for me that I stepped away from him and called a halt. That was going too far. Especially that kind of kiss.

The next day I gave Tom a lecture about homosexuality and how wrong it was. I had had a very tormented sleep and had distanced myself from what had happened. I was now blaming Tom for the attraction, the hug, the kiss, and the words of affection. He took my lecture with equanimity! Maybe his journey towards acceptance of himself and his acceptance of his own way of loving helped him to understand my turmoil and denial. I had a number of years to go before I could admit that I was lecturing myself as well as him! Now I thank God for having had such a good introduction to the beauty, power, strength, warmth and awesomeness of a man's body. I am grateful now for Tom, for his brown eyes, his affection, his playfulness, his courage and compassion. I am grateful that Tom was a gay man and a person of deep faith in God. The years after meeting Tom were years of conflict, guilt and shame, but these gradually were to lose their power over me. Initially I persuaded myself that those days with Tom were not at all about me and my sexuality. Gradually this lie gave way to a beginning trust that God was present in whatever was my sexual orientation.

And so I set out on a journey. I had a deep, deep hunger for self-knowledge and self-understanding. I had a deep desire to face and accept the truth, wherever that led and however frightened I might be. I read voraciously anything that would help me to understand myself and especially my sexual self. I had picked up beliefs that homosexuality was the result of arrested human development and that it was a flight from our attraction to women. I dug deep and could find nothing to support these beliefs. But I kept looking for years before I concluded that these beliefs were, for me, lies. More and more I began to participate in retreats and seminars for gay men. I spent many years in psychotherapy with a great woman therapist and at the same time a lovely old priest as spiritual director. The question of my being gay regularly entered into these sessions, but so did so many other issues. These sessions were about living life fully in every area of my being. During these years I found a capacity to make friends, both among men and women, gay and straight. The intimacy I discovered with gay men was mostly about friendship, companionship and being relaxed with like-hearted companions. Especially in the company of gay friends I grew to accept that I was gay and came to like the gay man that I was. Some of the intimacy had a very strong physical component. I loved to hold and be held. I loved to give and receive a massage. People told me I was a natural at massage. And as I became more comfortable in and accepting of my own body I found many of my straight friends, male and female, seeking out one of my 'great hugs'! My body and my very skin craved touch and revelled in it. I felt more alive and nourished and balanced.

Over these years there were times when the intimacy became sexual. The genital involvement — however good in itself — was problematic for me. In general it pushed me to re-examine my Church's teaching on sexual intimacy. I grew up with the teaching that sex is for marriage. My own sexual experience made me question how adequate such a teaching is for heterosexual people, not to mention gays who don't even get acknowledged in such a norm or rule. But these sexual experiences also had me question seriously my priestly vow of celibacy.

I had at that time a passion to be faithful to God. I still have. I loved being a priest. I still do. While I knew many would disagree and some would — if they knew — be scandalised, and others would judge me, I came to the belief that I needed to be unfaithful to my vow of celibacy in order to find out who I really was and what God was calling me to. It wasn't that I was going to suddenly start seeking out lots of sexual experiences. No, but I needed to trust deep in my heart that having some sexual intimacies over the years was not contrary to truth and love in the eyes of God. This was a very lonely road. Almost everything and everyone was saying that this would be unfaithfulness, rationalisation, self-seeking, lust, etc. I did not start off this journey with a permissive attitude or a lax conscience. You can decide for yourself how I developed. I know I can fool myself and make mistakes. However, I think the way my conscience developed and my behaviour are more Gospel-based now than they ever were. I also came to the conclusion that if God is worth his salt, all this sex-negative and sex-restrictive talk in Church (and in society, however disguised) is making of sex a false god. In the overall plan of creation and daily life, sex is far from the central concern or value.

One day early on, after an experience of a friendship becoming sexual, I felt disturbed. I felt at the time as if I had betrayed friendship, God, priesthood, and my Church. I felt guilty and ashamed. And then a friend, David, phoned me. He asked me to come to the funeral Mass of his aunt, who'd killed herself. I said yes, because of our friendship. However, as I travelled to the church I felt terrible. I felt so unworthy to be dressed as a priest. Words like 'fraud', 'hypocrite' and 'Judas' echoed through my mind. It was going to be difficult to concelebrate when all I wanted to do was hide. But then I thought, 'What if the parish priest asks me to preside and preach?' I dreaded the thought. But that's what happened. And I agreed to help. I preached out of my own pain and darkness and invited the family and friends to leave this woman's suicide to the mercy and love of God. I also invited the congregation not to judge themselves for their own range of feelings and reactions in the face of such a death. I concluded by saying that the greatest tribute we could give to this woman was for each of us to live our lives as fully as possible.

As I journeyed home the accusing voices tried their chorus again. But something of what I'd preached to others I had also heard. But the deep belly-dread of guilt and shame were still active. I still felt unworthy. When I reached my room my answering machine was blinking. I listened to the message. It was David. He said: 'Brian, I have received many wonderful gifts in my life but the greatest I ever received was this morning when you did my aunt's funeral. You touched all our hearts. You brought deep healing and love to everyone. Thank you. You are a great priest. A great man. A very special friend.'

All I could do was burst out crying. I sobbed and sobbed for nearly an hour. And in the midst of the sobbing a question arose for me: 'Where was God most likely to be heard — in the voices of condemnation arising within me, or in David's message of support?' I began to sense which.

During these years I met quite a few gay priests. Some I did not like. The vast majority I had great respect for. Some had clearly come to a deep acceptance of themselves and some were only beginning to face their truth. Some were dating secretly. Some had had no sexual experience whatsoever. Some were in long-term relationships. Some had been in significant relationships and moved into deep friendships without sexual intimacy. Some were terrified of Church and of society and were living severely restricted lives, slaves of the acceptance/disapproval of others. All had something to teach me. What began to emerge for me, as the most important value I looked for in their lives, was how available they were for others, for ministry, for their parishes and for their religious communities. Availability is far more profound than whether or not one is sexually intimate or in a relationship. I find myself being unsure about what is best in terms of sexuality and sexual morality for gays and everyone else. But when it comes to priests and religious, the clearer value to me is whether or not this person is open to others, can touch and be touched by others, can be vulnerable and feel for the pain and brokenness of others, and can be courageous in challenging destructive behaviour in self, in society, and in church.

Having spent a good number of years discovering a lot of who I was, I decided that I needed to take time out before making a commitment to the future shape of my life. I moved away from active priestly ministry for a number of years. They were graced years. God sent me a number of boyfriends to open my heart, my mind, my body and my spirit. They were each unique, sometimes tough, but blessed teachers and friends. I now had greater freedom to explore life. I face my God every day and I will face my God one day in eternity. While my externals may not have been what the Church wanted or told me was the right way, I have very little doubt but that God has been with me every day of my journey, even when I messed up and was driven by fear or anxiety or self-seeking.

One day in a group of men and women to whom I had grown close and to whom I had come out, the facilitator asked me one of the most important questions of my life. He said to me: 'If you were free to choose right now, would you choose to be a gay or a straight man?' I waited for the response to arise from deep within me. I did not know what it would be. And then the simple answer came and I replied: 'I would choose to be gay because that is who I am.' That was an epiphany for me. I had finally come to choose to be as God had created me!

A lot of water has flowed under the bridge since that day! I have never found myself changing my answer, however. Thank God! Since then I have returned to ministry. My provincial and many of my fellow priests and brothers know that I am gay. I came out to my family, most of my friends, and when it seems right I come out when I think it is important to.

The most important person to come out to, to admit I was gay to, was myself. I've said already that this took years, but it was truly worth it! It is one of the rocks in the foundation of my life. During that time some close friends and fellow priests asked me about my sexual orientation. I went from saying that I wasn't sure, to saying, some years later, that it seemed more likely that I was gay rather than straight. Finally, when I decided there was no evidence whatsoever to the contrary, I said: 'I am gay.'

Once I reached this important statement, for me it was clear as day that I needed to tell my family. I wanted them to know this important part of me. But I absolutely dreaded telling my parents. Sex wasn't talked about in my home! Being gay...oh my God! But I felt I owed it to them and myself, and with the help of my counsellor and spiritual director I prepared and went home to come out. I asked Mam and Dad could I speak to them together. And when the three of us were together in the sitting room I told them: 'Mam and Dad, I have something important to tell you. I am a gay man.' Very little was said after that. We just all three hugged and cried for some minutes. My tears were partly relief at having revealed this truth to two of the most important people in my life. I couldn't begin to do justice to what this meant for Mam and Dad. Mam asked me not to tell the rest of the family. I hadn't anticipated this, but, probably against my better judgement, agreed to this at least for a year. My mother expressed her concerns for my health, especially since it was the early days of AIDS. She also showed her love for me and her acceptance. She did not show me much of her pain and anguish. A few hours later I was out doing some gardening and my dad came out and sat down beside me. He was a man of little formal education yet with a great heart and sense of humour. He addressed my coming out in his unique way. As I remember it now — fifteen years later — I still can feel the warm glow I felt then as he spoke. He said: 'Son, I can understand two men being best friends and always wanting to be together, seeing each other, talking and listening to each other. I can understand the love they'd have for each other and how they would want to sleep together and hold one another through the night. And that is alright as long as they don't waste any seed.' While Dad held to his traditional teaching, he was so big-hearted and wise in his acceptance and embrace of me, his gay son. It thrilled my heart and spirit!

And so I did not plan to tell my brothers and sisters for at least one year. I was going to keep my word to my mother. But I have a sister who asks unexpected questions! A few months after coming out to my parents I was visiting this sister. She asked me a question she asked over the years: 'Are you in love, yet?' This time she had hit the bull's eye! I was, and my face gave the game away. She wanted to know everything. And so I told her. The fact that I was in love with a man didn't seem to faze her for a minute. She was just so delighted that I had found the capacity within me to fall deeply in love! That evening she told her husband and their family, who all took it in their stride also. Then she went on to tell my other brothers and sisters. That annoyed me at first, but then I thought maybe I might have wanted her help to come out to them. And then to round things off my same sister phoned my parents to ask them why had they wanted to keep this important news a secret!

One of my sisters struggled with the news. She couldn't accept that I was gay. She wanted me to change. She sent me prayer cards and mass bouquets. Everything from her had the underlying message: return to the way you were. She could not realise that I was her gay brother from when

I came out of my mother's womb! This sister's husband had even greater difficulty in coping with my being gay. He had always been friendly beforehand. Now he cut off all contact, wouldn't talk to me, and even pulled away if I went to shake hands. It has taken them over ten years to come to some level of acceptance and comfort with what is not likely to change. My brothers were not as warm or as articulate as my father, but they seemed to move quickly to trust me and my self-knowledge and never backed away from me.

Word spreads and I often find priests, brothers, sisters, and parents and gay and lesbian couples contacting me and coming to talk about being gay. It is heartbreaking to come across the sense of isolation and worry many parents feel when they suspect or are told that their son or daughter is gay or lesbian. Often they don't know where to turn or whom they can trust. Most often they love their gay son or lesbian daughter and even value deeply the love and care they have been shown by them. While it is changing in places, they often tell me that their Church has prepared them so poorly to deal with this reality. Sometimes the parents want to try and protect their sons and daughters from the likely hurt and judgement they are likely to experience. It repeatedly strikes me as a scandal that parents in this situation often feel as if their Church, mainly in its official positions, has made a natural, loving and accepting response to their gay sons and daughters more difficult.

A couple of years ago I heard a Methodist minister give a talk on young people, their values and struggles. He described how after a lecture in a university a young man approached him. The young man said: 'I am a gay man. Would the doors of your church be open to someone like me?' The minister replied spontaneously: 'If not, my church should close down altogether because it would no longer be the Church of Christ.' The minister went on to talk of his own sons and daughters and how he would dread to think that if any of them were gay or lesbian that they would feel rejected by the very church he's given his life to serve. His words were good news to my ears! Imagine if one were to apply that standard to the churches, mosques, synagogues, temples, and their civic counterparts throughout the world! How many places of worship and of commerce would stay open?

Nothing of my past history — in its frozenness, guilt, shame, fear, crushes, intimacy, sexual exploration, lovers, dissent from Church teaching, anger at the Church and at society, fighting homophobia, and continuing to grow into being the man God made me — is ever wasted as I sit and listen to others. And the stories and struggles of others gives me lots of energy and courage to keep being true to myself and my way of loving, blessed by God. Many priests and religious, parents, families, friends and colleagues, together with a good number of bishops and cardinals (but usually unofficially) have looked into their own lives and found within them the capacity to understand and accept that being gay is the way many of us are called to live and love and follow God.

At this stage of my life I don't find myself drawn to have a lover. In the first few years after returning to active ministry there were times when I fell madly in love. A lot of soul searching went on each time. I came to the conclusion that I couldn't manage an intimate relationship and be really fully part of a religious community. I couldn't be fair to either and would have a divided heart. Not that I believe there is any contradiction between being in ministry and being in a loving relationship. Hopefully one day this blessed change will come about in the Church! So there hasn't been anybody 'special' in my life now for over ten years. Thank God though there are lots of very good friends whom I deeply love. Sexual intimacy is not what I seek now in my life, but I still love a good hug and a massage. I really love the sensation of holding and being held, of touching and being touched. At times I long for it as dry land longs for rain. Some would probably see even this as contrary to celibacy. I think they are wrong, but again walking such a path can be lonely. Many would find my desire to touch and be held as a prelude to or cover for sex. I have come across this attitude widely, in church, in the media, which is supposed to be liberal, and in some of the gay community. I think it is overly suspicious and narrow.

I also wonder from time to time whether or not I should come out more publicly. There have been times when I completely disagree with what the Church is officially saying and I would love to say in public: 'What is the basis for your saying this? Is this the truth of experience or the lies of prejudice and a seriously faulty and outdated sense of God's gift of sexuality and relationship?' At present I have the idea that if I were to come out I might suffer a rather strong reaction from the Church authorities. I am not sure how able I would be to cope with that. I have a lot of strength but I am not superman. I pray that if this is what God is calling me to do, then he will show me the way and give me the courage to do what he wants. In the meantime, in my preaching and all kinds of ministry I speak of gay and lesbian love as much as I do of 'straight' or heterosexual love. Maybe the day will come when I need to go further and take a greater risk.

As I conclude, I am feeling a sense of gratitude for the opportunity of writing this short account. I regret that I am not free to sign my name but I hope something of what I describe may help others not to feel so alone or wrong. I remember the first time I picked up *Embracing the Exile* by John Fortunato and read about gay Christian men and my heart leaped for joy! And then I faced into John McNeill's *The Church and the Homosexual,* which helped me begin to form a radical critique of my Church's approach to gays and lesbians. Those writers were liberators. We need gay and lesbian truth to be told. The risk factor for young males killing themselves in Ireland increases when they are gay. In other words, for all its advances Ireland has still a long way to go before our Churches and our communities rid themselves of homophobia and cherish our gays and lesbians.

I am not perfect and have not figured out all the answers. I have strengths and weaknesses. I struggle with the typical dynamics of minority groups who set a higher standard for members of their group than for the majority. I know that some gays and lesbians see gay priests as living a lie. I know that many Church authorities would be happy to throw me out of ministry. All I can do is try to live and love and be as truthful to self as I know how and as I have the courage to be. I am God's son and He has called his gay son in out of the cold!

my teenage friend coming out to me

Peter James

I HAVE ALWAYS BEEN grateful that I met a gay man for the first time when I was young and impressionable. It's almost thirty years since one of my best friends told me that he was gay. We were in our late teens. Liam made his announcement to my brother and me, as we sat around the kitchen table. We had just come back from the pub. We knew something was troubling him. It was ages before he plucked up the courage and blurted it out.

'I'm queer, gay, a fairy, a homo!'

Initially, we were stunned. Neither one of us thought that we knew any homosexuals. In our innocence, we thought that they existed only in jokes or in British TV sitcoms. It had never once occurred to us that someone we knew, let alone one of our best friends, could be gay.

Liam informed us that earlier in the pub, while we were searching for talent among the girls, he was ogling the young men. He hastened to assure us that he didn't fancy either of us!

Even though Liam was quite effeminate in his mannerisms and had a nickname in school that reflected this, it had never crossed our minds that he was gay. He had had girlfriends and this compounded our puzzlement. He did not seem to fit in with the image of 'queer' that we had. He was far more popular with girls than we were and we were always jealous of his easy manner with them.

That night, we spent hours well into the night listening to Liam and learning what it was like for him to be different.

Now that I knew a real live queer, my perspective changed

completely. Homophobic jokes weren't funny anymore.

At that time, Liam was only beginning to come to terms with his sexuality. He found the pressure of living a secret life too much. A year later, he moved to England, where he felt he could be himself.

I know people who are caring, kind and enlightened, except in their attitude to homosexuality. Almost invariably, they don't have friends who are gay. Is this the cause or the result of their of their prejudice?

Who knows what my attitude today would be if Liam had not confided to us that night. His story formed me in a positive way before stereotypes had a chance to take hold.

my grandmother, god and i

Leah Bools

I WAS SUITABLY HOLY when I was in school. I joined prayer groups, enjoyed the masses we had, liked and admired the nuns who taught us. How was I to know that this was more a comment on my to-be-discovered 'lifestyle' than an attraction to the world of vocations? I enjoyed wonderful and close companionship and discovered the nature of friendship as a result of the world that my school life nurtured.

My difficulty with the Church, Catholic as it happens, began when I was in sixth year and we invited a couple of Mormons in to talk to us about themselves. In truth all we wanted to know was why they didn't drink tea and could they really have more than one wife. Unbeknownst to us our principal was embroiled in 'talks' with the bishop regarding the removal of the Dutch Catechism from the classroom. My understanding is that she didn't particularly want to comply but that old vow of obedience was going to get her one way or the other.

Enter two very smartly ironed and charming Mormons to be met in the front hall, in one of those unbelievable coincidences, by the two local curates. Of course all Catholic hell broke loose and, following incredible military dances involving a multitude of students being manoeuvred around, we were thrown into a room to be cleansed. Being head girl (mentioned to help confirm the Lesbian Theory on same) I was heavily involved and complicit in having to 'get rid of them'. The two boys were perfectly charming and as we sipped orange juice on the way to the front door I recognised both true faith and dignity. As an aside: Book of Mormon — one, Dutch Catechism — nil.

For me this episode was the beginning of some serious questioning and indeed the awareness of my lack of respect for an institution that was blatantly unchristian. It was too strange and probably too radical for me at the time to turn away from the Church, but I quietly no longer accepted the hierarchical set-up and began to deal directly with God.

My grandmother, who came to live with us when she was well into her eighties, facilitated this path. Grandma had raised a family of six children and my mother was the youngest. I'm not sure that I could ever effectively describe the presence that the woman had, but a measure of her demeanour is to say that my mother remembers only one 'fight' in her home ever and that was two siblings arguing over a cherished wooden coat hanger.

Calm gently plunged itself into my life by virtue of the fact that some things were going to have to be taken a little more slowly. The walk to mass now took three quarters of an hour instead of ten minutes and in that time I had no choice but to relax and enjoy the scenery. There were never great philosophical discussions between us but rather a curious innocence in wondering would God smite the woman who had worn an off-the-shoulder dress up to communion?

We had a number of years of this wonderful journey before I became a minister of eucharist — as Grandma was no longer able to leave the house I brought communion to her every Sunday and at Christmas and Easter. Against this seeming duty and regular Mass attendance I was having difficulty finding my own place in the church, being doubly afflicted as woman and lesbian. I am now at the stage where I am not at all bound by indoctrination but can still enjoy a good funeral.

I was lucky though in not having to become too agitated about the whole issue. When I felt like I was on the outside looking in I simply returned to a world of calm and of 'something' else where I had no choice but to relax and pray. This was not a chore by any means. I eventually began to realise that this something else was the presence of God and the instrument — to be clichéd about it — was now a 99-year-old woman who simply believed. That was all it took and I was lucky to have caught onto the hem of her skirt.

Grandma died with the sound of women's laughter ringing around her bedroom — this is a whole other story in itself but it was a suitably appropriate passing. Her funeral was for me a strangely uplifting and happy occasion. I now understood what the waiting was all about and the fact that I was bawling throughout belied the inner belief that she at least was heading in the right direction. Grandma will have spoken to St Peter and in her gentle way will have convinced him that, despite the fact that I love women and have 'sinned', I will meet God.

two ordinary lives

Seán

T HIS IS A story of ordinariness, of two very ordinary (some would say boring) men, working in public service occupations, living in the suburbs and loving one another. It also seems an extraordinary story of a journey and of a life that would have seemed impossible to me twenty-five years ago. I write it in honour of those countless ordinary gay men and lesbian women, your brothers, sisters, colleagues and neighbours.

I was born in rural Ireland in the 1950s. I remember one day before I started school feeling very strongly attracted to a man who was a neighbour. I remember on my first day in school I really wanted to touch one of the bigger boys who was in first class. At fourteen I felt a really powerful attraction to a man. It was many months later that I first read an explanation of the word 'homosexual'. What a relief! I was not the only one in the world.

Who do you talk to about being homosexual (the word 'gay' hadn't yet reached my part of the country) when you are fourteen, fifteen or sixteen years old and Catholic in rural Ireland around 1970? You go to confession! Most priests were kind enough to listen, even though none gave any helpful guidance. However, one priest told me he was widely travelled, had worked in New Zealand and had known of a homosexual who had ended up stabbed in the hold of a ship. I wonder did that reflect on New Zealand, on gay people or on the shipping industry? I can laugh about it now but at the time it hurt a lot. At one stage I contemplated suicide — such a feeling of isolation and alienation when all around me the only norm (or even the only possibility) was to get a girlfriend. And what if people found out?

At eighteen, in desperation, I wrote to Angela McNamara who had a 'Problem Page' in the *Sunday Press* newspaper. She put me in touch with a very understanding Redemptorist priest. It was a great relief to talk to someone face to face. But the 'problem' remained. I went to the dances — danced with the girls and looked at the men. I dated some girls. The prohibition on any kind of genital contact was a great cover. Sure you can kiss anyone if you put your mind to it!

At twenty-two I made contact again with this Redemptorist priest. He led me, as gently as he could, to an acceptance that I would not be getting married, that I would be a gay man all my life. He advised me to stop trying to have relationships with girls. He said I could have a better camera and better holidays than everyone else if I was not going to be married and have those kinds of financial commitments! It sounds both awkward and funny now. But it was delivered with kindness and it was a huge relief.

My relief was soon followed by a sense of loss and loneliness that was physical in its intensity at times. I now know that I was going through bereavement. Gone were the accepted expectations of marriage, children and the bungalow down the road (the ultimate aspiration in 1970s Ireland). Would my life always be one of being totally alone, cut off from my family and friends by their not knowing the real me? I was so afraid of the ridicule and rejection that I felt would follow if I revealed who I really was.

Age twenty-three. I write my pain to Angela McNamara again. By return of post she tells me of a day retreat for gay men and lesbians. The following Sunday, 1 October 1978, I lie to my mother, telling her I am going to a trade union meeting in Dublin. I arrive in a room full of people. It's scary. I hold my nerve. People don't have two heads. Some of them even talk to me. People listen and share experiences and stories. They are so ordinary really! By the end of the day I have made friends with a guy of my own age who has remained a good friend ever since. He told me all there was to know of gay venues in Dublin. I started to come up some weekends. I spent vast amounts of time in Rice's, Bartley Dunne's and the Hirschfeld Centre.

My mother had heard on the *Gay Byrne Radio Show* about the opening of the Hirschfeld Centre, its discos and the fact that dozens of people came up regularly from the country to attend. She asked me if I had a problem. I knew what was coming. I asked her what she meant and persisted with my stonewalling until she was forced to ask 'Are you homosexual?' I know I can't lie. I say 'Yes'. I add 'I am in a relationship which is very good, so please don't ask me to end it because I am not going to.' She runs over, hugs me, tells me she wouldn't dream of asking me to end it, cries and asks for forgiveness for being so bad a mother that I felt unable to tell her.

My mother was quite upset though. She didn't sleep that night. When I got home from work next evening my brother and his wife were very worried. My mother had stayed in bed all day. I insisted on taking her to her doctor. He listened sympathetically, advising her to tell my sister (who has proved to be very supportive to me ever since) but not to tell my brother and his wife. Mother and I lived with them and he was afraid they might react badly. The doctor prescribed valium for her and suggested a local psychiatrist as the only one he could think of who might be able to help me with 'the problem'. I went to the psychiatrist to please her, but we both knew in our hearts that it was a waste of effort. She learnt to live with having a gay son and was very supportive and protective. When my relationship ended she was sympathetic, and talking of it to her was a great help. A couple of years later, when she was dying, she rubbed my hand one day, saying 'poor Sean'. I asked her why she said that. She said she felt afraid that I would have a lonely life. I do so wish she had lived to see me in this long-term relationship, and to get to know her wonderful son-in-law, Colm.

That first relationship ended after a short time. Two hundred and forty miles proved to be an insurmountable obstacle. We still exchange Christmas cards. I went to the gay bars and discos whenever I could get to Dublin. Through Dublin contacts I made some gay friends near where I lived. After some time I became tired of the bars and discos. I am not a pub person; I dislike smoke and loud music. I decided that I would have things in my life other than looking for a man. If one came along though that would be great! I developed some close friendships with both gay and straight people to whom I felt able to 'come out'. I continued, and still do, in the gay Christian group I had encountered on that first retreat. It is nowadays called Reach. It is a good space where people can relate to their god (whatever way they perceive god) and still be who they really are.

On 31 December 1983 I met Colm. I was spending New Year's Eve with a friend. Colm was also a friend of his. He had heard of me as being a member of the gay Christian group and thought that as a Christian I might be worth getting to know. We were attracted. The next day, An Post, to mark its becoming a semi-state commercial company, was offering postage for one penny. To cover my shyness I used the penny post as a joke excuse to write to him, saying it would be nice to meet him again some time. Our letters crossed in the post. What a thrill! And so began a relationship that is still going strong after nineteen years.

After knowing Colm for six months his work brought him to my part of the country. By now I had my own house and he moved in. After another year and a half we both moved to Dublin for reasons of our work/training. I also felt that as his widowed mother lived alone in Dublin, and as my parents were both dead, that our relationship probably stood a better chance if he could visit and look after his mother easily.

We lived in rented houses for the first few years in Dublin. We were quite tentative with neighbours, with Colm's family and with others such as work colleagues. There were the things left unsaid — what I sometimes think of as lying by silence or by implication. We hid the Christmas cards that were addressed to both of us. We had some very fraught patches in our relationship due to this lack of openness. An example was one Christmas when I felt I was being dispatched down the country as he felt unable to suggest to his mother and sister that we both spent Christmas with them, and yet he felt he had a duty to be with them. But we weathered the storm. We love each other dearly.

Slowly, tentatively, we made changes. I was included at Christmas and at his mother's seventieth and then eightieth birthday parties. I was invited to the homes of some of his relatives. His sister read the one giveaway Christmas card we forgot to hide. She was fine. We have since attended her wedding together, with Colm 'giving her away' and later becoming the godfather of his niece. We visited my family together occasionally. We found ourselves beside my sister and her husband in the front pew at their son's wedding a few years ago. I had come out to my brother shortly after my mother died and he was really accepting and pleased that I had told him. Country people should definitely not be typecast as conservative. My sister-in-law thrust her young children on me, and on us, as convenience dictated. They came to stay with us many times, and still do, now in their teens. We took Colm's mother on holiday to various rented houses. Mind you, she always got the double bed while we had the singles or even the bunks. Some instinct always led us not to talk about being gay or our 'coupleness' to her. Maybe one senses that some people are better suited to a gradual dawning of unspoken recognition. And recognition has come! By now she has acknowledged implicitly our de facto relationship, e.g. in matters of domesticity, holidays, etc. We get on well. She even tries to influence her son through me — presently thinking aloud to me that our house would be greatly improved by a conservatory!

When we moved to our present house we met a married couple with two young sons who had moved in next door only a few weeks beforehand. We knew someone they knew. This link, and their friendliness, made life great. They invited us in for a drink and a chat along with other neighbours at Christmas. As it happens, this gathering consists mainly of couples, including Colm and myself. It has become an annual event. Through this connection we have been invited to other people's homes, birthday parties, etc. And we have of course returned their hospitality. We have truly become the suburban couple! Recently the teenage son next door invited us to his table quiz in aid of the Scouts. We attended, but our team didn't win!

About eleven or twelve years ago, having been a weekly Mass-goer all my life, I heard a sermon in my local church that I considered to be sectarian. I wrote to the priest in protest. When I got no reply I felt very angry. Perhaps I was also carrying anger from years of feeling truly connected only to the unofficial (some might say underground) part of the Roman Catholic Church. I felt my anger was so negative and was coming between God and me. Having been brought up in a home that had particular respect for our one neighbouring family, which was Quaker, it seemed like a natural step to try Quakerism. This particular branch of Christianity had, in my experience, a reputation for truth and openness. I was not disappointed. A lot follows from truthfulness. Most

Quakers I know, now numbering hundreds, instinctively seem to realise that you cannot aspire to truthfulness without being prepared to accept the truth of people's lives and of their individual journeys towards God. When I had been attending Quaker worship for a couple of years, Colm decided to come along too. I recall one lovely occasion. We always seemed to sit in front of a very elderly couple. The wife had failing sight. One Sunday, because of a task I had to do, I sat separate from Colm. When worship ended the elderly woman leaned forward and asked 'Where's Sean?' He explained that I was present but sitting near the door. She said 'Oh, that's all right, then. I was afraid you had got divorced.' Our experience of love and acceptance within Quakers has strengthened our relationship greatly.

In reflecting on our life together I think there are two themes that reflect the sort of people we are and the journey we are on. We have taken a gentle pace with other people — taking time to get to know them and letting the fact that we are a gay couple seep into their consciousness before ever getting to explicit mention. In return we are accepted. Presumably, having discovered our similarities to themselves first, people are not overly frightened or embarrassed if our sexual orientation is different to their own and thus feel they can continue friendships with us. The result of this is a social support system that strengthens and supports our relationship. People ask 'How is Colm?' / 'How is Sean?' Neither of us feels that the other's presence in our lives is something to be embarrassed about. In contrast to what some gay couples experience, the social pressure that exists for us is to stay together, to be a couple. And just like married couples the social climate can be either a negative or positive influence. It can encourage or discourage a relationship. For us it is encouraging. Social support is important in helping any relationship. I thank God for it, and for the blessing of having Colm in my life.

While many people nowadays feel able to establish same sex relationships, I believe that the continuation in our legal codes of the notion that same sex relationships are of no value and do not need recognition is damaging to society and to individuals. Actions really do speak louder than words and the state is making a very strong statement by its continuing unfavourable treatment of gay and lesbian relationships. It sets a very poor example to people whose behaviour its anti-discrimination and equality legislation seeks to change. Heterosexual marriages and parent-child relationships are given protection and status by legislation. People in gay/lesbian relationships need and deserve these too. The absence of this type of equality of treatment continues to drive relationships underground, into the furtiveness and denial that works to strongly discourage commitment, security, permanence and thus social stability. In 2003 an Inter-Departmental Committee on Reform of Marriage Law was inviting submissions. I will finish with the submission I made.

Submission to Inter-Departmental Committee on Reform of Marriage Law

March 2003

Subject:: Gay Relationships Need Fair Treatment

Having lived with my partner since 1 July 1984 I feel acutely the unfairness of the law as it applies to us. As a couple (in public service occupations) we are part of a family, neighbourhood, religious, occupational and voluntary work network where we are acknowledged as a couple (joint invitations, etc.). However, in several important areas the existence of our relationship and home together over almost nineteen years is dismissed as being without value. Fortunately I now have the maturity that comes with age and years of patient struggle to be able to live with this.

Our existing equality and anti-discrimination legislation would have more moral credibility and would thus be more effective if the general legislative framework supported this aim by example. At the moment the areas of discrimination that exist in law serve to undermine, by bad example, the equality that these anti-discrimination laws were designed to ensure. The discriminating legislation is experienced by people as a justification for negative attitudes and treatment of the significant minority of gay people in the state. People who wish to discriminate against gay people use the legal situation as justification for their behaviour. The decriminalisation of male gay relationships, a laudable move by minister Maire Geoghan-Quinn in her day, went only some of the way to redress abuse of rights.

Even today too many people live lives of quiet desperation. I believe that a considerable number of young male suicides are due to inability to come to terms with the pariah status that our legislation seems to confirm. It is hard to be different. It is harder still to have that difference confirmed as inferior status by the law. Still today young people, because of fear of a stigma reinforced by our laws, enter into heterosexual marriages, thereby causing years of unhappiness and pain to themselves, their spouses and children. Still today people live furtive lives and engage in serial short-term and destructive relationships in order to avoid the visibility as a gay man or as a lesbian which commitment to a long-term relationship brings.

If you are a heterosexual reader of this submission you may think of 'out' gay people like Peter Mandelson and be tempted to dismiss what I say. Please try to imagine what it would be like if heterosexual marriage had no legal recognition and carried a social stigma. Would that be conducive to human contentment or happiness? Would driving large numbers of people underground in their relationships produce a healthy and well-ordered society?

The following are some practical examples which are pertinent to myself and my partner and which underline our inferior status and the inferior value of our relationship in legal terms.

1. Right of access to and information about partner: Total absence of legal right if he should become mentally incapable. Access and information would then be dependent on the goodwill of his legal next-of-kin.

2. Pensions: My pension prospects resulting from my public service occupation are considerably better than those of my partner. Despite having paid the compulsory widows and orphans portion of pension contribution, I will not be able to make pension provision in any way for my partner. His financial circumstances in retirement would become very difficult should I pre-decease him. In contrast, under the social welfare code cohabitation is taken into account in assessing entitlement for many benefits.

Meanwhile there is no entitlement such as a spouse would have regarding free travel, etc. Surely this is a double standard of present regulations.

3. Inheritance tax: Having bought our home jointly in 1989, and our present home in 1992, I find that I would be liable for inheritance tax on half the value of our home should my partner die. On a modest semi-detached house in the Dublin suburbs, which we bought for £80,000, this would now amount to about €47,000.

There is in existence a 'hardship clause' which eliminates this liability, but only on condition that the 'inheritor does not have an interest in any other residential property'. My own situation is that I inherited a small family house, which for family reasons I intend to keep. I am therefore ineligible under the 'hardship clause'.

This situation is in marked contrast to the situation of a married friend whose circumstances mirror my own. In addition there is a huge irony in the fact that had I inherited millions of euro or a large tract of land without a residential property I would still be able to avail of the 'hardship clause'.

4. Adoption: About ten years ago my brother and his wife were involved in a serious road traffic accident. As I had always been very close to them and their children, with frequent overnight visits, I was relied on heavily to care for the children. I realised then that had the parents died my relationship with the children could not be secured in law by adoption. Anyone who disapproved of my 'lifestyle' could have had those children removed from me by legal process.

5. Local authority housing: This concern is not personal to myself or my partner. For people whose only chance of security of tenure is in local authority housing they should be considered as a couple if they wish to be, including rights of succession to tenancy.

Summary Recommendation

In summary I ask for true equality of treatment. There are different models available among our fellow EU members regarding partnerships. These include both marriage and civil registration of partnerships. Registration of relationships, call it marriage if you wish, accompanied by true equality of partnership rights, would eliminate real and practical difficulties experienced by those of us who have the good fortune of having the family and social support and the personal courage to make it into the couple-hood experience. It would make a real difference in ending the type of furtiveness, unhappiness and tragedy I have described, giving many more people the opportunity to live in dignity and make a real contribution to Irish society.

It would also be a powerful signal of moral leadership by lawmakers.

I would gladly participate in any discussion or forum on this subject that you may consider it useful to organise.

Thank you for consideration of this submission.

Yours faithfully, etc.

mary, my daughter

Ann Dillon

MY DAUGHTER MARY was a proper little tomboy because a few years ago boys and girls here in a town in the south of Ireland would be forever playing together. But as she started her teen years I began to worry a little, especially when she wasn't taking much notice of her appearance by the time she was sixteen. She has three older sisters and Mary was totally different in that there was no experimenting with make-up, or no boyfriends mentioned. She did have friends but no special boyfriend even though at that age she was quite pretty. Then she started to get very quiet in herself, going to the church every day. I tried to cheer her up, asking her was she going to the church after the young little priest we had back then. The problem was, as I found out later, that she liked a girl in school but of course could not tell her.

Anyhow, I decided to send Mary to America to one of her brothers, for a holiday. That would do her the world of good. She told her brother and his wife, because she said she couldn't tell me; she said she tried to tell me a few times but she failed. It was just as well, because I would have tried to make her believe she was confused and making a mistake. I would only have made her more unhappy. So my son phoned my eldest daughter and she told the family, who all tried to explain it to me. So I borrowed the fare to America and off I went, to fix this problem as I and some of the family thought I could. But no, I'll always remember her waiting for me at the airport, my baby, my poor baby. I looked at her, brown as a berry and seventeen years old — I thought the pain in my heart would give me a heart attack. I've been a reader all my life since I was eight years old and I knew from all these books I've read that life would not be easy for Mary.

She returned to our town after a few weeks and I took her to an expensive qualified doctor counsellor, who had done a course in homosexuality in America. But after an hour with Mary she told me that about five out of a hundred would be making a mistake about their personal sexual life and that in her opinion Mary was not wrong. She said Mary knew for years she was different, God love her. She was seventeen and had spent those lonely years. I hated myself because she felt she could not talk to me. Anyhow, her father cried when my daughter Angela told him. But a few weeks later when we were at a wedding he took Mary out dancing and gradually they have gone back to their old relationship.

Even though Mary has been asked to leave at least three premises in the town because she is homosexual, she still had the courage to go on the radio here in our local radio station. She was the first person to 'come out' in the town and for a long time some of the girls who went to school with her would not speak to her, but gradually things have got a little better here, quite a few people have 'come out'. But I am quite proud to say that Mary was the first and in a town like ours that took courage. I myself have always believed that to face the problem shrinks it a little.

People will say it take all sorts to make the world so why don't they stand by this and live and let live. Forty years ago when I was young if a girl had a baby she was an 'outcast'. Now it is totally accepted because everybody's daughter is either an unmarried mother or in danger of becoming one. So I think it is best to let everyone know in the most pleasant way that there are gays and lesbians in so many families now, either sons or daughters, or nephews or nieces. They are born that way and are just as beautiful and just as wonderful as the people we call 'normal'. That is one way of helping. Writing this story for you has helped me.

gay in the shadows

Patrick O'Brien

I N THE RECENT past, a number of psychologists and social theorists averred that homosexuality was not an innate characteristic of gay people but was 'acquired' due to social conditioning and 'questionable' forms of parenting. The pendulum has now swung more towards the idea of nature versus nurture and, of course, homosexuality is no longer considered a form of deviation from normality. However, I (and a lot of other gay people from my generation) can personally vouch, from the circumstances of our early lives, that homosexuality is definitely innate.

During my early years — indeed, in practical terms, right up to my early adulthood — positive images of a 'homosexual lifestyle' were barely visible in Ireland. From both the religious and social points of view, the practice of homosexuality in any form was considered anathema and the terms used to describe it (e.g. gross indecency or the peccatum nefandum) certainly did not make it seem attractive as a sexual orientation. Even when it was viewed in a non-pejorative way, homosexuality was imbued with an exotic, even dangerous mystique. However, because of the rigid censorship that then operated in the English-speaking world, positive images of homosexuality were few and far between.

Looking back on it now, my first memory of childhood is infused with a gay resonance. I can recall drawing pictures of girls wearing voluminous dresses. My father's reaction was: 'Don't be bold now! Boys don't do this.' About a year later, I was similarly taken to task for holding a cat in my arms and stroking it: 'Don't do that — it's not manly.' The importance of the inculcation of 'manly values' in the minds of their male children was a constant preoccupation for my parents, both of whom, having come from poor backgrounds, hankered after economic success and social respectability. In this context, any signs of a gay sensibility were considered anathema, although in most other ways my parents were good, kind and generous people: they were not religiously conservative and were in fact quite liberal as far as heterosexual relationships were concerned, even outside marriage. But their viewpoint on normality was strictly straight down the line, reminding me of a confessional observation I heard in a Gay Sweatshop production at the end of the 1970s: 'My parents were straight and when I say straight I mean straight as in lace, as in arrow, as in jacket.'

My father, by dint of sheer hard work and an astute commercial flair, eventually became quite a wealthy man. Although generous, often to a fault, towards the disadvantaged in society, he never relented in his abhorrence of homosexuality. (I have often thought that he inherited this attitude from his own rather stern Victorian father.) At any rate, homosexuality was always conjoined in his mind with weakness of character and a tendency towards criminality. Whenever he wished to cast doubt on someone's trustworthiness he would routinely and — I think — unthinkingly say that 'so and so was lazy, unreliable, light-fingered and probably homosexual as well'. My mother's viewpoint was also a homophobic one, but one that was based on the notion that most male homosexuals were also, potentially at least, pederasts. However, it must be taken into consideration that at that time homosexuality in the movies was still, as late as the 1970s, being tackled in a very narrowly stereotypical and often quite negative way. Harvey Fierstein maintains, in *The Celluloid Closet*, that any gay visibility in the movies is better than none at all. I would agree with this proposition but, nevertheless, there are some negative images of gay people in films that, even many years later, haunt me still.

I am not, of course, referring to the old comedy sketches that some people now find discriminatory and offensive. But comedy is, by its nature, not amenable to political correctness and I for one find the campy capers of Dick Emery (to name but one famous comedian) hilariously funny and oddly endearing. (I still recall one of his sketches when he tells a bespectacled interviewer that he calls his house 'Henry the Eighth Cottage' because six old queens live in it.) But the studied malignity with which the gay antagonist in a filmed thriller was invested — up to about twenty years ago — was often of a pruriently one-dimensional nature. Although I can't remember the name of the film (which I saw but once, about thirty years ago), I can well recall the details of a movie about criminal shenanigans in the British horse racing industry. It turns out, at the end, that the villain of the piece is in league with a younger man, who is also his boyfriend. This 'unnatural' relationship serves to blacken the villain's character even more.

The first twelve years of my life were spent in an urban suburb, in a street full of terraced houses. My parents led busy lives and we used to see the neighbours quite often. Even though I felt different from most other boys, I didn't stick out a mile back then. Nobody seemed to notice that I read Louisa May Alcott and that I fancied the hunky teenager in *The Waltons*. But all that changed when we moved out to the countryside at some considerable distance from neighbours. My parents gradually spent more time at home and began to be concerned by my eccentric behaviour. At the age of thirteen I was sent to a psychiatrist to be 'straightened out'. My parents assured me that visiting a psychiatrist was a normal part of growing up, but this psychiatrist told me that my parents asked him to 'cure' my 'effeminate' outlook on life. I was warned that 'to be neuter gender' was not a viable option in life. However, various attempts at aversion therapy proved ineffectual. I think my parents eventually became reconciled to the fact that I would always be different. However, my parents periodically, for several years afterwards, also used to say things like: 'You had better walk and talk in a more manly way, otherwise all the homosexuals of the county will be after you.'

During term time, six days a week, my younger brother and myself journeyed the ten miles to school. This system did not seem arduous to us and indeed I had more freedom of expression at school than elsewhere. I was always regarded as odd but I did make friends and most people treated me kindly. But how innocent I must have been in many ways! Nothing of an even vaguely sexual nature occurred to me while I was at school (although, I later found out, this was not the case with some of the other boys). It was not until I was seventeen that I finally admitted to myself that I was gay, although everyone else knew that I was. Looking back, it is the general invisibility of my gay contemporaries that strikes me now. I only found out years later that at least three of my classmates in school were also gay. It seems incredible, but in all of the houses that neighboured mine in that terraced street many years ago, there was at least one gay resident. As one friend recently said: 'There must have been something in the water!'

lesbian mums and their baby boy

Jay and Alex

PAUSING TO TAKE breath from clearing the attic — our four-month-old son is propped up on the bed watching the mayhem.

Where to begin — Jay told me she wanted a baby approximately one year after we started going out together. Not just a vague 'I'm thinking about...' but a definite proposal. I thought it was only six months into our relationship, but I 'lost' six months after my dad died, so that's how it felt. Today is the ninth anniversary of Dad's death. We started seeing each other the same year after he died in the March. I was thirty and Jay thirty-two. She said that she wanted a baby now because she had met me. That was great to hear, but a bit perplexing too as my feelings were in a whirl.

I can't remember exactly how I felt — Jay says I was 'pleased but then angry'. I felt it was too early in our relationship. We went to see a couple who had had a son by donor insemination and I remember feeling quite unhappy in their kitchen. I felt like I was being bounced into a decision. Jay, once she has decided to do something, takes steps to make it happen. I live with ideas if I'm not completely moved by them. Maybe we're not that dissimilar. I just wasn't so taken with the idea.

I had talked about having children with my previous partner, but I can't remember if we ever decided who would be the birth mother — maybe we hadn't got that far. Since coming out at the age of twenty-five I always thought I would be involved with children, but not as the birth mother. Probably by meeting someone who already had children.

Jay and I began by thinking of who we could ask to be a donor — Jay couldn't think of anyone — well she could, but the men she really wanted to be donors she didn't think she could ask. Partners of friends — men she liked. A friend of ours offered her partner — he said no. It was quite amusing. We talked a lot about donors. I remember sitting in my hairdresser's chair, he and I discussing the situation. He said he'd like to be a donor — in a non-specific way, i.e. he didn't offer to be our donor, but then maybe that's what he was doing! It was all very strange. I was quite shy about it all.

I never really considered having a baby at that stage, because it was so definitely Jay's thing — I can't really describe how much it was her thing, and I'm not being negative about that, just that it was.

After some time of this, we decided to use an unknown donor service, and did so for eighteen months. I remember how exciting it was every time she inseminated — and how disappointing when she failed to conceive. At first not so bad, but gradually quite wearing. Jay did not conceive — eventually she saw her doctor, who confirmed polycystic ovaries. She has very irregular periods, and the condition makes conceiving very difficult. I think this is when we decided to go to the NHS. Jay's doctor was brilliant — the practice paid for Jay to be treated with drugs to regularise her periods, and we paid for artificial insemination (intra-uterine insemination) for a further eighteen months. We were interviewed by a consultant for suitability, and I believe the unit had taken a vote on whether to treat lesbian couples or not. I remember that I wore a suit and that he addressed the entire interview to me — halfway through I turned my chair to face Jay so that he was forced to talk to her! I remember having to be quite brave about all this.

Those visits were very hard in some ways. Painful for Jay. And the monthly cycle of insemination and waiting, disappointment and anticipation was wearing. I feel tired and tearful thinking about it.

I feel quite guilty that I let Jay pay the £180.00 per treatment. That says something about my decreasing level of commitment. As the years went by, I really went off the idea of having a baby with Jay — I was angry with her for the situation. This may be a factor in why she decided not to proceed to IVF. But she also became very tired of the whole process, and felt ill with having her periods artificially controlled. She lost weight.

In the end she decided to stop. We went to a local authority adoption meeting. Babies, if available (which was rarely), were offered to straight couples under thirty (by now we were thirty-four and thirty-six). We had heard that lesbians could adopt children over eight, or sibling groups. We came away knowing that it was too soon for us to be thinking about adoption. It was a totally different thing.

We went to America for eight weeks, and I think that is when we decided to stop. We had a great holiday — so relaxing and adventurous.

Some time later, we were on a bus back from a weekend visiting friends in London, when I said 'let's go abroad — let's move'. To cut a long story short, and having looked at many options, we moved to Dublin. To get away from the town where we were going to raise a child. To get away from friends and their children. To get out of a rut.

Last August, we were in the car and I said 'I want to have a baby'. I'd been looking at toddlers and babies, and the phrase 'I want one' kept coming into my head. Very strong and passionate feelings — overwhelmingly so. Most unusual for me, I would have said. I think in some ways I am the one who 'carried the torch' over the three intervening years in Ireland — I think Jay was reconciled in many ways to us not having children, or maybe thinking about fostering or adoption in the future.

So we began to talk again. We put an advert into a lesbian and gay paper for donors. We asked a man — a new friend. I nearly asked one of my best and oldest gay friends — well, I did ask him in a roundabout way — I asked did he know of anyone, and he said 'no'. I wanted the man to be a friend, or at least the friend of a friend. This was going to be a lifetime commitment. Jay felt the same way. There was a factor, in that we are intending to move back to the UK, and this was a problem for most of the men we asked. They, of course, wanted continuing contact. We understood this. I was thirty-eight by now. We both wanted to start insemination soon and I was worried that it could take one or two years for me to conceive.

After six months of looking, we decided to once again go with an unknown donor and I conceived our son at the first attempt. He is beautiful and I have never felt so much love for another human being.

There is so much more I could say — about my experience of 'mothering', about our experiences as lesbian parents. Our families and friends. My feelings since the birth. Our relationship. This article is a snapshot in time, and a brief history. It by no means tells the whole story — that would take too long.

– Alex

****

I think I'll start by writing about the time since our son was born. We've received a huge amount of positive attention: loads of presents, offers of support, a real outpouring of what feels like love towards our child and so by implication towards us. This has been really special but I've often felt quite removed from it and like it's not really about me. I think part of me is still badly damaged by all the years of not being able to conceive. By the invisibility of that, particularly since as an infertile lesbian I belong to a not very well publicised sub-group. In fact I've never actually met anyone else of that description. So freak among freaks I'd feel on my bad days.

So my reactions to Alex announcing her intention to have a child and then very quickly, and apparently easily, producing the goods have always been mixed. I think I am mainly delighted, feeling very lucky. Certainly much luckier than straight women friends who on having found out they cannot conceive, have very few other options left whereas I had access to another whole womb.

It was a huge surprise to me when Alex said she wanted to try for a child. I'd been convinced, from everything she'd ever said, that pregnancy was not in her plans for herself. When she told me I felt terribly excited but then I cried as if my heart would break — what felt like ancient tears.

Since our son has been born I've continued to have wildly fluctuating reactions…veering from a quiet, pleased excitement to waves of anger, from shy pride to real panic. Sometimes I feel incredibly close to Alex and so lucky, sometimes I feel like the baby takes up a space in her life that used to be mine and I resent him (even though he is only four months old: I didn't say I would be rational here!).

I think some of the anger is around us trying to sort out our roles as parents. As one of my friends with grown-up children said to me: 'Oh dear, he's going to have two Mammies!' As a couple, we've always had great battles around certain areas like DIY (who can drill the best), gardening (my great love, part of her job), cooking (she follows recipes, I don't). So I had already thought we would have some good fights ahead of us in the new arena and was anticipating them with a wry smile. However, our conflicts have actually been both more frequent and more raw than I'd imagined. It would be interesting to know if this is the case for other same sex couples. And in fact we do have straight friends who have similarly fierce arguments so maybe it's just about wanting to be an involved parent (and being stroppy).

Anyway, enough angst. Let me write about the joys and realities now! I was trying to type with the baby on my knee because he was getting a bit bored but this does not improve creativity or lucidity so he's back in the baby gym. However, I know my time is now being grudged. This is one of my days to look after the baby: we do half the week each. It is fun but I have to be very organised and often forget to take crucial things with me (nappies, teats...even on one horribly memorable occasion, the whole changing bag!).

At first I wanted to rush around visiting, showing him off, shopping and combining walking the dog with getting me and the baby some fresh air and exercise. After two exhausting and stressful days I realised this was not possible or sensible... he hated being carted around so much and I wasn't enjoying the visiting, being too concerned about his needs. The same thing was true when I took him to a work meeting: I felt vulnerable, distracted and a bit foolish. Not a good combination when trying to convince someone I am worth my money as a freelance trainer!

I am intrigued by people's reactions to him. They inevitably say: 'Isn't he big?' which I finally worked out must be a compliment. They then say: 'Is he good for you?' which I worked out means does he sleep all night? So I say 'He's great but he doesn't sleep much' — goodness and sleep not seeming to have much to do with each other when you are talking about totally instinctive needs.

I have also been surprised at the way other lesbians address him. 'He's going to be a real heartbreaker,' and they mean little girls' hearts! Compulsory heterosexuality is alive and well and kicking in the lesbian community. Me and his other mum are just the same though, careful to dress him in real boy's clothes and anxious to spend time with men so he gets male role models. It's as if we feel ourselves to be out on a limb in terms of our own sexuality and are terrified that our choices will impact negatively on him, specifically in terms of his sexuality.

On my bleakest days I hope he won't be gay because the scene feels so narrow and obsessed with appearance. On my sunny, all's right with the world days, I think he'll be okay whatever he chooses to do or be. We often sing the Flirts' lullaby 'You can be anybody that you want to be' to ourselves as much as to him. For of course he'll get most of his messages about the world from me and Alex these first few years so I need to keep my self-image, as a dyke, a woman and a parent, in good shape.

Invisibility does seem to be a theme in my half of this story: first my history around trying to bear a child and now my role as a... well, as a what? Non-biological parent, co-parent, secondary parent? Yuk! I have often been assumed to be Alex's sister or her strangely involved but extremely supportive friend. When I am with him on my own of course I am seen as his (only) mother. Which is fine unless they want to know how the birth was or am I breast-feeding him.

At different times on the same day last week I had to decide whether to come out as: a lesbian (with some young people at work), as a mother (in a taxi without the baby), and as a lesbian mother (to the older lady in the local café who thought he was my baby). Well, he is, but sometimes it's just too difficult, and often actually frightening, to have to explain.

The acuteness of this fear is new to me. I've been out for twenty years: at work, where I live, to my family. It's not always been easy, or safe, but I've only been deciding for me. Now my answers implicate our child as well, and may affect the way he is regarded and treated.

In many situations, the option to come out is denied me anyway because I simply do not exist. I am not his parent in any legal sense, not for passports (Irish or English), not in Temple Street, not on child benefit or tax forms. I was moved almost to tears when our GP (a sussed and sensitive woman) said I could sign the permission slip for the baby's jabs as his parent.

In the UK I can start to apply for parental responsibility so I can officially share in decisions. We are keen to complete our wills so I will be able to continue as the baby's parent should Alex die.

Rereading this I see I have moved from my emotions before and immediately after his birth to my daily experiences as one of his mums. It's good to talk about it and, as Alex says, there is loads more we could say. It's both surprisingly ordinary and completely amazing to be living this life now. I do feel blessed and very alive.

– Jay

a bad story with a good ending

Brian Sheehan

Seven

WELL, HE WAS the sexiest thing on legs. Tall, dark and handsome. Not that I knew how to say or even think that then. Though I felt it. Strongly. And this was big 'B' Bad. This was serious trouble. There were loads of weirdos out there, and look, I was now one of them. I knew what they were called. Didn't know what they did, but I was in mortal danger of becoming one of them. So, just don't say anything. Fantasise in my head only. Studiously make it look as if nothing was happening. Only accidental, casual looking at him. Watch other people watch me watch him. Allay any hint of suspicion. Still wanted to be in his company all the time. Shame. He was my cousin. He was about nineteen. I was seven.

Fourteen

Now in boarding school. Now I knew exactly what I was. But if I didn't think about it, it just might not be true. But it was. Block it out. But there all the time. What if they knew? They'd hate me. This was the worst thing possible. Look at all the names people were called. I'd have no friends. My family would get rid of me too, have to, because of the shame. This is too awful to even contemplate. And there's no one else. Literally no one — apart from Shakespeare and Wilde. And they're dead. So there must only be a very few at any one time. And I was one of them. And I wasn't a writer. 'It' was only ever referred to, obliquely, in school as 'bad'. Only hinted at — rules in place to prevent any of 'that kind of thing'. It was too much for them to mention it. Utter invisibility, yet the strong and clear message that it/I was bad. Whatever happens, don't let it show. You'd get the crap beaten out of you by others. I had a big crush on John. I wanted to be with him all the time. I fell in love. I needed to be near him all the time. Craving any casual contact. Wanting more, wanting to be tactile. Those scary moments when it just might possibly be reciprocated. Could it be possible that he was also like me? Never really thought so (it was just me who was weird and bad). Just fervently hoped. So it was just me. Hide. Not just different, but bad. Make them like me. If it ever got out, they might just remember that they did like me once. And what of the rest of my life? Could I just disappear somewhere? Could I just get married to someone and pretend? What if I didn't? Only a lonely, miserable, alone life ahead. Exhausting. Shame. You're letting everyone down. Zero prospects. Why bother? Fear. I was fourteen — this was too much.

Twenty-one

Dublin, finally. There were gay magazines. So I knew there were others. In Dublin too. And it was cropping up in the media and music and foreign films. But scared. Really scared. Fear constant. Know I have to do something about it. Wanting to meet someone else. Wanting sex. Wanting relationships. But crushing fear of losing everything — friends, family, home, carefully built security. Fear breeding utter inactivity. Paralysing. All strategies to avoid thinking worn out. So constantly in my head. Casually walking past the gay pub, constantly. No one could suspect if I was caught. But they would 'know'. Better not get too close to anyone, because then I might let it slip. No point anyway, as friendships would end when they found out. I was going to get caught sometime. Could I possibly hide it forever? Long browses in the bookshops from the gay press. Surreptitiously got out gay-ish videos when everyone else was away for the weekend. Gave some connection. But what if I was caught? What would happen at work? Career over. Still don't know anyone else. And in work or pub conversations it's never mentioned, or only mentioned as bad/scary/weird, a joke, an offensive joke, certainly shameful if you were a fag, queer, bent, pervert. Equality my eye. Angry too. Why was I like this? Why is it so bad? I can't get rid of it, despite my very best efforts. It won't go away. So that's what I am. Why would I be ostracised if it came out? If I came out? Why were people so awful in the media? And what happened to a bit of Christianity from the Catholic Church? What were they afraid of? I picked up those fears by osmosis. Confirmed, compounded my own. I couldn't be as bad as they all made out. Have to do something or just crack up. Immense pressure. Dublin, freedom, at twenty-one was crap.

And then…?

I was twenty-one, and I had to accept I was gay, and had to make some sort of life for myself as a gay man. Somewhere within, I knew I had to be open about it, that I couldn't go through life without being open. The challenge, without exaggeration, the life challenge, was how to become comfortable, and possibly even happy, about being gay. I knew it was going to be hard, particularly given the entirely pejorative, shameful and invisible space it had already occupied in and around my life so far. This was also the 1980s. HIV and AIDS had come along to scare me even further, less HIV than the horrible and virulent reactions of many against gay men. Yet, I wanted love, I wanted life, and I wanted sex.

I started with Gay Switchboard Dublin (GSD). I knew I couldn't ring them, as I 'knew' that they'd know who I was. And I'd have to say that I was gay. And then someone else in the world would know. And then it was too late. 'It' would be named. 'I am a gay man.' (I am what I am.) It would be out then. So I thought of a compromise. I'd ring GSD and get the name of a counsellor or psychiatrist who I could go to and this wouldn't really be naming anything. Rang. And hung up a million times before they answered. Finally after a few more days, spoke to someone. Avoided any other conversation except getting a counsellor's number. This was a missed opportunity. If only I could have spoken to GSD then, if I'd not been as sweatingly scared as I was, it might have been easier, or at least quicker.

So, I went to this counsellor, who suggested that I face the wall in sessions, because I wouldn't say what was up. That didn't work either. So I blithely wittered on, not fooling either herself or myself, but serenely wasting my money. I eventually copped on, and stopped going.

More months passed, angst-ridden months. Eventually I had a conversation with a woman friend, who was lesbian, and who knew I was gay, though it had always remained unspoken between us. There, it was said then. Gay. There wasn't any going back now. So thus began a slow process of talking to her, obliquely at first, then more straightforwardly. I spent some time with her and her girlfriend. Normalising. And there were bits of sex, furtive really, and mostly abroad, balanced precariously between fear and excitement — though they were always disassociated from mental goings on. This was the beginning of the shift from being gay inside to being gay outside. This was coming out. It was a bit like getting on a treadmill. There wasn't really a way off, and while you were always moving forward you could at least control the speed.

I had never knowingly talked with another gay man, so that was arranged through my lesbian friends. Walking down Grafton Street, with them, towards the pub was a marker moment. It was all going to be different. And it was. 'They' were now 'we'. I began to have a visibility, at least to myself, where I had wanted it, needed it since I was seven — with other gay men. There was no big 'I have arrived' moment, just a gradual familiarity with gay people, and pubs and clubs and events. Dispelling the entrenched fears was slow, but they were displaced by a growing confidence and pride in who I was, and a strengthening sense of belonging, somewhere, finally.

I had gradually whittled down my friends to those I was reasonably confident wouldn't reject me for being gay, while also resenting that I had to put myself through those thought processes constantly. Over a few months I told them all. (Why does a gay man or woman have to cope with that burden too?) All except one were very positive, had already known in fact, and the only difference that telling them made was to strengthen ties of friendship by increasing vulnerability and honesty.

Then came the family. I have three sisters, and telling each of them took a bit of strategising. It was important to me that I was secure about being gay, and that I had strong gay and lesbian supports and friendships before I told them. That was my safety net. Still it was very difficult, and somewhat embarrassing. I felt a bit ridiculous, and I was tired of this. I was putting myself out for their judgement, and that irritated me. However, I went through with it, and all was well. They, of course, had sussed years before — though the fact that they never said or at least hinted at it rankled. And then my parents. This, defying all logic, was the difficult one. I went to Clare, reversing into the driveway so the car faced out, in case a quick getaway was required. Conjured an excuse for turning up unannounced midweek, then hummed and hawed for ages, and finally thought, just do it. So I did, and said that I was gay. And, irrationally, in my head I had given them just a few seconds to be okay with that — I had them on trial. And they passed, admirably. Their first reaction was to say that they loved me and it didn't matter what I was. I didn't have any real sense of relief; I somewhere must have expected that reaction. I can imagine that it was hard for them, but I also felt that they had to get over that themselves, with my sisters' help if necessary. I had enough to do minding myself without minding them too. The new honesty though was good. It allowed me to include my family in my life, and me in theirs in a different way. And they were all welcoming towards gay and lesbian friends and boyfriends as they got used to the idea.

Prompted by my experiences of isolation and exclusion, I started volunteering with Gay Switchboard Dublin. GSD is an amazing organisation. It's the oldest gay or lesbian organisation in Ireland, around since 1974, and entirely voluntary. The volunteers run a helpline that is open each day. They also run coming out groups, a youth group and work closely with Parents' Support, a support helpline for parents of lesbians and gays, run by other parents. GSD gets up to 5,000 calls per year on the helpline, and the volunteers hear the most difficult stories of people's lives. And equally importantly, they hear about the often remarkable coping skills that people develop to deal with the impacts of being lesbian or gay in Ireland.

The profile of callers to GSD over the years has changed. With the increasing visibility of lesbians and gay men throughout the media, and a changing legislative environment (decriminalisation; Equal Status Act; Employment Equality Act), the climate has improved somewhat. Many people are able to acknowledge and talk of their sexuality at ever earlier ages. GSD regularly get calls now from fifteen-year-olds and younger. The issues are still similar — no support within education or schools, anywhere. No protection from bullying or harassment. No accessible or welcoming youth services. No local visibility of lesbians and gay men, and poor national visibility. Very few role models. And no or very poor connections to other lesbian and gay people — the lesbian and gay community infrastructure remains under-developed.

After a number of years working with GSD, it was clear to me that tackling the causes of the stresses and difficulties and inequalities that people daily experienced was critical if there was to be meaningful change to people's lives and expectations. Many lesbians and gay men are excluded from or have difficulty in accessing education, health, youth services, employment and training, the police, and very importantly, linking with other gay and lesbian people. It is easy to relax into the comfort of being very 'out' in your own life, with the confidence and means to avoid most of the difficulties. However, that isn't the experience of very many lesbians and gay men. Unless equality is achievable for all lesbians and gay men, it's not real equality.

I now work with lesbian and gay organisations who are trying, and succeeding, to change the bit of the world that is Ireland, to make it a better place for lesbians and gay men, and through that to make it a fairer, genuinely equitable society.

I am what I am. And getting to the point of realising that, of being that, was very difficult. Let's not make every gay man or woman go through all that again. It's such an unnecessary waste of effort.

Now on to love, and life, and friendships, and families and relationships…and, just maybe, meaningful equality…

david

Louise and daughter

DAVID AND I met in college and married in our early twenties. Our life together was good for years and I felt very secure and loved in our relationship. David was a great dad to our four children and was very involved in their lives. Careerwise he was always restless and dreaming of the benefits to him and to us as a family that a change would bring. This culminated in a decision to make a career change in his early forties. I fully supported this, wanting more than anything to see him happy and fulfilled.

As time passed, however, I began to gradually feel that David was becoming less connected to the children and me. For quite a while I convinced myself that it was a period of adjustment to work changes and life would soon get back to normal. This didn't happen. Things got worse. I no longer felt loved, special, important or secure. That sense of loving partnership had somehow managed to disappear. I felt completely shut out of his life. Our sex life became almost non-existent. I assumed the fault was mine — that I must be responsible for his lack of interest. My brain was scrambled with confused thoughts. Something was wrong and I couldn't make any sense of it.

When I shared this with David, he didn't have any answers and we agreed to start couple counselling. I recall a conversation we had about this being like there was a Pandora's box waiting to be opened. For the life of me I didn't know what could be in it. At this point David seemed as confused as I was.

At our initial counselling session we were both asked about our sexual orientation. I considered this to be a daft question to ask a married couple. We both responded that we were heterosexual.

However, unbeknownst to me, this question raised serious questions and doubts for David. A few weeks later he dropped the bombshell — he wondered if he was gay. That progressed to considering the possibility of bisexuality. Within days though, he had decided that he was gay. It seemed to make sense to him and explain a lot to him about himself.

Nothing could have prepared me for or protected me from the impact of this disclosure. My world imploded. I couldn't make any sense of it. This couldn't possibly happen. He was my husband and my children's father. Gay people do not marry. I honestly thought it was some kind of brainstorm. Perhaps he had a brain tumour or was having a mid-life crisis, but that he might be gay was unbelievable and surely not possible.

My life became a living nightmare. I couldn't talk to anybody about this. If I said anything I could never unsay it. So I carried this secret in silence.

David, however, was growing into the idea of his newfound identity. He attended some meetings of the gay married men's group and accessed support groups on the internet. The reality of the existence of these groups shocked me, but also brought me to the realisation that maybe this does and could happen. This, however, did nothing to lessen my pain and confusion.

Months of hell followed. I got through the days in an acute state of panic and anxiety. The idea of my children knowing this was overwhelmingly terrifying. How could they, who were trying to find their own identities, cope with the knowledge that their father was not who or what they rightly assumed he was? I found the idea devastating, so how could they possibly cope with it?

Physically I was disintegrating. I yearned for the unconsciousness of sleep, but even that eluded me. My racing and pounding heart kept me awake and in a twenty-four hour state of acute panic. My appetite went and my weight rapidly fell. Each new morning following very little and very disturbed sleep brought the momentary hope that it was all a bad dream, but the new reality quickly surfaced to consciousness. It felt as though there was now a third party in our marriage.

As a woman I felt neutered. My new status as the wife of a gay man robbed me of my sexuality. I felt like a freak.

Life had to go on. Work and children's needs don't go away. So a mask had to be worn every day to hide my secret from my family, friends and colleagues. All I wanted to do was scream but I couldn't. I felt if I started I would never stop — the scream would devour and consume me. I had to hold myself together, or at least appear to, for my children's sake. People started commenting about my weight loss. I found this very distressing. It was as if my body was betraying me and somehow drawing attention and speculation which I didn't want. I didn't want anyone to notice or suspect that anything was amiss in my life.

Meanwhile it was becoming very difficult for David and I as a couple. The façade of a happily married couple could only be dropped when others weren't around. Then it was an endless round of talking about his being gay. All the time at the back of my mind was the idea that if only I could find the right words I could bring him to his senses. No words I found ever had this impact. I struggled to understand but I couldn't. Neither of us heard or understood the other.

During this time I felt totally alone. I desperately wanted to talk to someone in the same situation. I scoured the Golden Pages to find somewhere I could be understood. There was nothing for people in my situation. I felt completely alone and different. In desperation I rang the Gay Switchboard. The man I spoke to gave me the phone number of a woman who had found herself in the same situation. Her way of dealing with this was to facilitate her husband living a dual life. I was so crazed at that time that I considered this as a possible solution and as a way of protecting my children. But some innate sense of my own value and worth kicked in and I rejected this as a demeaning model for me. Instead I begged David to hold off on exploring his new identity until the children were independent adults. He felt unable to do this, saying he would be too old then.

In the smallest and most subtle ways he was becoming a stranger to me. While I was desperately trying to hold our family together, he was trying to break free to honour his identity. His mantra became: 'I want to live alone and be responsible only for myself.' This was shocking to hear and absorb. Who was this man? How was he, as a parent, able to square this with himself?

Panic attacks, acute anxiety and sleeplessness eventually became so debilitating that I had to go to my doctor. He prescribed anti-depressants and sleeping tablets. Never being one to pop pills, it enraged me to need a chemical strait-jacket just to get through each day. That my beloved husband was responsible for bringing about a situation to cause a physical and mental disintegration in me was unbearable.

Dying became a very attractive option. Physical problems prompted medical tests. I hoped for a cancer diagnosis or anything terminal. This would, I felt, offer a legitimate and unsuspicious way out of this hell my life had become. Not able to cope with the reality that my marriage was built on a foundation of lies, I yearned for the release death might offer. Then David would have to honour his responsibilities to the children. He wouldn't be able to land this on them. The tests, however, were clear.

I strongly considered suicide. I was in a dreadful place and couldn't see anything but black all around me. But I knew suicide would create other problems for the children, and hurting them like that stopped me. Perhaps though, fate could intervene. Another car could plough into me. Some tragic accident could befall me. None of these things happened.

David was also finding it very tough. He was attending a therapist and was also put on medication to help him cope. I think I cried enough tears for the whole country. My search for answers was fruitless. Our life together became intolerable and too intensely painful. We agreed that separation was the only option.

Even when he left I couldn't comprehend it. I honestly thought he would be back — that he would realise our marriage and family were more important then anything else. It took months for me to realise and accept that this wouldn't happen. In many ways David was gone long before he ever left.

This was two years ago. My children have all been told. However, they don't want to talk about it. It is as though when David came out of his closet the rest of us found ourselves in one. This is our secret, which we individually share only with trustworthy friends and family. Time hasn't eased my sense of difference, stigma and shame. I neither want people's pity nor to be the subject of gossip. Counselling has helped me deal with the pain of loss, grief and intense anger. In time, hopefully, my children will feel ready to deal with its impact on their lives. Maybe then they will feel more comfortable talking to each other, to me and to David about it.

Sometimes it takes a desperate situation to realise the blessings one has. Mine have been the constant support of my friends and family, who are always there for me. The mutual understanding and friendship of others in the Straight Spouse Support Group facilitated by the MRCS has been incredible. It is so helpful and comforting to know you are not alone. While all our experiences are different, we are united and affirmed by being with others who have walked the walk. The breakdown of my marriage has brought with it lots of losses. Gone is my partner, fellow traveller, best friend and my dreams, hopes and plans for our future together. Gone is the stability and security of a normal family, structure and life for my children. I grieve for what might and could have been.

Following our separation I assumed that David and I could have a working relationship, at least as parents. Unfortunately it hasn't worked out this way. I felt absolutely battered and bruised mentally and physically. I was really angry and couldn't cope with David's response to my distress. I couldn't tell him or reassure him that it was okay. It just wasn't. He seemed always to be so angry and defensive with me that he actually frightened me. He could never hear or acknowledge my pain and perhaps was unable to deal with my obvious devastation. He didn't understand where I was and I didn't understand where he was either. But it didn't work and I decided that for the sake of my sanity I would not see him. My children didn't need to see me like a basketcase all the time. Now we are both getting on with our separate lives.

Our contact now is minimal. There is nothing familiar about him anymore, even his physical appearance and dress have changed radically. While I accept that this way of dealing with my situation is far from ideal, for the children it is, for now, the best I can do.

Self-doubt is my constant companion. I don't trust my feelings anymore. How can I when I was so wrong about the most important relationship in my life? Who can I trust? Are people really who and what they claim to be? There is safety in armouring and protecting myself from further betrayal and duplicity. But I grieve my loss of trust.

Three years after disclosure and I still have days when I wake in a panic hoping it has just been a bad dream. The shock of realisation is akin to a very forceful blow to my stomach. It still has the power to take my breath away. I yearn for answers I will never get. I yearn for the day when it won't be my first and last thought and I don't torment myself questioning what our shared lives, loves and intimacy meant. What did it all mean? Is sex all that matters? So many questions — no answers.

– Louise

****

David's Daughter Adds Her Story...

Previous to two years ago I had never heard anything, or even imagined gay people having children — a bit naïve I suppose but the subject isn't really broached much in society.

My parents were always your typical 'happy couple' with common interests, rarely arguing.

When they dropped the bombshell that they were separating, it was totally unreal. I can't begin to explain the confusion, worry and sadness I felt. My little bubble of security and certainty (that I had never appreciated or even acknowledged before) had been burst, and now I was left open and bare. I felt vulnerable and totally lost. I could not work it out in my mind and the whole thing just didn't add up.

Months later, when my Dad told me the truth, that he is gay, the devastation that I felt was huge. This man, my male 'ideal' that I had grown up with, who when I was a child I was convinced I was going to marry, was now telling me he is gay!

I was ashamed and embarrassed, but confused. Society is changing and encouraging people to accept homosexuals (which I always have done), but now when it hit so close to home, I was unsure, embarrassed, but ashamed of my embarrassment.

I find it hard to look on all this as a hopeful situation and would not wish this experience on anybody.

I felt, technically, I am not supposed to be here; had my Dad figured out his sexuality earlier in his life I would not exist.

It is not a subject I can talk about with my friends, nor do I want to. It makes me feel uncomfortable and I suspect it would make them uncomfortable as well; after all, what can they say?

My dad has changed significantly over the past few years and in a way I feel I don't know him anymore. I don't question him, afraid of what else he might reveal.

being gay – it's only part of who i am

Padraig O'Brien

I MAGINE WHAT IT'S like to feel so utterly alone that every shred of sense and logic you've allowed yourself to follow throughout your life means absolutely nothing. Of course, this is a premise based on complete denial, so who am I kidding?

I'm at the stage in my life now where everybody that's important in my life knows that I'm gay. I mean, it's not as if I want to brand myself with a hot iron poker declaring to the world 'I'm gay', now is it? Being gay is not everything I am, it's only part of who I am — a big part, yes, but not everything I am. I know guys, on the other hand, that make it everything they are. The overly camp, overly effeminate, overly gay type. The image that the muggles, so to speak, have in their mind of the stereotypically gay man.

We can all stand back and take a look at what happened throughout our lives that made us into the people we are today. Unfortunately a lot of us don't, and this is why we're doomed (as a race) to make the same mistakes over and over. This is where our current lack of perspective in life emanates from — our inability to perceive the past, our inability to learn from past mistakes. So, what happened in my life that shaped me into the person I am today? For each of us it's different, but there are moments in our lives that we can pick out and say, yes, it all makes sense now.

I grew up in an all-female environment, with the females being both the matriarch and the patriarch of that environment. Strong women, whom I love very dearly today, but who at the time had a massively influential part in moulding me. Times being hard, my parents had decided to leave me at my Gran's, temporarily of course, but that ended up being nearly eight years in total. I'm very aware of how the interaction between genes and environment are thoroughly interconnected and how together they make an individual who they are, but what science does not yet fully understood is the variable that adds that extra 'umphhh' to human nature — emotion!

As a child I was very emotional, almost to the point of empathy — influenced I think by the fact that I was raised in my early childhood predominantly by women. A lot changed after I moved back in with my parents. I was about eight. They'd got a council house and wanted me to move in with them. What I remember of the next four or five years was that I was like an emotional bottle of madly shaken fizzy orange, at any moment ready to be unscrewed and popped. Stuck between what seemed like a veritable rock and a hard place. As children do, they adapt and survive, move on. During this time, between the ages of say ten and twelve, events occurred that were to change me and in essence mould me into the person I am today.

Imagine a new street, new families, new people, new home, new parents, metaphorically speaking of course. Everything and everyone was new. I can't remember exactly how it happened but I befriended this guy, about three years older than me. I don't know, maybe he befriended me. We became friends, as kids do. Our parents were good friends too, so hey, everything was good, wasn't it? I remember one day he asked me to go to his room to play, something I'd done many a time and didn't think twice about doing. This time was different though. 'Let's play mammies and daddies, it'll be great.' At the time I was thinking nothing out of the ordinary was happening here, we were going to play an innocent game of mammies and daddies — sure, what the hell could possibly be wrong with that? So we played. He was the mammy and I was the daddy, probably so as not to cast suspicion on the whole thing. If he had suggested I be the mammy then I probably would have said, 'no way man'. I don't know, at the time I was thinking this is wrong but at the same time I was thinking, this is what most kids do so why should I be any different? Boy was I wrong. What we were doing was different, what I was feeling was different. And so began a life outside of the norm, a life filled with self-doubt and confusion, a life that made me the man I am today. It is only today that I find myself in a position to confront those feelings and emotions. To rationalise how it was to be a child on the verge of realising he was gay.

I have a problem defining what happened in those years because of what occurred in the years to come. Simple childhood exploration. We all do it. That other guy went on to abuse young children, far younger than I was then. He was classed as a sexual deviant and shunned by his peers, family and community. He now lives a life of loneliness. A life outside the norms dictated by society, shunned by all. Alone. So you see, we can all look back on our lives and pick out some of those key moments that define the very essence of our being, and still be a little confused as to what they meant and how they fit into the grand scheme of things. I wanted to blame this guy for doing what he did, but at the same time, you can't help but think, maybe this is what I wanted to happen as well. Maybe it's time to stop pointing the finger of blame at individuals and events throughout our lives that made us who we are, and start accepting who we are, exclusive of our own sexualities.

Then came the dreaded teenage years. Once again, it was a time of new beginnings and new people, not to mention emerging bodily changes. Confusion was not the word to describe what the hell was happening — complete bewilderment maybe!

Humans as a race have one fundamental thing in common and that's our ability to adapt, whether that is to a new environment or new circumstances, etc. So, what was my way of dealing with my emerging gay self? Denial, of course! What is it they say about ignorance being bliss? Well then, I was blissfully ignorant by all accounts.

And so it began, the teenage quest to define oneself. I easily fit into the quiet, bookworm niche, thereby only drawing attention to myself by way of academic achievement. This niche remained my security blanket for the next ten years or so, right through college and up as far as a few months ago. I now realise that there's no need to categorise myself into any group or niche, I am who I am and if ya don't like it, well then...

Even at this stage of my life I have a lot of things to work on. I have outed myself to my family, which for me — and most gay guys and girls — is probably the hardest thing they're ever likely to do. Being gay is not everything I am; it's only part of who I am! I think if we can get people to look beyond the established norms and bias against gay culture, then maybe we can wake up some day and be totally happy with who we are. I mean, isn't that the human condition? Everyone everywhere seeks happiness, but searching for it and achieving it are two very different journeys!

Having faced my fears I have now found someone who means a lot to me, whom I can call my own, whom I love. It's one hell of a road to journey on, but if and when you can reach the point where you can look in the mirror and smile back at the person who's looking back at you, then...

a chat in the kitchen

Walt Kilroy

SOMETIMES A GOOD deep breath is the only way to start the process. It's a kind of a first step, a way of launching into saying the thing you've been working up to saying for so long. You've already taken other 'first steps' on a road that leads out into sunlight and fresh air, but this next one is the biggie.

So here I was, sitting in the kitchen with my mother, about to change things forever. We remember the details of it differently; it may have been at one in the morning, when we might have easy chats about the big questions in life (or indeed inconsequential things), unworried by the way time slipped past unmeasured at that hour of the night. Or it may have been the early evening in winter, when she was preparing the dinner in a steamy kitchen with a comforting Radio 4 on in the background. Either way, we do agree it was in the kitchen, where so much chat and family banter took place, in December with the dark pressing in at the windows.

But even a deep breath wasn't quite enough, so it had to be half step: 'Mum, I've something to tell you.' A way of putting me past the point of no return (I'd have to think pretty quickly if I was going to change my mind at this stage), and a moment's warning to her that something big was coming.

Of all the hurdles I'd jumped so far, this was the hardest. I had already come out and met openly gay people for the first time in my life, just a few weeks before. After years working up to it, that was the easiest leap into the unknown I'd ever made. I was nineteen and in my first year in college, and it was an idea whose time had well and truly come. I was now meeting up with other gay and lesbian friends at the Gay Soc in UCD, finding a huge weight had been lifted off my shoulders as I found new friends and personal liberation. It was even possible to think that having a crush on someone could actually lead to something. Suddenly life was full of even more wonderful possibilities.

But liberating and important as all the other steps were, talking to my mum was a serious business in another way. I was about to ask her in a roundabout way if she still loved me, even if I suddenly might seem to be a different person than the one we all thought I was.

Well, after my opening line, I had my mum's full attention. The concern was written all over her face, as she dried her hands on the tea towel. Was it drugs, she asked? At least I could offer reassurance on that. The only thing left to do was to summon up all my available courage, and fudge it.

'I think I'm bisexual.' I suppose that in my rather confused thinking, I imagined that this might be less of a shock. Maybe she'd be relieved that at least her youngest son wasn't a fully fledged homosexual. It didn't quite work that way; for this was 1981, and I found myself having to explain to a well-educated woman what exactly I meant by 'bisexual'.

I tried to reassure her about how wrong the stereotypes were, and how this was the right thing for me. I told her I had known for many years that I was destined to fall in love with men, and that I was happy and relieved that I did not have to keep it a secret any longer.

And the warm-hearted and open-minded person who had always taught her four children to be tolerant and to think for ourselves did not reject me. Nor was I told to go to a psychiatrist, and at least she seemed to believe me when I said that this wasn't just a phase — it was a blossoming after years of denial and hoping that my feelings would go away.

I was of course enormously relieved that I had finally unburdened myself of the great news; but the following days and weeks were no doubt worrying ones for her. She now had to follow part of the daunting journey that I had taken years to make, while she tried to get to grips with what I'd told her. She wanted me to be happy but was haunted by the popular beliefs about the life I was going to lead. There were hardly any positive images of gay people, so I probably seemed destined to end up as the stereotypical Sad Old Homosexual, despised and lonely, who would die unloved and alone.

So I went back to college in the New Year, and headed off excitedly down my path of exploration. My crush on my best friend in my psychology class turned out not to have been another pointless exercise: one day in a lecture, I saw the date, time and venue of the Gay Soc's coffee afternoon written on his folder. It might as well have had flashing yellow arrows pointing at it. A few days later, I waited in a state of unbearable excitement for him to walk into the meeting. He finally did screw up the courage to come along about two weeks later; soon after, we became each other's first boyfriend.

My mother's journey meanwhile took her to the family doctor, who at least said that I was not going to change and become straight. My studies in Logic in UCD helped me to understand just why the beliefs and false reasoning that condemned us were so flawed — the generalisations, the failure to distinguish between 'some' and 'all', and the muddled thinking that so often takes the place of reason when we think about a hidden minority. But unassailable logic and convincing arguments on their own were never going to change minds. The best thing I could offer was to let her see that I was now happier and more fulfilled than I think I had ever been. And there was no longer an unspoken secret between us, something to eat away at the trust and communication that are so vital to any relationship. She knew me well enough to see that I was finally daring to be the person I really was, and was so much happier as a result. We were already lucky to have had a wonderful relationship; now it was even better.

In many ways, my father had a more difficult journey to make, in that he was coming from a more conservative outlook. When I told him a year later, with the support of the rest of my family, he rose to the occasion. He could hardly have been delighted. But he still accepted me as I was; in time, he showed his openness and acceptance in his own unequivocal way. The way we tried to take on board each other's needs and fears was the basis for a renewed relationship — one where the respect, appreciation and love was mutual. Those feelings may not have been alluded to openly very often, but they were never in any doubt. I feel so grateful that I had what I always feel were those 'extra years' with him, a valuable and wonderful time that will stand to me for the rest of my life. It's now more than ten years since he died, but my appreciation and gratitude continues to grow, for the journey he made in order to accept me as I am. If I had been born a little earlier or in a different place, I doubt if we would have had the opportunity to enjoy a renewal of our father-son relationship.

My mother, of course, was soon reverting to type. She was always a person who would speak up for what is right, even if feathers got ruffled. It wasn't too long before she got involved in what was then called Parents' Enquiry, a support service for other parents who've just received the wonderful news that one of their kids has turned out to be homosexual. This was a pioneering group of parents, who had nothing to gain by giving up their time and privacy. It was at a time when attitudes and laws were so much less forgiving. Taking phone calls, going to meet people, giving talks, and appearing on radio or television — they worked away steadily. They were in a unique position to change people's minds, and the ripples they sent out reached far and wide — parents, their lesbian/gay children, young people who had yet to come out to anyone. I couldn't have asked for any more from her as an endorsement or a badge of acceptance.

Soon my mother's presence on the activist circuit matched my own whirl of meetings, poster-making, marching and writing. In 1983, just over a year after I came out, a protest march was held against the suspended sentences given to the men who beat up and killed a gay man in Fairview Park in Dublin. My mum went on the march with the placard she had made herself, after struggling to come up with the words that would express her feelings. It simply said, in her own distinctive lettering: 'Parents of Gays Love Their Children.' It was an emotional gathering, and I felt touched and proud at what she had done. I still have the picture of her with it. When she couldn't walk any further, the placard was carried the rest of the way by Phil Moore, who had already done so much to help parents of gays (and their children) to come to terms with having a gay son or daughter.

In time, my mum's profile grew within the lesbian and gay community, and the inevitable started to happen: it may sound rather Freudian, but I found that wherever I went on the gay scene, I was being preceded by her. Friends would ask me constantly to pass on their regards to her, or tell me how wonderful they thought she was. (I couldn't disagree — literally — nor did I want to.) Complete strangers would come up to me in bars, not wanting to talk to me, but to tell me that they'd loved what she had just said on television or radio, or how Parents' Enquiry had helped them when it came to telling their own mother and father. I would find that Mum was good friends with lesbian or gay figures who were just a name to me. I even found myself at Áras an Uachtaráin, when Parents' Support (as it is now called) presented its booklet to President Mary McAleese. As we were introduced one by one to the President, what else could I say, but that I was only there because I'd tagged along with my mother. Perhaps parents get used to being overshadowed by their children in some fields; I certainly took a special pleasure in all of this. I am proud to have an activist mother.

I know how lucky I am to have parents I was able to talk to. They gave me enough belief in myself to take that risk, they listened and were open-minded enough to change the way they thought. Love and hope triumphed. And we all benefited from the heroic work done by the people who went before us by coming out in much more difficult times. They helped us, as parents and children, to become one of the first generations who would see difference and diversity become something that brought people closer together.

i was so lucky with my gay son

Patricia Kilroy

WHEN TALKING WITH distressed parents, I often ask them have they recently looked into the eyes of their gay son or daughter. I know that if they did this, they would see the exact same child they have always loved. It is not the son or daughter who has changed, but the parent's perception of them.

I was so lucky with my gay son, Walt, for he did me the honour of telling me that he was gay, looking me straight in the face, that night, standing at the kitchen table. Well, I was a massive jumble of ignorance, one of my strange notions being that there might be as many as six gay men in the whole of Ireland, maybe even seven or eight. And lesbian women didn't exist. It all sounds very funny, but this was more than twenty years ago, when being gay was not talked about; in fact, a great veil of secrecy covered the whole subject. However, what I did know, from looking into those eyes of his, was that here before me was the selfsame son I had loved for nineteen years. In the following weeks, he set about educating me in his lovely, kind way. How sad if he had never shared with me and the rest of our family something that was such an essential part of him. How sad if I had never met his gay friends, nor met the different members of the gay community whom I like and respect so much.

About two years later, a young gay man was murdered in Fairview Park, Dublin, apparently for no other reason than his sexual orientation. When the gay community organised a protest march, and with Walt in mind, I simply had to join them. Because I'm bad at any kind of walking and would never reach the end, I thought I would compensate by making a placard. It was a small one on a long stick so that, hopefully, everyone could see the message. It declared, with idiotic simplicity, that 'Parents Love Their Gay Children'. It was really perfectly silly, but I'm glad I did it, because that is how I met Phil Moore and Rose Donnelly, also on the march. They, with their husbands (Harry Moore and John Donnelly), were the founder members of Parents' Enquiry, as Parents' Support was then called, and that afternoon they asked me to join them.

Parents' Enquiry at the time was a part of the English group of that name, but there did not seem to have been much contact with them. At a later stage, we changed the name to Parents' Support, because the word 'enquiry' seemed to have connotations of a trial, in the dock, that is, for bad parenting. We did not go in for titles, but if we had, Phil would have been our secretary, because she was our organiser and did great work. Her gay son was known in the gay community as 'the gay guy with the mother'.

The way we have always operated is this: parents who have learnt that one of their children is gay or lesbian, and who have questions or seek reassurance, contact us through the telephone helpline, Gay Switchboard Dublin. Parents are given time to unburden their worries, and the volunteers staffing the helpline are kind and understanding to parents, as well to the gay people who call them. At this stage, I have to say that none of our work could have been done without that vital link to the outside world, Switchboard. Their different members over the years have never been anything other than pleasant, helpful and positive — giving us a little nudge forward now and then — so it has been a real pleasure to work with them. They post our booklet to the parents who call and give them the first name and phone number of any two of our volunteers. It is actually a wonderful thing to speak with parents when they take in the information and we sense them relaxing by the minute. Generally, though, it takes time, for the whole thing can be such a shock that a couple may be unable to eat or sleep for days on end, or may feel that the family has been disgraced. You can imagine what this last does to a gay child. Often, we will spend an hour or more on a first call and, of course, we invite the caller to ring again. If we feel it would help, we also meet them confidentially on a one-to-one basis. We reassure the 'new' parent that having a gay child is absolutely nobody's fault, neither theirs ('where have we gone wrong?) nor, of course, that of the gay child. We make sure they know that gay people do not choose to be gay, but are born gay. Sometimes a child may realise it as early as seven or eight years of age, but generally it is in their teens. What worries parents is sometimes seeing a gay son/daughter become depressed at that time, and the parent does not know the reason for it. The cause (with a gay child) can be that the child is going through the process of accepting his/her own sexuality, and this can be extremely difficult, if being gay is the last thing that a child wants. Usually, when a gay child accepts himself or herself, and 'comes out', the black cloud lifts. In fact, it is like a light to see the newfound confidence of a gay person, just 'out'.

It is only when that self-assurance has grown even stronger that we would hope a gay son/daughter would tell their parents. In any case, actually saying those three words, 'Mum, I'm gay', can be so difficult. Then, if the parents find it hard to accept, a great deal of patience and understanding is needed on both sides, and plenty of time. Parents will naturally have hoped over many years that their child would lead a happy life in a loving marriage or heterosexual relationship. One can imagine, therefore, what a long process of readjustment some parents have to go through. The terrible old myths about gay people being sinful, wicked and degenerate are certainly no help. But the situation is even more difficult for very religious parents, because of the old condemnation by the Churches. At the other end of the spectrum are the parents who need nothing more than a little information.

During this time of readjustment, rather than leaving the parent unhappy and confused, not knowing where to turn, it is a great help if a son/daughter takes the time to help. Information being the cure for parents' worries, we always hope gay children will gradually pass on the information that is relevant at any particular stage. Parents' Support is always glad to hear of gay children passing on to their parents a copy of our booklet, If Your Child is Gay or Lesbian (of which more later). In reaching toward a more informed understanding, the love between parent and child will be the great impetus that can make the seemingly impossible happen. And it is all worthwhile. I've known many parents say, after the turmoil and sadness were over, that they actually felt closer than ever to their child. When this happens it is important to the child, as parent acceptance still seems to mean a great deal to the gay child, even in this day of independent youth.

Another piece of helpful information is the fact that being gay is in no way unique, since about 10 per cent of any given population is gay: therefore, neither are parents of gay/lesbian children unique. We are all over the place, in a pretty large sisterhood and brotherhood, did we but know it. Parents' Support likes to reassure parents that their gay child need not have a sad, lonely life (as I had feared for my own son). There are many gay groups that they can join, each with different interests, such as 'OutYouth', lesbian discussion, Christian study, a gay choir, hill-walking, etc. More details may be found at the back of the booklet, or in lesbian/gay publications. But apart from this, the gay community in general is so supportive that it is often felt to be a second family. It enables gay people to make supportive, lifelong friendships, quite apart from partnerships.

Sometimes, parents find it hard to accept their child's partner, if they meet them early on in the process. We try to ease them around this hurdle by asking them would they really want their gay son or daughter to live life without a lasting and caring relationship? And so on.

The parents' process of adapting may be very quick, or may take a long time — a few months, a year, or longer. This can lead, nevertheless, to an excellent resolution. Keeping communications open is essential. We can also reassure parents about where their sons can get information to protect themselves from HIV/AIDS — something parents do naturally worry about. Another worry is, at times, greater than all the other worries put together. It is the fear that the neighbours will find out about their gay child. We point out that if the neighbours should find out, they are likely to be sympathetic, in this more open age, rather than hurtful. It is quite possible, too, that a neighbour will even say that they knew it all along. In any case, in so many places, people today are aware of that one-in-ten figure. Younger people, especially if they live in cities and towns, generally have no problem with gay issues. Older people and parents in rural areas are more inclined to be shocked and unhappy to find they have a gay son or daughter. But why do people get so upset? It seems to be due to an unspoken message in the air around us.

In the course of their lives, and without even thinking about it, most people used to pick up the notion that homosexuality was wicked and sinful and, to a lesser degree, this still happens. This was not their fault. They simply took on board the age-old unspoken message that it was so shameful it must never even be spoken about. This was all so hurtful and damaging to gay people who, of course, do not choose to be gay. Unfortunately, it was reinforced by the attitude of the church, whatever the denomination. If one considers the old doctrine that even heterosexual sex was sinful — and that was not 100 years ago — the church's condemnation of homosexuality is not surprising. Yet even as early as the 1980s, one would occasionally hear of a priest or pastor with a more informed outlook, who was helpful to gay people, and prepared to ease parents towards greater understanding. As a result of the work one of our members, Eileen, we can now pass on to parents the names of such priests.

In order to counteract the general beliefs that led to so much lonely unhappiness, Parents' Support has from the beginning pursued publicity (as keenly as a would-be pop star, but without quite the glamour). Early on, Phil Moore organised appearances on the Marian Finucane radio show and on *The Late Late*. We also took part in a short Louis Marcus film, and were interviewed and photographed for articles in newspapers and magazines. Unendingly, we each told the story of our gay children 'coming out' to us, and how we had found it was not such a terrible thing once we got used to the idea. In fact, it was quite all right. Now and then I felt an interviewer might have been a bit disappointed not to get the drama of broken hearts and get-out-of-my-house scenes. But if we had not been fairly calm people, ready to adjust, then we would not have been speaking out for Parents' Support. Naturally, every time we went public, we invited parents to contact us if they felt the need.

In 1993, a great change came about for gay men in Ireland. Until then, a law had remained on our statute books from nineteenth-century English legislation declaring sex between men to be a crime. I don't think it was actually acted upon in its last years, but it remained a threat and an injustice, and some dedicated members of the gay community worked hard to reverse it. They succeeded, gay sex was decriminalised, and President Mary Robinson — always so keen on justice and equality — signed the new law. Then she invited representatives of the gay groups to

Áras an Uachtaráin to celebrate, including Parents' Support.

Later that year, Joan Rippingale and Jim Egan joined our number. When Jim's son was just out, he had asked his dad to come to a gay 'Tea Dance', and Jim was the kind of father who did just that. On the next Saturday afternoon, watching gay men dance with one another, he was at first amazed, but after an hour or so, decided it wasn't such a big thing after all. Not long after, our four founder-members retired, sorely missed, especially Phil and Harry Moore, who had always been such faithful workers. So the three of us (Jim, Joan and I) carried on with the work as best we could.

Having seen how rural families seemed to have particular difficulties — both the gay child and his/her parents — we were always concerned to reach them. With this in mind, I wrote an article for the Irish Countrywoman's Association journal. The ICA, however, did not publish it. By 1994, the article had expanded into the booklet we use today, as I took advice from Walt, from Switchboard, and from people with special knowledge of theology and/or HIV/AIDS. It is regularly updated, and is intended to help not only parents but their gay children too.

The trouble was we had no money for printing, so for the next four years both we and Switchboard posted it out in its early format of 22 photocopied A4 pages. Naturally, it went to parents who had contacted us, and to other gay groups. But we were keen to reach parents who needed help but did not know where to find it. This had to be done through other voluntary organisations and, hopefully, through Department of Health sub-sections. For this we needed to have the booklet printed. It was only after four years of applying for printing funds that, under the wing of the two then Switchboard directors, Brian Sheehan and Ciaran Wallace, our application at last bore fruit. In March 1998, the Eastern Health Board paid for the printing, and even undertook to distribute the booklet through their health clinics.

So, with this seeming success, and as a result of sending out our printed booklet in all directions, I was under the illusion that we would be flooded with calls. So I enlarged our committee from three to nine in order to deal with the expected flood. A little later, I asked President McAleese to launch the booklet, which she kindly did, and out of that developed a positive windfall of new articles and radio and TV interviews.

We even felt we were really getting somewhere in reaching rural Ireland when the Jesuits recorded an interview with Jim to be passed on to all the local radio stations, and when *The Irish Farmers' Journal* printed a full-page article on gay issues, with a good section on Parents' Support.

Confidently, we waited for that flood of calls. Not a bit of it. The number of people ringing us had always been small, and small it remained. Was it because so few parents knew where they might get help, or because they felt so trapped that they dare not speak of it to anyone? If we considered that it might be because parents no longer needed help, that thought was swept aside by the evident distress of those who did call. The only answer seems to be simply to carry on and try to break that old enemy, secrecy. There was still plenty to be done. Now that the booklet was in printed form, we sent it to the various sub-divisions of the Department of Health and to the Health Boards of other areas in Ireland. The National Social Services Board distributed our material to their members, and in the end so did the ICA. We also made contact with many relevant voluntary groups.

For many years Jim Egan was our faithful chairman, who never said no to any call to go to any corner of Ireland, while Joan Rippingale continued to share in taking calls. Our 'new' volunteers, since they joined us in 1998, have made great contributions to the work, each with their own skills. Eileen, a gifted comforter, also became our treasurer. Nick and Mary Knox saw to the second printing of the booklet, Vincent Moorehouse became our new chairman, and Doreen Moorehouse has taken on the job of posting out our video. When I decided to retire from the secretaryship in 2000, to my great joy Louise O'Donovan agreed to become our new secretary. She has brought our group into the modern age by means of the Internet, has created the long-dreamed-of video, has organised the launch of the second edition of the booklet at the Equality Authority, and much else besides.

All my life I have sworn not to become prejudiced, but it has not worked out. I find I'm prejudiced in favour of gay people. One could not meet a nicer bunch of people. And it all came about through Walt. Recently, I was asked did I not worry about the neighbours knowing I had a gay son. It is very hard to answer. Did the questioner, a nice young African, imagine I would put a neighbour's approval before Walt? Gay is what he is, courageous and warm, with a huge love of life, and a wonderful friend to me. I love him exactly the way he is.

ennisocence

Bernard Lynch

I HAD TURNED FIVE when I started school at the local Convent of Mercy in Ennis, County Clare. A town which, our teachers reminded us, was not only the capital of our county, but the one that elected Daniel O'Connell, Charles Stewart Parnell and Eamon de Valera to parliament and the Dáil. Fame and fortune were in our bones, as it were, having sprung from a people so hell-bent on the freedom to carve out their own destiny in whatever limited way they could. I loved the nuns, especially Sister Mary Malachy, who had a big doll's house in her classroom, which I always wanted to play with. I cannot quite remember when I was first called a sissy. This name-calling and bullying would accompany much of my school days and indeed reach into my adult life. I cannot say that I ever got used to it, but it did foster in me a deep sensitivity for the underdog, accompanied by a very strong desire to prove myself. I would run a mile at the very mention of competitive sport, as any attempt on my part to participate ended in unabated name-calling and inevitable humiliation.

My earliest memories of hurling and football send a shiver down my spine. I never fitted in. My father came from a well-known hurling family and he himself enjoyed the sport very much. Consequently, of course, I was expected to follow suit. Nothing could be further from my truth. I would feel more comfortable in a tutu than with a hurling stick. The horrors that boys of my ilk went through, as we stood there in the pissing rain, not being picked for anybody's team, still gives me nightmares. If one was picked at the end of a long, humiliating line, it was usually as a substitute player. We were far more suited as cheerleaders, like those girls one sees in those colourful miniskirts at American football games, than hurling players. I usually prayed like hell that I would never be brought onto the playing team, lest my already tattered ego would be torn to shreds as I heard my more butch classmates shout, 'You fuckin eejit, hit the ball...What are you? A girl or something?'

I knew from the start that cowboys and indians were way down the scale in preference to dolls and prams. It was this sense of dire despair at my not so impressive masculinity that eventually drove me into the arms of cross-country running and track and field sports. Quite by accident, I was asked to stand in for a boy who was ill in the cross-country annual race in the grounds of Dromoland Castle. I won the race and absolutely shocked everybody, but most of all myself. In fact I actually thought that I had come second place. I did not realise that the boy way ahead of me was sent out before the start of the race as a guide on the course for the competing runners. When I arrived in to cheers and was carried shoulder high by my comrades, I thought that I had had the first successful soul transplant. I was a real boy at last. I immediately buckled my newfound male identity steadfast by joining the local Ennis Shamrocks cross-country team. From that day to this, running has been and is my greatest physical love. It is even better than sex.

I dreaded making my First Communion, because I knew that after that I would have to go to the all-boys school at the Christian Brothers. I of course enjoyed all the fuss around First Communion and getting half crowns from some of my 'rich relations', and shillings and sixpences from the poorer ones. On the morning of the Communion itself I almost choked myself in trying to dislodge the host from the roof of my mouth without letting it touch my teeth. We had been warned by the Sister preparing us not to chew the host under pain of sin. It would be like chewing Our Blessed Lord Himself. We were to allow the wafer to melt and then Our Lord would disappear into our souls, which would be full of sanctifying grace. The sanctifying grace was imagined like pure, snow-white liquid that made us as close to God as we would ever be. It was a wonderful feeling when I eventually succeeded in releasing Jesus down my throat. I knew and believed that He now lived in me and I could be closer to him than anyone in the whole world. The real presence of Jesus in the

Holy Communion would be central to my Catholic faith all of my life. There were no two ways about it. Jesus was really present in this wafer, because the priest had consecrated it at mass. How could anyone get closer to another human being than to be somewhere in that person's stomach? That somewhere we call your soul.

I devoutly prayed all the prayers I had been taught. I believed that Jesus was now within my breast with his body, blood, soul and divinity and that nothing in my life or death would ever separate Him from me. I asked Him to bless my parents, my brother Sean and to please give me a baby sister. When I was eight years old, my prayers were answered. My mother was pregnant with her fourth child. As she got bigger I remember her beginning to talk about us getting a new baby. In my child's mind I was not sure where the baby would come from. I was taught that all babies were delivered by stork to Sheehan's back garden. There the midwife, Nurse Duggan, would pick them up and give them to whatever family wanted one. I told my mother I very much wanted a baby girl. I already had a brother but I wanted a sister. I made no secret of the fact that the reason a sister was so important to me was that I needed a sister in order to have dolls and play doll's house. I thought that there would be nothing like having a little girl of my own that I could take care of and play endlessly with to my heart's content. I started praying to Saint Martin de Porres, who was called Blessed Martin at the time. He had been introduced to me by a sister of my mother's when I was two years old. His picture hung over my bed until I left my home for the noviciate in 1965. I saw him as my special protector and patron and still do. So in answer to my prayers to Saint Martin, my sister Mary was born on 10 April 1955. I was thrilled, delighted, beside myself with pure and utter joy. At last, I thought, I would not have to play rough and tough with other boys. I had my own little girl all for myself and we would share everything. I took care of her, washed her, walked her, clothed her and helped my mother in every single way. I could not wait to get home from school to see her and take her out in her pram for walks.

Mary was a very good baby and easy to take care of. The other boys did not seem to bother me about pushing her in her pram with my brother Sean holding its handle by my side. It was not at all unusual for the eldest child to take care of younger sisters and brothers in the large families that were quite common in the 1950s. I suppose one could say that this conscious identification with my first sister was the genesis of my gayness.

It was no surprise to anybody when as a young boy I started to practise saying mass. I would borrow one of my mother's more colourful dresses, together with a scarf to use as a stole, and begin to play priest. I would mimic what I could remember of mass in the church, giving out little pieces of Marietta biscuits for Holy Communion. It was then that my father decided that it would be a good idea to have me join the altar boys. I jumped at the idea, and felt so very proud when I was sent to the local dressmaker to be measured for my altar boy outfit. I looked like and felt like Shirley Temple, with my beautiful blond curls, red soutane and white surplice as I headed off to serve my first Mass.

Again, as an eight-year-old altar boy I had no conscious awareness of being sexually different. I knew I was different, but it was much, much later that this difference took on a sexual connotation. I loved the church and was the best little altar boy in the world. I could rattle off the Latin responses without a bother, even though of course I did not understand a word of them. Everything in the church, especially inside the altar rails, was beautiful. God lived there in the tabernacle, as did Our Lady, the angels and all the saints, including Saint Martin. I served devotions as often as I could, from the confraternities of the Holy Family, the Stations of the Cross, Mass on Sundays and at least one Mass on weekdays before I headed off on my high nelly bicycle to school. This was my mother's bike, which my father rescued from a fire in the café Iris and brought home. Of course it was far too big for me and I nearly castrated myself in trying to ride it.

By pubescence, I was prefect of the altar boys and had the say in who would serve what Mass, as well as which part each one would play in the high drama of the Easter triduum. These services were the high point of the church's liturgical year. They were magnificently camp and nothing I have seen on Broadway or the West End have replaced the beauty and splendour of the Tridentine liturgies of those pre-Vatican II days. I was in my seventh heaven.

After one such celebration I came home to our back garden to find two of my older pals ensconced in a makeshift tent of potato sacks that I had erected the day before. I was just turning thirteen years of age at the time. One of the boys was already fourteen and the other was sixteen. We started playing a game of truth and dare. The older boy dared the fourteen-year-old to try and put his hand up the leg of the older boy's long pants. The fourteen-year-old responded and succeeded. So the game went on. The problem was I was still in short trousers, so that when the dare came to me, I was of course an easy feel. That incident I believe was the first dawning of real awareness of my sexual attraction to my own gender. Innocently enough at the time, I believed that it was a sin only to touch a girl, but not a boy. That would soon change.

That September, I entered secondary school at Ennis CBS. Like all first year students I was full of beans and at the same time very apprehensive about mixing with the big boys. The brother in charge of first year students tried to give us something of a sex education. When he mentioned the word 'penis', one of the braver boys started mimicking piano playing. The brother gave him six of the hardest slaps on the hand with his leather strap and so ended our sex education. Fear, not love, was the rule of the day. We learned to fear everyone from teaching brother to the Garda Síochána, from the local shopkeeper to our fathers in our homes. 'Spare the cane and spoil the child' was the unwritten motto of both our primary and secondary school education. One of the few Brothers who showed us great kindness was also the one who sexually molested us at age eleven. It could certainly be said in the words of George Bernard Shaw that my schooling spoiled my education.

Through some kind of uneasiness I eventually mentioned in confession that I had put my hand up another boy's trousers. All hell broke loose. The priest told me that this was perverted and against human nature and it would have been better had I done it with a girl! I was from now on to seek him and him only for confession. When in future I would enter the box, instead of the usual greeting, 'Bless me Father for I have sinned', I would say: 'I come to you Father' so that he would recognise my tendency was to sin against nature. I was too afraid not to go to this priest for confession. Years later when I reflected on the endless questioning and inquisitorial manner that this man would engage me in when I confessed anything sexual, I was convinced that it was his perversion that led him to such voyeuristic and abusive use of the sacrament of reconciliation.

Eventually, after many rosaries and many more warnings from my confessor, I stopped playing truth and dare. Tangential to this was the fact that I had now for the very first time in my life fallen in love with another boy.

He looked like John Lennon and wore his hair in the same Beatle style that was hitting the hotspots of Ennis at the time. This gorgeous hunk was sixteen and I was just one year younger than him. We were in the same class at school and because he and his father used to attend mass every morning for Lent, I of course had to do the same. Getting up at the unearthly hour of 7.15a.m. was nothing to catch a glimpse of my Romeo as we caught each other's eye on our way back from Holy Communion. After Mass I would rush home and gulp down my breakfast and hop on my high nelly bicycle and just catch him as he rounded our street corner so we could cycle to school together. He of course had a proper boy's bicycle, as his family did not live in a council house like us.

This upward mobility of my very first romance convinced my mother that I had acquired some of my father's airs and graces. She kept asking why one of the kids of the estates that surrounded us was not good enough for me. I could not exactly tell her that this guy was more gorgeous. Instead I gave her religious reasons for my sudden interest in the other side of the railway track. I informed her that his father was in charge of the Legion of Mary and that they both went to mass every day for Lent. My father, on hearing this, said that his father must be a terrible old dry balls, which of course immediately ended my religious fervour.

The Beatles came to stay in Dromoland Castle and my newfound love and I hitched a ride from Ennis to try and sneak a glimpse of them in the castle grounds. One of their hits was 'I Wanna Hold Your Hand', and when Rick and I started holding hands when singing the song all my dreams started to materialise. But this was a short-lived pleasure, as one of the older boys saw us and called us queer and that was that.

I now spent countless days and nights wondering how I could have some kind of physical touch with Rick. More than anything in the world I wanted desperately to kiss him. I could not have him stay over in our house as there was not room enough for ourselves. So I thought that the best thing to do would be for us to try and get away to Lahinch for a camping holiday and there maybe, by the grace of God and our own hormones, we might just end up in an embrace. Of course Saint Martin was employed on the double to try and make this happen. Seeing that there was no sexual contact between us or consciously desired at the time, I believed that my good patron would not mind helping me out in loving someone. Eventually, after much negotiation and weeks of doing jobs around at home to convince my mother that I was not getting above myself going off with dry balls' son camping, I was released to the wilds of Lahinch.

Lahinch village was the favourite seaside resort for the people of Ennis. Located in west Clare, with a famous golf links, it had at the time a resident population of less than a hundred people. Rick and I had a wonderful time and kissed passionately every single night before we went to sleep. I was as happy as Larry until Rick's hormones suddenly, like a Paul of Tarsus conversion, turned heterosexual. Up and until now he had shown little interest in girls and I of course had absolutely no interest. I was what they now call at the extreme homosexual end of the Freudian scale. Despite having been told by the priest in the confessional that homosexuality was a phase that I was going through, it was 'a phase' that would last all of my life.

I tried to pretend that it was alright and that maybe I would meet a girl myself. I did try, but it was like kissing an ashtray. Eventually, on return to Ennis with our Lahinch accents, Rick started to go out with his newfound love. I was mad with jealousy and spent nights crying and wishing and praying that God would make me different. It did not work. I could not tell anybody that Helen had stolen my boyfriend. I could not even tell Rick. We still kissed and held hands occasionally but eventually that ceased. My mother thought that I was going through one of those teenage phases when she would catch me moping around the house or crying. How I wish I could have told her or anybody. She was again pregnant with my youngest sister. I urged her with all the powers of persuasion at my disposal to call my new baby sister Siobhán after Rick's sister, but my father beat me to it and she was called Ruth. I then pleaded that it would be wonderful if Rick were Ruth's godfather. Anything to get close to him. Anything to hold onto him. Even a spiritual relationship would do. But to no avail. A first cousin was chosen and my romanticism dismissed without a question. I was lost in an abyss of perpetual doubt and despair. There was no future to love for me. I probably was the only boy in all the world that felt this way. I used to lie awake in bed at night thinking of him and talking to him in my mind. His Beatle haircut, brown eyes, drainpipe pants, duffle coat and winkle-picker shoes are as clear today as they were then.

The priesthood, which was never far from mind, became more and more my desired future. Forget about loving another boy or man. That did not happen in the real world. I would be a priest and love everybody. I thought and believed that I would never again fall in love and that giving my life to the church to help others would be the cure all for these feelings I had. In fact I would give my life to the poorest of the poor in Africa and there all these feelings would be submerged and channelled into bringing souls to Christ. I could never be more wrong.

On 15 September 1965, I boarded a train for the African Missionary Noviciate in Cloughballymore, County Galway, for what was to be the happiest nine months of my life. I was seventeen years of age. Here in the novitiate, as later on in seminary, I flourished in my studies. For the very first time in my life I was free of fear. The priests and teachers were kind, gentle, encouraging and supportive of our learning. It was a night to day difference from school in Ennis. The monastic life we led was highly structured. Every hour of every day had to be accounted for. From dawn to dusk we had a daily horarium to follow and this was the unquestionable will of God for us. In fact there was more emphasis placed on holy obedience than any other virtue, including charity. In the noviciate certain boys had crushes on certain boys, but of course such crushes were totally frowned upon and any Particular Friendships were forbidden. The word 'homosexuality' or any sexuality was never mentioned, either here or in the major seminary afterwards, but the big no was 'PFs', which was the acronym commonly used for Particular Friendships during the years of our formation. I very quickly developed my own PF, but of course did so with all the skill and cat and mouse tactics I was fast learning in order to hide my true feelings and nature. Even though I am sure that the Dean of Students knew of Jay's and my relationship, he never did say anything directly to us. He simply made sure that when we were together, there was always someone else in our company. Again our relationship at this time and throughout the noviciate was completely non-physical. It was later that this aspect of our love began to express itself.

This happened in the major seminary during our philosophy years. Up and until now we modelled our relationship on Jesus and John the Beloved Disciple. We were both very athletic and spent whatever free time we had either playing sport, weight-lifting or running. After one such workout we decided to give each other a massage. One thing led to another and almost inevitably the juices started flowing. When one of our confessors found out about it he threatened to kick us out, but then relented. We were both so innocent and ignorant of sexual matters that when questioned as to whether 'we had ever entered each other from behind' I responded, 'O no Father, we always come in the side door.' The priest told me later, after my own ordination, that the reason he did not ask us to leave was because we were so naïve and that he had fancied Jay himself. We were told that we could stay on the condition that we would never again touch each other sexually. We never again went to confession while in seminary and continued our relationship until Jay eventually left and married. I was ordained in December 1971 and left for a two-year stay in Africa the following year. This was the most difficult time of my life up and until now.

Although celibate for several years now (since Jay left the seminary), I was still in a lot of pain about my sexuality. This fact was exacerbated by my presence in a foreign country with a people, language, customs and culture that was as different from where I came from as Mars. I loved the people and got along with them very well. But ultimately I had no one I could talk to about what was going on inside of me. I knew intuitively that no one of my confrères would understand, so at the end of my second year I requested and was given permission to go for further studies in psychology at Fordham University in New York City.

This was to be my true apotheosis. I fell in love with New York straight away. I had already worked there as a singing waiter in 1969 in order to pay toward my training for priesthood and my ordination reception. I had worked in the Catskill Mountains in what they call the Irish Catskills, as distinct from the Jewish, Italian, etc. I located myself in a little town called Leeds, Green County, and had one of the happiest summers of my life. I worked hard waiting on tables all day and in the bar at night. As well as that, I was available for singing on request with whatever band would happen to be in residence for the entertainment of the customers. My singing career took off quite by accident, like so much in life. On the first evening of my arrival I was invited up to give a song from the old sod, seeing I had just arrived 'off the boat'. From then on I learnt more Irish songs and ballads within a week than Christy Moore in a lifetime. Of course my efforts were richly rewarded and I became the popular Irish lad who was studying for the priesthood. I can still hear people calling for me to sing 'Boola Boola' because they could not pronounce Boolavogue. That time I had no consciousness about my gay identity in any liberating sense. I still believed that it was a sin and for me a cross I had to bear. The fact that there were many beautiful and very attractive young girls around, in whom I had no interest, did not raise an eyebrow. After all, according to local lore I was watching my vocation. This I completely accepted myself and never once got involved with dating either boy or girl.

That was then. This time it was going to be different. I had no idea where the path would lead me. My mentor at the university insisted that I go into personal psychoanalysis while I was studying for my masters degree and then my doctorate. I could no longer hide. Having practised as a psychotherapist over the past twenty years I can say unequivocally that there is no magic whatsoever in being either patient or therapist. But what the experience can do is allow one to freely express without being judged what one is truly feeling. This was and is an extraordinary gift to someone bred in the Catholic clerical world from such an early age. All human behaviour in such a world is looked at from the point of view of being right or wrong. Feelings are similarly judged. The result and consequence of this is that sexual feelings, where every thought, word or deed is at least a venial sin, are rarely if ever expressed in an honest and healthy way. One is reduced to infantilism, psychosexually speaking. The results being that few if any leave this system without serious sexually arrested development. The fact that I was nearly thirty years of age before I could admit to myself that I was gay is only one aspect of this. Knowledge is power. There is no place in our entire educational system where an absence of basic information was more obvious than in the area of human sexuality. Human sexuality is to my mind the seat of our relationality. It has as much to do with how one celebrates mass and relates to God, as it has to do with the love we sleep with. If not treated with the care and nurture it deserves, then it can and will result in very unhealthy relationships and even more unhealthy and bizarre preconceptions about who we are as human beings.

Therefore, trotting off to this very classy Fifth Avenue shrink every week to pour out my soul became for me not only a way to get my own degrees in the field, but more importantly still, a kind of rebirth. I was very afraid that I indeed might discover I was gay. I am sure at one level I was as obvious as a fairy on a fairy fossil, yet there was no way I wanted to accept this. After all I was still praying to Saint Martin for a cure. I did not at all realise that the answer to my prayer was acceptance of facts. This was not helped by my erroneous belief that what the Church taught about homosexuality was from God.

New York at this time was having one of it many fiscal crises. Abe Beam was mayor, and the lesbian, gay and transgendered communities were very vibrant and alive with all kinds of promise. After all, it was less than ten years since the Stonewall riots that gave birth to the whole liberation movement, so gay bars and clubs flourished everywhere. As a priest I was flung in at the deep end of this newfound freedom and for the first time in my life began to seriously question my vocation. Very soon I was part of and theological advisor to New York's Catholic lesbian, gay and transgendered community in an organisation called Dignity, the largest then homophile group in the United States. I was no longer the only, lonely boy with these 'unnatural' feelings. There were thousands of us and we were everywhere. With fear and trepidation at first and then with more and more confidence I became part of that self-liberating, other-liberating mass of queer people who had had enough of shaming and hiding and pretending to be something that we were not. I saw my faith in Christ now as a challenge to be who God created me to be in love. As an extension of that baptismal covenant I saw my priesthood as a vehicle to be used for the liberation of others from the same self-hatred and denial.

I have written extensively about where this commitment to the freedom of 'my own people' has led me, and also about my work with people affected and infected by HIV and AIDS in my book A Priest on Trial (Bloomsbury Press, 1993). What I would like to do now is continue that story from my departure from New York City in 1992 to the present time.

The most momentous and significant event in my life is that since 12 September 1998, I am a happily married gay man. Billy and I met at a mutual friend's birthday party in March of 1993. At that time there was not a bone in the soul of my body left unbroken. I had been forced out of the city I loved, after the most ignominious and shameful trial brought about by the Archdiocese of New York and the FBI. On top of that I had witnessed person after person fall ill and die of HIV/AIDS, amongst whom were some of my closest friends and associates. I was in no fit state for loving. The trial had left me in shreds.

Billy from the beginning did the chasing. I, initially, was flattered that someone so young, vibrant and with an extraordinarily winning personality would find someone like me so attractive. I passed it off and never really took Billy's attentions seriously. What I did not realise at the time was that Billy was most serious and indeed hurting that I would not give our relationship a chance. For almost four years I played this game, until eventually the penny dropped, the hurt healed and I fell for what would be and is the truest and most beautiful experience of God in my entire life. On 12 September 1998 we had our relationship solemnly blessed and affirmed by a Cistercian priest friend of ours who flew to London from the United States to be with us. Both families were present as well as many of our friends.

I continue to remain as priest, celebrating and ministering where and when I have the opportunity. I am still very focused on the particular mission that my love of those affected and infected by HIV/AIDS has gifted me with. As the Lakota Sioux Indians put it, 'When life gives a burden, it also gives a gift.' I pray I am worthy. Gratefully, through some good fortune in our youth, our hearts were touched by fire.

so far along the road

Braveheart

MY FIRST SEXUAL encounter with a man took place when I was nineteen and in college. He was twenty-two and training to be a priest also. I was besotted by him — late nights, climbing stairs in the dark at forbidden hours, the sense of danger, the risk. It was wonderful, new, exciting and definitely love. We never spoke about it, it just happened. We never called it homosexuality, we never saw ourselves as being gay. We just spent these most intimate of times together. I was sure that we were the only two guys in the world who lived like this and I didn't care.

Then, the inevitable happened, he was ordained a priest and ended our relationship of six months. My world fell apart. He told me it was over and moved away, he had become a priest and this new responsibility literally changed his attitude to me overnight. He just walked out. It devastated me. I lost sleep, weight, my sense of fun and confidence. I had no support, none whatsoever. I was alone. I could tell nobody, especially my family and friends. There was nowhere to turn except inwards. Inwards and downwards it went like heavy lead, poisoning my system. I pined and pined for my lost love. Looking back on it now I was grieving for the loss of love, the loss of that person to hold and touch and connect with — the stuff of love songs.

And yet there was a hope in me that made me determined to survive. I was going to become a priest at all costs. But I was definite that I would never be intimate with a man again and I could now deal with being gay by completely ignoring it.

I was almost thirty years of age before I began to look seriously and honestly at being gay. By then I had begun the journey out of priesthood. I faced a new reality with a sense of uncertainty and fear but also an inner optimism and strength. It was a difficult journey for me. Having hated the very thought of being gay and having had so many negative thoughts around it, I am not surprised that my life was filled with shame. I 'above all' could not be gay; how could I be gay? I believed in God and worked hard for the Church, so how could I be gay? I wasn't sexually abused, my family upbringing was the same as any so-called 'normal' Irish family, so what made me this way? I was always a sensitive child and was very close to my sisters and loved them dearly and learned a lot from them. I was always conscious that I held strong opinions about fighting and bullying and war, being opposed to them. I never fought at school, never, and apart from the occasional fight with my brother I never hit anybody in my life. I preferred playing with the girls because they were more real and kind and able to listen. So was this part of being gay? Or was it the fact that I loved art, and cooking and gardening and plants and flowers and liked all things French, including fashion — did this make me gay? Or was it because I loved my mother and took her side and could see her point of view and found my dad to be so lost for feelings and expression and warmth at times that I disliked him? Or was it because my dad once called me a sissy and I never forgot that? Or was it because my mother minded me too much and smothered me under her apron? Or was it because I inherited it from my parents' genes just like my two gay cousins?

I never found out what made me gay and I don't expect that I will, but I am gay. The moment I accepted that I was gay and could act no more was a new beginning for me. I could not live in conflict. I needed intimacy and a relationship if I was to develop as a man and nobody was going to stop me.

I had little or no support on this journey apart from counselling sessions, for which I am indebted. I knew few gay men, which is still the case as I live in rural Ireland. When I left the priesthood I received no support whatsoever from the Church I worked in — and I mean none — and to be honest I didn't expect any. There were a few good men in the diocese and these remained supportive when I left. There were a few gay priests in the diocese and, as I found out to my surprise later on, some were 'half out', attending gay clubs and pubs. Word always leaked out about who they were and, while they were always friendly, very few were prepared to discuss the core issues affecting them as gay men. I believe that the failure of gay priests to support one another as gay men and talk out their issues is a lost opportunity for the development of the Church of the future. That same Church is the one that I have now let go from my life and no longer believe in. I cannot trust an organisation that condemns me for what I believe so strongly in. I beg to differ and respectfully leave it behind me on my journey.

For me there was the double shame of being gay and a priest. At times I nearly felt responsible for the priests who were abusing young boys and girls, until I realised that there was the world of a difference between paedophilia and being gay. I will always be grateful to my therapist for giving me the safety of her counselling room to discover this awareness. The sense of relief was unbelievable; at long last I could be gay without the shame.

One of the most difficult and disappointing experiences for me, having left the priesthood, was the lack of support within the gay community. The 'scene' was mostly a 'meat market' then, and I am sure it still is, although I don't go there anymore. Sometimes I 'binge' on the chat lines but they too can be tedious and addictive and there is often a sense of loss associated with them, grieving the friendships that never came to pass.

I lived in Dublin for a short while and there I slowly moved into gay circles, joining a support group and meeting some guys. But I found it difficult. I didn't like being confined to the gay scene with everybody watching everybody else (heads spinning like prairie dogs), the suspicion, the infidelity, the promiscuity, the rows. I saw one poor guy slapped so hard across the face one night that an earring was knocked out of his ear; and all because he smiled at me in front of his partner. I found it difficult to find guys who were looking for more than sex and a one-night stand. And I didn't want to be classified as being a member of a gay walking group, a gay art group, a gay wine taster's group, or whatever. I could see the value in them up to a point, but it just wasn't me. Much of the gay support scene is almost clandestine and underground, and society still has a long way to go to accept gayness at a level where it will be safe for gay men to express their affection in public.

I have fallen head over heels in love a couple of times and that has been good, and I have been hurt a few times and that has been hell, and through it all I have had two good friends who have allowed me to stand on their kitchen floor and laugh and cry about it all.

But I know who I am and that is important to me. Most of my family know that I am gay and I remember with great clarity the day I told my mother. I knew the time had come to tell her. I was always close to her and once I had accepted that I was gay to myself it was almost automatic that she should know. So I sat with her in our kitchen one day, having planned to tell her for a week beforehand, and seized the opportunity. 'Mum,' I said, 'I have something to tell you, but I find it difficult to say.' I struggled to say the words and became sick with fear. She asked me if everything was okay and I replied that I had something difficult to say to her. She encouraged me but I couldn't say it. She asked me if it was cancer and I replied no, was it some other sickness and I replied no. It was so difficult that I couldn't speak. Then she said 'Oh I know...are you gay?' and I replied 'Yes...' and I cried and I said that I hated myself for it. She looked at me and replied that she had only one worry and this was that I would hate myself. She didn't care what I was and loved me very much. It is what I expected from my mother and it was a good lesson for me, to learn to trust those with whom I had journeyed throughout my life. I saw her in a different light from that day on. She was now my peer; always mother but a good friend too. Her acceptance allowed me to tell other family members and my closest friends.

I remember sitting beside her once as a politician ranted on the TV about homosexual acts being heinous crimes. She knew I was gay and I felt sorry for her as she listened to a man condemn her son, to the applause of some of the audience, and I felt sorry that I had brought her in to all this pain. But she didn't see this as pain, just another silly politician and laughed.

Living alone in the countryside has great advantages for me, but finding the partner of my dreams is a challenge — not impossible and I live in eternal hope. I am conscious of the loneliness and isolation of rural gay men and how some of them must be living in hell. Gay men need to talk and need the opportunities and safe spaces in which to talk, where there is no competition to look good, no alcohol to drown the pain and no one with a twinkle in his eye expecting you to sleep with him tonight.

I feel that my life is now just beginning and I am full of hope because of this. I am looking forward to meeting somebody, someday, who will bring fun, support and companionship into my life.

'til deceit do us part

Sinéad

'TIL DECEIT DO us part' (a title I came across) applies to my situation. My husband is gay. He didn't choose to be gay, but he did choose how he reacted to it. He decided not to face up to it. This has ended in tragedy. He knew he was gay as a teenager, yet when he was thirty-five he married me.

After fifteen years of marriage and two children I found out he was homosexual. I look at my husband now and see a stranger. He was unfair to himself and unfair to me.

Who's to say what anyone will do in certain circumstances. Nevertheless, to marry when your sexual orientation is in question or, in my husband's case, knowing you are gay, is wrong. To deceive a woman in this way is immoral. To bring children into the world and cause them so much upset is selfish.

How do I tell a girl of fourteen and a boy of nine that their father is gay? And if I don't, I risk them finding out in an inappropriate way. There is a huge stigma attached to it. They won't be able to talk about it; they will wonder if they are the same. Friends will shy away from them. When there are gay characters on television, I watch uncomfortably. My children watch, oblivious of the heartache that lies ahead.

I'm devastated mainly because of the effect on the children. They will have to deal with having a gay father. They have been robbed of a normal family and will suffer the financial and emotional consequences. For my part I was duped and used as a cover. I have been sexually rejected. My husband was having sex with men for some time before I knew, which raises the HIV business. It is bad enough that he has been unfaithful but with a man…if it had been another woman it would be totally different. My husband has had and continues to have sex with numerous men.

My marriage was based on lies and deception. It never really existed. In legal jargon it could not be sustained because my husband is not by nature heterosexual. It was contracted under false representation and fraudulent concealment and but for that I would not have consented to marry him.

We have separated. The cause of the marriage breakdown is my husband's sexual orientation. The family unit has been fractured. This has been shattering. It is difficult for children to cope with separation. My father was killed when I was small and I'd hoped my children would experience having a father living with them. Alongside the emotional, parental and financial issues associated with separating there is the added torment which having a gay husband brings. It would have been easier if he had died; others in my position feel the same.

The secrecy is the hardest part. It is a huge burden to carry. When a gay married man comes out of the closet, his spouse and children go in. The cause of our separation is no one's business, yet I can't tell people even if I want to. Despite my reticence, the help I've received from family, friends and colleagues has moved me to tears. Our separation came out of the blue with no lead-up to it. As a couple we got on well. Everyone is stunned. Family, friends and colleagues are naturally curious and concerned, yet I can't talk about it even to the few I would like to. Not being able to tell the truth (because the children don't know) makes me uncomfortable. It also makes people jump to erroneous conclusions. The pressure of the secrecy, medical issues, separating, finances, the dread of the children finding out, etc., takes its toll. It affected my work on one occasion. This I deeply regret. My manager, for whom I have enormous respect, made allowances for me.

Having a gay husband is not dissimilar to being physically or sexually abused in that it 'doesn't happen' and is not spoken about.

My life (so far) has been extraordinary. As well as happy times I've experienced poverty, physical and emotional pain, and abuse. These and other experiences make me know that I am strong and that I will move on.

My husband knows by my words and actions over the years that I am not homophobic. Yet to pretend you are something that you are not is wrong; to mislead innocent people is wrong.

My husband knew he was gay yet he still married me. The deceit was wrong. My marriage was a sham. My past and my future dreams have been wiped out. Yet I refuse to carry resentment. I live in the present and don't dwell on the past. Despite everything, each day is a joy. I have my health, family, friends, work and interests.

Gay men saying they 'didn't realise' or they 'hoped it would go away' is a euphemism for cowardice. My husband and men like him have lost out. Nothing can repair the damage that has been done. The repercussions devastate lives. By living a lie all their relationships have being irreparably damaged. Their friends and family never really knew them. Any perceived trust between them has been betrayed. Their sexual orientation inevitably means that there will always be a chasm between them and their children.

My husband didn't choose to be gay. He did choose his reaction to it — to betray the very essence of his being and ruin many lives.

being different in a rural area

Paul Allen

I DIDN'T KNOW UNTIL I was forty, although everybody else knew. I certainly had those tendencies as a teenager, but I just thought it was all part of the exploration of growing up. I had no interest in exploring the opposite sex while I was at school. That was because I had always been at a mixed school and so took the opposite sex for granted. I kidded myself. I always dreaded the school dance, as that was crunch time — I had to find a girl. If not, I was the class 'wallflower'. I didn't know at that time that being the class 'pansy' would be worse. It was possible also that I could have been asexual, but I didn't know either that such a word existed in the late 1970s. At that time to be 'gay' meant to be 'happy', and if a guy liked guys he was a 'queer' or a 'homo', and had at all costs to be avoided. For another guy to walk along the corridor or to be alone in a room with 'one of them' meant an awful lot of slagging for a number of weeks afterwards. The law of the country didn't help either — it was 'illegal', despite patriot Roger Casement's suggested tendencies.

In Leaving Cert class little bits of advice were given out by masterly teachers to beware of those who decided they wanted men, not women. One so-called expert said it was all a matter of discipline, and anyone with such tendencies was urged to mend their ways, to confess it to the priest and to find a woman. Some years later my younger brother told me a nun came to his class in first year to talk about sex. Students, to save embarrassment, were given the chance to write down questions anonymously and the questions were then read out in class and discussed. That night at a parents' meeting one of the questions asked was read out and described by a nun as a 'nasty set-up'. A disappointed nun said that while she didn't take the question seriously, she felt that parents should be aware of the type of ideas that were in children's heads. The question directly asked 'Am I gay? I'm fourteen and think more about boys than girls and wonder what certain fellows look like with their clothes off.' I didn't confide that I felt the same when I was that age, but didn't have the 'late 1980s' courage in the late 1970s.

I remained in perfect celibacy and went to Dublin in 1980. I had heard whispers about the 'jacks' near the Green and the ones on O'Connell Bridge. I went to assess the O'Connell Bridge situation and went into a cubicle. I always had a problem with urinals. Behind the door was graffiti by the ton, each note gave credentials and said 'make date'. I refrained from doing that. I thought of all the pretty girls in the office — surely one would have feelings for me. I ignored the graffiti invitations with disgust. Graffiti was illegal, I felt, but that was just a surface thought; an underneath layer of the mind told me that these were the guys I was told to watch out for at school. The inner self felt sorry for such guys and for me, as I had the same tendencies. Perhaps I was one of them. A mixed-up teenager caught the Friday evening train home.

Over the next few months/years there were two attempted 'rendezvous' in Dublin. One Monday morning I entered a toilet in O'Connell Street and stood there. An older guy stood beside me. I left, he followed me and asked for a 'light'. I didn't have one but he chatted away and admired my jacket. He then asked had I a safe haven. I pretended, trembling, not to know what he meant. He apologised and disappeared. I had missed an opportunity. A later encounter with another guy spelt disaster. At the same venue I accepted his invitation and went a step further. He said he heard someone coming and left in a hurry. My wallet went with him.

For personal reasons I had to leave Dublin and return home to rural Ireland. It was hell! I don't know what happened, but the youth of my locality knew my secret. I don't think they were told, I think they just guessed, but it happened. Ten years of hell! I was afraid to go into town after dark or during school lunch hour. Teenagers were everywhere, yelling out my name across the street followed by all the usual comments: 'Queer', 'Pansy', 'Faggot' ... 'Why have you got your hand in your pocket?' Innuendo in pubs, someone I would have a drink with would be remarked to: 'Are you not afraid going home with him?' My youth was destroyed. Living near the road and lying in bed on a summer's night, abuse was shouted as youths who had had one too many passed my house. Gardening was almost impossible on a summer's evening as vicious comments were made by the youth of the town as I dug a flowerbed. By mistake when attending mass one morning I found I was at a school mass, and as we left, abuse was hurled at me by name. The teachers didn't hear or were incapable of doing anything, and hopefully the older people there didn't know what a 'queer' was. The worst came as I walked with other family members behind my father's coffin down the main street of the town. Three youngsters sat on beer barrels outside a pub and as the hearse passed by they looked at me and shouted 'Queer'. I couldn't trust anyone. Fortunately for me, Ireland was in economic crisis and the emigrant train took away a lot of the culprits to London and things quietened down publicly after ten years. But in private the mind was in greater turmoil. I told my secret to no one. I didn't even know that I had a big secret. I just about coped and got on with life.

One day I opened a newspaper with an article about gay men in Ireland. One guy told his story and of how eventually he learned to cope. He said he began life with a prayer 'Please God don't let me be gay', but he then realised he was and made the best of things. It gave a contact line. I phoned it but it was confined to Dublin only and the person answering knew of no rural support systems. I was no further forward except that I now knew of someone else who felt like me. His prayer became my prayer, but it wasn't answered. Sometime later when in the capital I bought the magazine In Dublin and there was an ad in it from my own locality. I answered it but gave no name because the advertiser was a nineteen-year-old. I wasn't much older myself but I felt I couldn't trust someone of that age. The following edition carried a message asking me to contact him again. I didn't, too afraid. Another missed opportunity!

A couple of years ago when I reached forty I realised that I was gay. I tried, in earnest — following up any contact I had, answering Buy and Sell ads, inserting my own ads, meeting guys occasionally on a once-off basis. They promise to contact me again, but don't. They often say not to ring them as the wife might find out. One particular guy clicked with me, he was unmarried and the same age. I had his mobile number and rang it a few times and got no reply. One day I did get a reply to be told that Daddy was gone out and did I want to talk to mother. I wonder how he explained that call to his wife.

Life goes on. I can't go public, the hassle would be too much. Despite equal opportunities my job wouldn't allow it. Some day my prince will come. Maybe! It can be very lonely waiting and also I know that for those assumed to be a little different, after ten years of bullying, life is not a fairytale.

changing through life's journey

Mike

I WAS BORN IN a working class area and brought up very Catholic. Sex was a taboo subject and whenever it appeared on TV it was switched off. My parents didn't really speak much about sex or relationships and I had an embarrassing two minutes while my dad tried in vain to explain the facts of life.

I was very religious, although not really in the Catholic or any specific Christian sense, and I spoke and prayed to God every day, mainly for help and support throughout the day, until I was about thirteen, when I got really interested in science and then decided that the universe was infinite in time and space and did not need a god.

I assumed I was gay from an early age, being attracted to boys in my all-boys school and not really having much success with girls. I had a few girlfriends but usually they asked me out.

When I was about twenty-three I rang the Gay Switchboard and they told me about Icebreakers and a gay youth group, which I duly went to and declared myself gay. The Gay Switchboard and Icebreakers were very beneficial, as I was at a very confused time in my life and they showed me an alternative to being lonely and unhappy, that there were other people out there with whom I could identify and who would not judge me if I told them about my sexual feelings.

I started going out with my boyfriend when I was about twenty-eight. My parents' initial reaction to my boyfriend was very negative — that he was a bad influence on me and that I wasn't really into men at all. I told them that they didn't truly love me, that their love was conditional on me doing what they expected of me. We all got very emotional and upset and they said that they still loved me but that they were scared of what the neighbours might think and of me being beaten up. They told me they would rather if I didn't bring my boyfriend to their house. This went on for a number of years but eventually they realised that my boyfriend was actually a nice person and nothing to be afraid of. Now things are fine — my boyfriend visits with me when I go to my parents' house and is very welcome. And his parents and mine get on well together also.

I can safely say that in the eleven years we have been together that, except at the beginning, everyone else in both our families have not treated us in any differently than if we were a heterosexual couple. And we get on very well with both our families now.

However, when I was about twenty-five or twenty-six I began to feel an attraction to women. I think I always felt this attraction, but was very shy and self-conscious. It wasn't until I discovered a group called 'Bi-Irish' that I realised that the term 'bisexual' was a term that I could be comfortable with and I could use to explain my own sexuality.

The bisexual movement had finally arrived in Ireland in the form of the Bi-Irish group in 1996 with four people getting together in a gay pub in Dublin and putting a listing in *Gay Community News* saying that Bi-Irish was a group for bisexuals in Ireland and that they meet each Friday in the Out on the Liffey pub.

I commenced going along to the meetings when the group moved to the new Gay Community Centre in Dublin, Outhouse, in 1998 and have been going along ever since. I am happy to use the term bisexual to describe my sexuality.

Meeting up with Bi-Irish has also been a very rewarding and positive experience for me. Being with my boyfriend means that most people would describe me as gay and I have no problem with that. However, I believe that because I am also sexually attracted to women, the term 'gay' does not truly reflect who I am or how I am feeling. I have found that a lot of people in the gay and straight community either feel threatened by or fail to comprehend that someone can be bisexual. It is great to be able to meet up on a regular basis with people who I can identify with and who have no problem with me being bisexual.

I began my interest in meditation in about 1997 when I was thirty, as

I was very stressed in work and someone said that meditation was beneficial. I went along to a meditation group, which I also discovered was run by a group of Buddhists called the Friends of the Western Buddhist Order (FWBO). They had just set up the Dublin Meditation Centre in Temple Bar, giving meditation and yoga classes. This led me on to read quite a bit about the Buddha, the four noble truths and the eight-fold path to enlightenment. I attended some Vassas in Cavan where like-minded people got together for meditation, yoga and general discussions on themes of spirituality and Buddhism. This was a breath of fresh air from my life in the hustle and bustle of Dublin and my 9 to 5 job. I found the FWBO to be open to people with alternative lifestyles like myself and I was also persuaded to become vegetarian, as they taught the way of loving kindness, Mettabhavna.

Coincidently, as with the reaction of friends of mine to my telling them I was bisexual, I have got a similar negative reaction when I tell people I am going to Buddhist classes or if I bring up the subject of Buddhism. Usually they just skip on to another topic or make jokes about me banging gongs and chanting. Again it is only when I am in the company of other people who have discovered Buddhism that I can identify and discuss the subject.

coming and going

Frances Bird

W HEN I WAS fourteen, I wanted to become a nun. Yes, I know, you've heard that one before! I clearly remember the first time it struck me, finding an incredible peace in the chapel of the Assisi Home and Hospital, run by a community of Franciscan nuns.

The order had been special to me since childhood. My parents, immigrants to New Zealand, made their lives deep amongst the Catholic community in the then small city of Hamilton. My earliest memories involve the Irish Franciscan sisters, their fundraising fair, and the temporary chapel in a nearby house that would eventually become the secular home of school friends (complete with older sister's stack of *Playgirl* magazines that were of educational interest, but not much else!).

I felt quite at home amongst the Franciscan community, and was moved by their members' simple lifestyle, wonderfully dry senses of humour and political debate. I was taught by RNDM religious, who seemed altogether more worldly and youthful — they were on the verge of shedding their veils. The stillness and reverence out at Assisi captivated me, as it did my parents, who themselves were lay Franciscans for years. I became big into basic living and shopping denial.

I was a fairly unusual teen for my time, as I spent much of my school holidays in the early 1980s attending daily mass at the local cathedral. My devotion would often result in a silent thrill when mass was also attended by Sr Christine RNDM, but more on that later!

By the end of my fifteenth year I hit my first emotional black wall, struggling with my life and its meaning. It was an experience that was to recur, and one I would discover that was painfully over-represented within the lesbian and gay/queer population. Later, when teaching, I was to be devastated by the suicide of a young gay man in my college.

Many of the significant events of my teenage years can be pegged around the pursuit of my dream to enter the religious life. At a diocesan youth weekend — a kind of grooming ground for potential priests and religious — I met other young people fired up by their faith. I became friends with a guy who was killed a few months later in a car accident. It was a kick in the guts, but God moved in mysterious ways.

My all-girls school had two senior balls a year, one with the Catholic boys and the other with the Anglican boys. As the ball with the Anglicans was first in the calendar, many of the single girls were snaffled up into cross-religious relationships. Having never received the slightest bit of attention from any boy, bar the rush of opportunities presented to me on my first visit to Ireland in 1980 (must be all that rural repression!), I found myself with a boyfriend. We were chalk and cheese: a national champion swimmer and a dog paddler, a dyslexic and a school first in English, a straight boy and a baby dyke. We dated, we walked, we talked for hours, we never so much as held hands. However, the mere presence of an historical boyfriend was enough for my hysterical mother to exclaim years later, 'You were normal once!'

My allegiances slowly shifted from the Franciscans to the RNDMs. The former were nurses in New Zealand, and as I couldn't stand the sight of blood it seemed an impossible career move. Besides, brown isn't my colour! I went on a reflective weekend at the RNDM's venue for postulants. It was especially exciting because Sr Christine, as an example of one of the younger nuns, came along. She practised her flute, a gift from the order for her final vows, and I thought it was heaven. Or perhaps I just wished I was the flute...

My last few years at school were dominated by Sr Chris. We developed a perfectly unhealthy, co-dependent relationship. We spent so much time together that I began to get a reputation, unknown to me, of being...you know. We walked, talked for hours, we lay on the banks of the river, we lay on the banks of the lake, we lay on a narrow bed at a hockey tournament, we hugged for hours, I cooked dinner, she made lunch... Of course, these were perfectly normal things to do, a teenager and a nun some eleven years older! It was quite innocent at the time, but hindsight and experience scream another story, and the jigsaw fell into place at university.

I headed away to university and Chris and another young nun, Ruth, became wandering retreat givers. I hardly saw Chris after that. For my first year I lived at the Catholic university hostel, where I was keen to be part of a faith community. I discovered I was pretty much the odd one out again, as the others were worldly wise, and I was exposed to life in a way I hadn't been before.

We had a gay lay chaplain, and it was the first time I'd knowingly been exposed to a gay person, although at first I found it hard to believe he could be gay. After all, he was a chaplain. I cringe when I look back on it.

The non-residential students who created the parish seemed very sophisticated and I enjoyed the vibrancy and depth of faith. I also got involved in the university cross-faiths political action group and this awakened my politics and liberalism. I was better able to handle myself around the gay members of this group! It was the year the Rainbow Warrior was bombed in the harbour at the back of my hostel and I denied myself the joys of French wines for years because of it!

I became friends with a trainee Dominican brother, and he introduced me to the liberal parish of St Dominic's, which made a lively alternative to the university parish. The church and my faith were very important to me, and I felt a sense of belonging and community that was incredibly rewarding. Having felt so different at school, having felt the difference of being the child of immigrants, not quite a New Zealander, it was wonderful to belong.

Chris left for Italy and then the missions. I saw her off at the airport and I cried, inconsolably, for hours. She sent me a postcard from Assisi.

By my second year at university my earlier feminist stirrings had been well developed. The Pope was heading to New Zealand and the arrangements, and his views on a number of matters, were causing some consternation for the leftish elements of the church. Sr Ruth, amongst others, was interviewed for a major national magazine, and spoke out boldly. I was increasingly questioning women's marginalised place within the Church and the morality of spending millions on a papal visit while the dispossessed I'd met on soup runs slept on park benches.

A friend asked me after Mass one evening if I'd go clubbing with him. He thought he was bisexual and wanted to go to one of the gay clubs. I thought it a supportive thing to do in the era of homosexual law reform and 'Heterosexuals Unafraid of Gays' badges. The churches were aligned in their fight against law reform, and massive petitions were organised up and down the country.

I had no idea one visit to a nightclub would change my life.

Across the smoky dance floor, in the downstairs of Alfies Nightclub (as bad as it sounds), I saw two women kissing. I felt a fire inside me. At last, I understood desire.

I came out through the dance floors of Auckland's two gay clubs. My first lesbian friend was also a first-generation Irish Catholic and we had much in common. It was a relief to step through those early doors with someone whose experience was somewhat similar to my own. However, my friend had moved away from the church and felt it had no place in her life.

I tried to make contact with the Catholic gay group, but received a response telling me they were in recess. I had no one I could tease out my anxieties with. I felt unwelcome in the church from the public statements made over homosexual law reform, and it only added to my growing political sense of disenfranchisement. I had had so much respect for my faith, and formerly for the church, that I felt I could not mock it or be a hypocrite, and thus my painful decision was made. I severed my ties abruptly. It felt like a huge loss.

Eventually the inevitable happened, and I had my first relationship. I thought it would be forever, looking at life with my Catholic framework. I had much to learn!

I came out to my mother as a church non-attendee the same weekend as I came out as a lesbian. I'm not sure which hurt her more, though both were not a surprise. My parents were always welcoming to my friends and girlfriends, not knowing who was what.

It took Mum years to find peace with my sexuality, and she eventually shifted when one of my brothers acknowledged he had known for years, as had all my siblings, and that God had made me as I am and therefore it must be okay.

After I came out, Sr Ruth returned to study at my university. She was a leather-clad, motorbike-riding babe, and sure enough, one of my friends remembered her from the scene! I nearly died every time I saw her. I wished then I'd had the courage to try to talk to her about politics, faith and sexuality, but I was too shy.

A gang of girls from my school came out after me. One told me later she had always been envious of my close relationship with Sr Chris. She was convinced I had 'gone further' with Chris than she had.

The 1980s was a time of queer political activity and AIDS activism across the globe. I revelled in grass-roots activism, and I look back with a fondness on nights of plastering billboards and power poles with posters, refusing to answer census questions that didn't allow for same-sex partnership recognition, forcing changes for future years, and staging sit-ins in New Zealand.

While living in London I took up a voluntary management position, chairing the board of an LGBT community centre that focused on providing health-related services and supports to the most vulnerable in the queer communities. How we, in the western world, had grown in a few decades, from community-based actions to being able to secure statutory funding for projects, looking for space to support the development of healthy identities.

In recent years I have lived in Ireland, my mother's homeland. I've enjoyed participating in Ireland's lesbian and gay choir, Gloria, which strives to educate and promote a positive image of what it means to be lesbian or gay, along with making a (generally) pleasant, uplifting noise. Not surprisingly, I get the most joy out of singing the sacred pieces that remind me of my youth.

I managed the Dubin LGBT community centre soon after the purchase of a ramshackle building with potential, and it is satisfying to know I made a really tangible contribution to developing both the physical and infrastructural fabric of Ireland's queer community. While I think it will always be important to create safe space for the support of lesbian and gay identity, evolution takes us to the place where we have become more accepted, attention turns to preserving history, continuing to diversify, and also to mainstream our agendas.

When I travelled through Italy a few years ago, the town of Assisi was high on the agenda. I wasn't disappointed. It's a magical place, even post earthquakes. I was reminded of my youthful enthusiasm for St Francis and the religious orders created to follow his road. I experienced a deep sense of peace and was incredibly moved.

I feel I've spent years looking to belong. I've found elements in a faith community, in the queer communities in the different countries I've lived in, and in searching out my Irishness. I'm happy now to accept myself as a hybrid, and I am anchored by my partner, with whom I am experiencing real love.

And what happened to Chris? She eventually left the convent with Ruth, and they've set up home together. They remain involved in the church, meeting regularly with a group of former religious and attending St Dom's, the liberal parish of my student days. Chris said to me recently, 'It's my church, too, and they can't force me out. There has to be room for all of us.' I admire her strength and sometimes wish I'd had more confidence in my youth to hold on. I have never again found an expression for my spirituality, and it remains a sadness. I contemplate revisiting St Dom's on my return to New Zealand. I'm not sure if the church and I would fit together, but it may go some way towards quelling that bit of nagging in my soul. Or maybe a return trip to Assisi is in order...

Epilogue

The bisexual friend I first went clubbing with decided he was gay and broke off his engagement. The last time I saw him he was a pre-op transsexual.

The trainee Dominican brother left the order and fell into unrequited love with me. He later married. His wife left him, after having four children, for their parish priest.

Fact is weirder than fiction.

a window on my soul

William Long

I STOOD BY THE window in the hospital ward, looking out at the general mayhem that was ordinary life. I couldn't admit that there was anything wrong with me and I felt I should be allowed go home, but they don't discharge attempted suicides that quickly. My life had begun imploding some months earlier and now all manner of horrible truths were struggling to surface within me. I pleaded with God to let the doctors continue to think I was sick, since I couldn't face being sent back out there where all those thoughts had been going round my head. But I'd brought the thoughts in with me, and now the psychiatric registrar was doing her best to pry into that very area that I'd buried, triple-sealed in lead coffins like a dead pope.

'Tell me about your childhood,' she asked. It was an innocent enough question, but one that could have unleashed a Pandora's box, if I'd let it.

It was a small primary school, just one teacher in fact, and when you're seven any interruption is a bit of welcome excitement. Today it was the turn of the district health team, and all fifteen or so of us boys were ushered into a room where we had to strip down to our underwear. The part that had us all agog was when the doctor felt our bits to see if our balls had descended. 'Imagine doing this to the girls!' said one of lads. I couldn't, and somehow managed to restrain my urge to say I'd prefer to be doing it to him. I knew then that I was, in ways as yet unspecified, different from the other boys.

Looking back, all the signs were there — playing with the girls in the playground, dressing up in my mother's old clothes at home (and having the photos taken to prove it!), being unusually interested in the Church's pageantry — but those were also the days when only the macho image was acceptable. I had a huge crush on George Harrison and used to try to will the camera round behind him to see his bum. Sadly, that didn't seem to work very often, but by this stage I was noticing more and more that other boys were talking about girls in a way I couldn't fully comprehend. Why didn't they talk about boys that way, surely that was the natural thing to do? So, gradually, slowly, the awful light dawned that maybe I was what they called a 'homo'. Indeed, it wasn't long before one or two of them started calling me queer, and each time it sent chill shivers down my spine. I couldn't be one of them, could I? I was in love with Dusty Springfield, for heaven's sake! Didn't I get on well with the girls in school, unlike other boys? My huge desire to be 'normal' allowed me to fool myself for many years to come. I was not a poof, I fancied not only Dusty, but Barbara Streisand, Bette Midler, Mama Cass Elliot, Diana Ross. Okay, so there was George. And Brian Jones. And Jimi Hendrix. And, later, Adam Ant, Abba, Boy George, Marc Bolan, Freddie Mercury, Lou Reed and Jimmy Somerville. But these were all ignored in the logical equation that made me straight: Me + Fancying Any Female = Definitely Not Gay.

I decided that stories of success at school and fun with friends would be much more acceptable to the shrink than the foul horror that was the real me. All sorts of childhood traumas were bubbling up from within me, things that had happened to me where I was clearly the victim. I felt so guilty about each of those episodes, and yet I knew they really weren't my fault. But surely this was a totally different matter, this evilness inside me? Wasn't this sick and sordid aspect that kept me thinking of other men an invidious disease that was entirely of my own making? But Crunchy, as I'd come to call her for no good reason, was moving on relentlessly and dragging me with her, kicking and screaming inside but feathers unruffled on the surface.

'Have you been having any unusual dreams recently?'

'I had a dream last night,' said Steve. He was my best friend and we were both thirteen. We'd known each other since we were three months old, and in the course of that lifelong friendship we'd discovered many things together, from potty training to puberty. We had a free house each

Wednesday evening and we made the most of the opportunity to watch anything even slightly risqué on the telly. Then we'd talk our animated, horny talk, desperate for something to happen. This particular evening, things were much the same as usual when Steve introduced his dream. 'You know the way we both like to wank?' he asked. Well, yeah, hello! 'I was dreaming that we could do it to each other.' A young teenager's body reacts very rapidly to certain stimuli and this was definitely one of those. I didn't need any persuasion and, only with the greatest of internal struggles, barely managed to keep myself from jumping all over him. I restrained myself enough to make it appear that I was prepared — somewhat reluctantly, even — to go along with his scheme, though in reality I was bursting at the seams.

So began our weekly ritual of getting naked, practising our kissing skills — just for when we met the right girls, of course — and investigating the fundamentally fabulous pleasures of mutual masturbation.

Boy dreams weren't unusual for me but I just knew that Crunchy would freak if she could read what was going on in my head, so I kept my counsel. There was no point in being locked up or being sent for electric shock aversion therapy. I was finally beginning to realise, aged thirty-nine, that I just couldn't continue to live as I had been. The choice was clear — I either had to own up and admit I liked sex with men or I had to die. On all counts, death looked the easier and more attractive option. Now my continuing stay in hospital could provide me with plenty of opportunity to develop a foolproof plan for my forthcoming demise, not for the first time.

I was fifteen and burning up with desire for more and more sex with guys, but there was also an equal and opposite compulsion not to allow myself to become one of those queers. It was something very definitely not approved of at home, and it was sneered at by my friends. I'd shared some forbidden pleasures with some of these same friends, but they were nonetheless vociferously opposed to tolerance for anything homosexual. And, perhaps most devastating to my self-esteem, it was a total anathema to the church. I could not summon up the will to continue living this painful sham, yet somehow I lost my nerve as I stood in the bathroom with the bottle full of pills and a glass of water.

The extent of my involvement with the church was obvious to Crunchy and others from the number of priests — even a bishop — who came to visit me in the hospital. My apparently sudden collapse (they didn't know of the suicide attempt) seemed to puzzle them and they were reduced to the 'never mind, you'll be out of here soon' type of fatuous comment that only served to remind me that most priests make terrible counsellors. If they couldn't understand my depression, how on earth could I expect them to have any empathy with my sexual preferences? No matter how desperately I wanted to talk to someone about my thoughts and feelings, I knew it could never be a priest.

As a child I had always wanted to be a priest. I used to dress up and hold masses for my siblings and I. The mysteries of the rituals fascinated and excited me even then, but I think the dressing up bit was just as much fun. I hero-worshipped several of the priests in my parish as I was growing up and I desperately wanted them to respect me. I knew that if I was 'one of those' there was no place for me in the church. I really, really wanted not just to stay part of, but to become an active member of the church, and the only way my narrow logic allowed for this to happen was for me to no longer be attracted to other boys. I took to reading texts on sexual behaviour, mostly found when abroad during summer holidays. This was the latter end of the 1960s and such writings were not very enlightened. One eminent book, stemming from Denmark in 1962 (which I still possess), talks not of homosexuality but of homosexual behaviour. The emphasis was on what you did, not the way you actually were, and one statement stands out for me even now, as it did then: 'Let it be said once and for all: homosexuals are very difficult to cure.' It speaks of domineering mothers, of boys being 'seduced' into what they called 'permanent homosexuality', and of helping a sad, misguided faggot into straight behaviour through psychoanalysis.

The church seemed obsessed with allocating blame, and penance for sins was offered as a route back to the centre of the fold. I wanted that route too, but I couldn't tell anyone in authority that I wanted to sleep with boys. This Danish book offered me hope at last. All I needed to do was meet the right girl and eventually, after marriage of course, have sex with her and then all these unacceptable thoughts would fly away. Even if they didn't, I could find a psychotherapist and have myself cured, no matter how difficult that might be. Surely then God would accept me. He (God was always 'He' in those days) would see just how hard I'd tried to be normal and stop being a sinner. I wanted God to speak to me and encourage me, to show me that what I was doing was the right thing. I never did hear God's voice, but She did send me — much, much later — many helping hands that I've never forgotten.

The clinically relentless way in which Crunchy was burrowing into my soul was unsettling, to say the least, and my private sobriquet reduced her in my mind to something altogether more human. It was a way of distracting myself from the almost certain knowledge that one day, perhaps even soon, I would have to face the music about my sexuality. Fortunately, she seemed to be totally oblivious to my hidden agenda and just continued asking her inane, straight questions.

'Did you have any crushes as a teenager?'

It was one evening when I was sixteen, standing in the centre of the room at the local youth club (so fashionable at the time) and chatting to my friend Peter, when in walked a trio of girls. The first two I already knew, but the third made me stop mid-sentence — not a frequent occurrence for me! I couldn't even see her properly, but I knew instantly that here was a very special person. I discovered her name was Mary and over the course of the next few weeks we had short conversations, obviously attracted to each other. Here, at long last, was my ticket to freedom, my route back to normality. I loved her from that first evening, and we started going out together within the month. This was nothing like anything I had ever felt before. My heart was on fire, my pulse raced every time I thought of her, and whenever I was with her I felt that complete inner peace that comes only when something is totally and fundamentally right. Obviously, sex was out of the question so I continued to masturbate just as frequently as before. Disappointed that my fantasies still concentrated exclusively on boys, I reasoned that things would change as Mary and I became closer physically. It was almost eight years before we got married and we were still virgins. I was still going solo every day and still imagining other men in my bed. The horror of finding out that the only way I could finish on our wedding night was to think about a guy I fancied was devastating.

Crunchy was delighted with my limited revelation about this first love.

She continued with trivial and meaningless questions into our relationship but never once came even close to touching on the closeted issues. Until, that is, the day when unknowingly she passed a comment about how Mary seemed to be everything I needed in life. Little did she know.

I was six years married when I met Neil. Younger than I, he was as tall, dark and handsome as the stereotypical Adonis of the fairytales. Now my life also had all the trappings of a children's fantasy — the beautiful stranger, a mutual love, and a belief that somehow we could all live happily for ever and ever. And of course it had the fairies! Neil found a sympathetic ear in me so whenever we met he would talk openly and at length about his life. I was approaching thirty, to him an older, wiser man, and he had never spoken like this with anyone before. Neil still lived with his parents, who were not the sort to encourage a young man to talk openly about his feelings. Maybe it was our relative youth, maybe it was the fact that here was, for each of us, the first time there had been a real, reciprocated attraction with another male, or maybe it was the continued mutual sharing of our hearts' thoughts, but after a time we both knew there was more to this than just ordinary friendship.

It was left to me to make the first move and things progressed rapidly to where we were having a full-blown sexual relationship. In spite of all the odds and the secrecy necessary given both our situations, our affair continued for over four years until that horrible moment when Neil's job took him overseas. Still following the classic fairytale line, he never returned, but met and married a woman in that faraway land, where he is now living with her and their children. My heart still breaks when I think of Neil and of what might have been if we had met earlier. But I was married with two children of my own and, in spite of all that had happened, I loved Mary and wanted to be with her. I was so confused and desperately wanted to talk to someone about it all. I couldn't admit to myself that I was gay — that was still almost ten years away — but I needed to talk to someone. There was nobody, nobody at all. Growing up as children we were taught to respect the gardaí and the priests and to go to one or the other if you were in trouble. This was trouble all right, but there was no way on earth I was going anywhere near a priest to tell him this lot. I'd need a calculator to count the number of sins I'd committed, let alone the penance. Haunted by my thoughts, hounded on all sides by the demands of a straight society, I turned to the only thing that I could think of to get by — obsessive subjugation, complete denial of these terrifying thoughts. Surely I could get through life without having to face the unmentionable?

I had many mixed emotions leaving the warm, womb-like hospital. I was spared further intrusions into my secret world, but three months of being Crunchied had left its scars. I tried to rebuild my protecting closet, that defence against the world that had seemed so effective in the past. But I was starting to question myself more thoroughly now, and I found my straight façade less and less comfortable as time wore on. Yet it was still my security blanket and I just couldn't bring myself to throw it away, so, shielded by my crumbling wall, I denied myself any incursions into the underground world that is gay Dublin. It doesn't surprise me now, but then it was something of a shock to find that it wasn't long before I felt the internal pressure rising again. Either I had to face the truth or accept the unacceptable fact that I would drive myself back into that agitated state from which I'd been saved not that long previously.

I picked up a copy of *Gay Community News* (*GCN*) — how did I know where to find it? — and read it avidly from cover to cover. There was a place for weirdos like me, I discovered, a place where they could meet other sad degenerates for coffee and conversation without fear of being judged. Could such a haven really exist? I quaked as I set foot on the outer steps of Outhouse and only by sheer instinct fuelled by desperate willpower did I manage to ascend to the coffee shop. Dear Sweet Jesus, it was true! There were two men near the window holding hands and the woman who smiled at me so warmly and took my order had just got to be a lesbian. The coffee was grand, the biscuit unremarkable, and I could just as easily have left after a silent encounter, but for Sheila. Sheila, who had brought the coffee, came back after a few minutes, sat down beside me and started to chat. Was this my first time in Outhouse? Had I seen *GCN*? Was I interested in any details of the pub scene? What about the clubs? A constantly gaping mouth gives a somewhat unattractive appearance after a while, so I struggled to close my jaw and formulate a response. Could I really be having a conversation with someone who, far from being embarrassed at being gay, was actually proud of her sexuality? Someone who introduced me to the various fags and dykes who popped their heads in and out like the weathermen? Yes, it was true all right, and I went back again and again, not so much for the coffee as the freedom of being able to greet another man with a kiss and not be mocked.

It was on one of those visits that I discovered something that was way beyond impossible, something simply inconceivable. There was in existence, in the very town where I lived, a group for married gay men! You mean there was another one apart from me? And suddenly I realised that I had said it to myself, though not yet out aloud. Six letters is all it takes, three little words. I. Am. Gay. I am gay. I'm bent. A poof. A faggot. A queer. Of course that's what I am! How could I be so stupid as to deny it all these years? And now here was a group of other, like-minded men who could help me deal with this blinding revelation, this lightning flash of the totally obvious. I was so excited by this discovery it transformed me. Everyone around me could see the change, including Mary. I had no idea how to tell her, but one evening she and I were watching a video — *Beautiful Thing* — and she remarked, innocently enough, that I was very interested in gay things these days. It was one of those heart-stopping moments when you have the choice to come clean or continue to deny. I'd had more than I could take of self-denial (I'd never have stuck being the priest I wanted to be as a child!) so, with cosmic courage, I just let the words trickle from my lips. 'That's because I am gay.' Mary smiled gently at me and said, 'I've thought that for twenty years, I wondered when you were going to tell me.'

It wasn't all plain sailing, however. It was one thing being gay and quite another acting on those instincts. That first couple of years after I came out to Mary were pretty rough, but I was helped enormously by the married men's group and especially by a couple of men from that group who were so helpful and supportive. Men who became my friends. Gay men. Married, gay men as my friends — it was astounding. After a time, Mary began to realise that I still loved her, possibly even more than ever, and that I wanted to stay with her. She gradually loosened her restrictions on what I could do and where I could go so that I was able to meet other gay people regularly and enjoy myself in a safe environment. Mary's acceptance of my sexuality has meant more to me than anything else. She is still my best friend and I love her to bits.

I never came out to any other family members; I didn't see it was any of their business. I never told any of my old friends, I just preferred to let them treat me exactly as before. Maybe that's still being in the closet, but it's a handy compromise that suits both me and Mary. I found no support at all in a church that wants to condemn people like me because of a 4000-year old rule in Leviticus, and I drifted away from its rules and regimen. Instead, I focused more on the plight of others ostracised by society for whatever reason. I took up voluntary work to help people who feel helpless, as I had done. My life today is very significantly different from my straight, strait-jacketed existence of years ago. I am so much more accepting nowadays of who and what I am. I am more at peace with the world and I have an inner contentment that would have been unthinkable ten years ago as I stood at that hospital window. I advise Mary on what to wear, I arrange the cut flowers, I choose the colours to decorate the home. And I walk down the street hand-in-hand with the woman I love, the woman who knows I'm gay and still loves me.

we're gay but still mums

Nuala and Deirdre

H EARTACHE IS UNAVOIDABLE when a marriage breaks down. For everyone concerned there's the pain of separation, the loss, and a huge sense of failure, rejection, and betrayal. However, imagine how much more intense that pain can be when the marriage comes to an end because a woman discovers her true sexual identity. After years of married life and giving birth to children, she has to face the fact she is a lesbian.

Deirdre lived in a small west of Ireland town most of her life. She and her husband met as teenagers and married in their early twenties. They raised three children, now aged between ten and sixteen, and by and large were a happy family. 'My husband and I got on great and we grew to love each other and we were best friends. I thought this was what marriage was,' says Deirdre, 'We obviously had a sex life,' she adds, referring to her adored son and two daughters. 'But it wasn't until I met Nuala that I knew what real love was about.'

Nuala, from a southern county, had known her husband since he was sixteen and they married young. They reared four lovely children, now aged fifteen to twenty-three. While she sometimes felt physically attracted to other women, she never acted on these urges, not least because she felt it was a terrible sin. 'I grew up in a very religious home,' says Nuala. 'The word "gay" wasn't mentioned, let alone "lesbian". But I reared my children to know about homosexuality. I think, subconsciously, I was preparing them for the day when I'd have to tell them I was gay.'
Admitting You're Gay

It was to be years yet before the women would meet each other in a gay bar. By that time Deirdre had accepted her sexual orientation and had told her husband. 'I loved him and had no intention of leaving him. But other issues came up that helped break down our marriage — his work, my work, the house, all the kind of things that can happen to any couple. Once the cracks came they just got worse. Then I had a nervous breakdown.' Deirdre used to visit Galway frequently, where there is an active gay community. She went to gay and gay-friendly bars, and even a gay bed and breakfast.

Nuala had also told her husband that she was gay, shortly before she met Deirdre, but he thought it was a phase she was going through. At first he even encouraged her to go out and meet other gay women, thinking she'd get over it. 'But he never realised the extent of what was happening,' she says. 'After twenty-one years of marriage, with four beautiful daughters that he loved, he certainly never thought I would leave him. As far as he was concerned he was going to grow old with me.'

'When I met Nuala for the first time it was a defining moment in my life,' recalls Deirdre. 'She was the first woman I ever held. I knew then that it was so very different from trying to be heterosexual. When I kissed her I knew this was what all the love songs are about, this is what violins are for.'

For Nuala the meeting had the same impact. 'Deirdre asked me up to dance. In the gay scene there are very few married women, and mostly they're all young. I said to her, "I'm married". And she said, "So am I. And I have kids." And I said, "So have I." We just stopped dancing and sat down and had a fabulous conversation. We clicked as if we'd known one another for years.'

While they had the joys of love on the one hand, they also had the torment of family commitments. 'This is a fabulous thing but is it too late?' they asked. 'We have responsibilities, homes and families.' They began meeting once a fortnight in Galway. At first they thought they'd wait five years until the kids were older and their husbands had got used to the idea that marriage was no longer an option. But it got too much for the women to bear. 'We couldn't function — all we could think of was being with each other.' 'It wasn't just finding a new love, it was finding your real self,' adds Deirdre. Their husbands came to realise this too, and knew they couldn't move on with their own lives until they accepted their wives' transition.

The time soon came to reveal all.

Telling the Family

Deirdre's parents took the news with total shock. 'They didn't understand why I had married if I was that way. But when I was young I truly didn't understand what being gay was. My parents have since come to terms with what's happened. They come to visit me but prefer not to come to the house because Nuala is there. If they meet her they are polite but they think that if they accept her then it appears that they approve and they don't.'

Nuala was worried sick about telling her 74-year-old mother. 'If she'd had a heart attack my family would have blamed me. My sisters were very supportive, and one came with me to tell Mum. I had her so worried she thought I was going to tell her I had cancer. "No, mum," I said and told her I was gay. "Ah no, you're not," she says. "Yes I am." Then she put her arms around me and said, "Why did you not tell me, why did you suffer like that? You are what you are," she said.'

Between them Nuala and Deirdre have seven children. The four youngest live with their mothers in Galway and go to local schools. The three older ones are at college or working. In general they don't talk about their lesbian mothers to outsiders but in the home environment the subject is quite open. Deirdre says, 'We discussed everything with them. I would say this is awful hard on you and how sorry I was about it, but they'd throw their arms around us and say it's okay, it's okay.' Deirdre's youngest through it was 'dead cool' that her mammy was being interviewed by *Woman's Way*.

Nuala's children took the transition a little harder. One daughter, aged nineteen, only recently told her best friend about her mother being gay. 'That was a big thing for my daughter to do.'

Deirdre and her husband are now divorced and he has since formed a new relationship. He comes to Galway to visit his children, and every other weekend they travel to the town he lives in to stay with him.

We're Not Perverts

Although their lives have changed for the better and the two women are in a loving relationship in which they feel fulfilled, it has been a difficult process. Both women have gone through an emotional wringer. Trauma, heartache, depression, barring orders, court cases, even attempted suicide, and most of all: 'Guilt!' they both cry in unison. They were told they'd ruined their husbands' lives by marrying them in the first place. But neither woman knew, no more than the men they had married, that they were wed because of social convention, not personal commitment.

'Who would choose to be gay?' asks Deirdre. 'To be discriminated against? It's who you are, it's something in your genes before you're even born. A lot of people have the idea that if you mix with gay people they can turn you gay — I spent all my life with straight people, and did it make me straight?'

'The other thing is some people think of gay people as perverts and paedophiles. But that's not what being gay is — it's just a different way of loving. Another perception people have of gay people is what they see on television and in the media. They're depicted as people who look very intimidating, with shaved heads and loads of piercings, but they're the extremists. Gay people are just ordinary — if you met them on the street you wouldn't know they're gay.'

In provincial Ireland in the 1960s and 1970s, there was relatively little information about homosexuality. Deirdre recalls, 'When there are only snippets of information, you have to assume so much yourself. And I was too shy to ask. What I understood was that I was having bad thoughts. I'd think that the devil was tempting me. I'd go to confession but then I'd come out without having confessed and I'd feel twice as guilty.'

Fear holds older lesbian women back, says Nuala. 'If you're a fifty-year-old gay woman, especially if you're married, and you've never told anyone, it's very lonely. You don't want to be condemned because of the stigma attached to being gay. But once you take that chance and get a bit of support, it gets easier.'

Happiness is What Counts
Nuala and Deirdre now run a gay bar in Galway because they want to provide a safe place for gay men and women to meet, socialise, communicate — and be themselves.

Aware of all they have gone through, they run it more as a club than a pub. 'It's a bit of a vocation for us,' laughs Deirdre. 'We pride ourselves on watching out for new faces to make people feel welcome. We have all ages, young and old, from all walks of life — teachers, doctors, nurses, lawyers, road sweepers, shop assistants — it's as varied as any pub.' The bar also acts as a community centre, running a monthly women's chat group and a monthly women-only meeting, both of which are particularly suited to older and perhaps married gay women who wish to discuss issues specific to them.

'We never meant to hurt our husbands. If we knew when we were young what we know now we would not have got married, but we're so grateful to have had a second chance at life,' says Deirdre.

growing up gay in the '90s

Geoff McGrath

T HIS IS NOT the first time I have talked about my sexuality to a wider audience beyond family and friends, having spoken to a religious group before and travelled from Dublin, where I live, to speak in Belfast, where they find it hard to get local gay people to speak because homosexuality is not tolerated as easily as it is down south. Each time I have questioned my suitability, wondering what my story offered.

When asked to contribute to this book there was an option to use a pseudonym, like many of the writers, to which I declined as a sign of defiance, not against those using false names, but because of bigoted people in society who have forced many contributors on similar publications to do this.

I also decided to tell my story from my earliest recollections about being gay to where I am now — feeling more comfortable about being this way. So I offer my story hoping it might enlighten readers about a gay man's experience.

Finally, it annoyed me to hear people talking about how easy it is now to come out as gay. Yes, homosexuality has been decriminalised, and it is easier even from when I came out a number of years ago, but teenagers and older gay people still find it hard to come out. The fact that many writers in this book have chosen not to use their real names shows that things are not quite as advanced as they could and should be.

Primary School (Age 8–12 Years)
My earliest gay memories go back to when I was about ten years old

walking home from school one day with my older brother and some of his friends. One called the other gay and the gang started to giggle. I didn't understand what the word meant, so Gavin explained. The idea of it sounded weird and not right; I even doubted if it was true. It certainly did not fit into my little world, which at the time were my mam, dad and brothers and my couple of friends whom I hung around with.

About a year later, on the way back from a school trip, I was sitting with another boy on the bus. He was leaning over from his seat, revealing the elastic on the top of his underwear. Innocently I snapped the top of his underwear and laughed. He told me quietly to continue on with my hand down his trousers. I felt about for a minute and then put my hand down his front with a schoolbag covering what I was doing so others on the bus couldn't see.

I remember thinking it was wrong, knowing my parents would not approve, but it felt good. A couple of days later he wanted to touch me in the school toilets. I really wanted to, but didn't because I thought it was wrong and I was worried about being caught and I thought I would go to hell, so I made an excuse that my brother was waiting for me to go home.

I left primary school two years later and we never mentioned what happened. Many went on to an all-Irish speaking school, while I went to an English one. So I left behind my old friends.

Secondary School (Age 12–15 Years)
In Old Bawn Community School I began to feel like an outsider — many did not talk to me and I remember one person slagging me by calling me Geoffrey in an upper class type of voice. One guy from my old school said it is because 'you are a bit posh, but I think it's okay,' he said. I now realise posh is not what he meant; it was because I was a bit camp.

My confidence plummeted and I began to dislike myself. Some of the lads just seemed to spot that I was gay before I really knew and said it. A friend in the school who got along with those who called me names told me why people thought I was gay. I was not aggressive and too polite, so I changed my gentle speaking traits, swore more and generally toughened up and got a new, more stylish haircut — well, stylish for that age. Looking at teenagers acting aggressively now, telling their friends to 'Fuck off, or I'll kill ya', or 'I'll box the head off ya' looks hilarious — these were the kind of things I used to say to try and pass myself off as straight.

While this pretence was going on I was experimenting with another boy from when I was about thirteen or so. Very innocent, we didn't even know how to make each other climax. Before anything happened we both sussed each other out, carefully asking each other questions about sex, each one being suggestive. Finally, we both justified what we would do by saying it was practice for girls.

After experimenting for about a year, I began to ask him whether he thought we might be gay, but it was very frustrating when he said no. I felt very alone and thought there must have been only a handful of gay people in Ireland.

Secondary School - Ashfield College (age 16–18 years)

I left Old Bawn after fourth year to do my Leaving Cert in Ashfield College in Templeogue. Still 'practising for girls' with Alan, I started to tell others in Ashfield that I thought I might be gay. While in Old Bawn I had told three friends but still felt isolated because they did not really understand.

In Ashfield some people said to me that they had thought I was a bit of a scumbag when they had first met me (this being a term to describe how toughish I appeared). This was great because nobody would suspect someone tough being a faggot; it was good to feel 'normal'.

Coming out at the same time as having the macho image helped. I think most kids that age put on the same act, gay or straight, so it was easier for them to be seen with me and I did not want to be an outsider again, like in Old Bawn, so the façade continued for a while. I was amazed at the support I got and my big secret was not such a big deal. Some even thought it was cool.

Being accepted put a lot of fears and anxieties to rest and helped me to tell more people, but I still feared not being able to take it back if I was making a big mistake. Deep down I knew I was gay, I was just too afraid to commit myself — complete admittance to myself would mean giving up the mapped-out life that heterosexuality offered. This being a chance to have children, christenings, a wedding and other formalities. Not knowing anyone gay gave me no hints to what gay life offered, and even then I knew I would still be living life outside the mainstream by taking the homosexual path.

Sorting this out in my head while I should have been studying for my Leaving Cert was difficult. Making the situation worse, everyone from my year found out after two friends passing a note mentioning my sexuality dropped it on the classroom floor and someone picked it up and passed it around. A friend later told me what happened, but the fear of people finding out led to great paranoia and I already had an inclination that people knew, but dismissed it as being overly cautious until I was eventually told.

Meanwhile my mother was diagnosed with cancer. Following a number of operations and complications that resulted from the cancer, chemotherapy followed. I sometimes feel guilty for not being as concerned as I think I should have been. In one way it was a typical teenage response, thinking nothing bad could happen. And with my mind working overtime with my sexuality, it was hard to empathise when I was feeling dreadfully confused and sorry for myself. I felt like I was living outside the living world as somebody looking in — I knew all these people but they didn't know me because they did not know my sexuality.

When people in my year found out, I decided to tell my parents a couple of days later. It was at the height of my mother's illness, but I still thought they may have been more upset if they were the last to find out. The Friday after the news broke in school my brother was getting ready for a night out. I was going to let him know after my parents, so I told him to remind me the next day that I had something to tell him. Knowing how curious Gavin got he would not stop asking me until he found out, therefore forcing me to tell him. Proving me right, he wanted me to tell him straight away.

The next morning I went downstairs and had my breakfast. My mother, sensing something was upsetting me, asked what was wrong. 'I want to tell you and Dad something but at the same time,' I said. After refusing to give in to her demands to tell immediately, she told me to follow her in to my dad, who was in the sitting room. Delaying the process, I started to clear away my crockery from breakfast, something I never did, and then ran into the downstairs bathroom. My mam had meanwhile gone into my father and I eventually came out of the bathroom and took what felt like a long walk down the hall to them.

I later found out that just before I went in, they were talking about a girl I had been going out with a couple of months previously and they thought she might be pregnant. How ironic — I was about to tell them they were never likely to become grandparents by me.

I went in and sat down in an armchair opposite the two of them, seated perched forward, eagerly awaiting what I had to say. Again delaying what I was about to tell them, I started off by saying, 'Well, you know how I've had girlfriends in the past,' which probably made it worse for them because they were thinking of pregnancy. I started this way to hold onto a sense of masculinity, still associating heterosexuality with machismo. 'Well, I'm gay,' I said.

I felt a rush of relief when saying it. No longer would I have to speak in code to friends on the phone in case I was overheard. No more pretending — freedom at last in the one place where most people can feel safe and almost be themselves. My house suddenly became home. Despite the interrogation that was to follow, it still felt better than it did before I told them.

My dad asked me if I had told others. 'A few,' I said, but did not mention those who found out through the note. I did not want to worry them and thought they might have been offended if too many people knew before they did. He said not to mention it to my brothers 'just yet', and told me not to tell people too liberally because 'people are not ready to accept gays'. He responded as well as could be expected, considering some parents never talk to their children after coming out.

Later on, my brother Gavin told me that he knew what I was planning to tell him. My mother had broken with my dad's wishes and told him. I was a bit embarrassed but Gavin was fine about the whole thing and asked questions like would I start to wear dresses. The idea seemed hilarious but it was good to know that he would have been fine if I did.

The normality and comfort I felt over the next couple of weeks was very weird, even with my parents bombarding me with awkward questions. At the time, I did not think about the fact that I had had years of adjusting to the idea, while my poor parents were expected to come to terms with it very quickly and at the same time my mother had cancer.

My dad later asked if I was molested and possibly confused as a result, or maybe I had been with a girl and unable to perform. My mother thought she had brought me up to 'respect women too much'. A mixture of ignorance because they too had never known anyone gay, and not wanting it to be true led them to say some of the things they said. I am surprised that I did not end up more confused after some of the personal details they told me about themselves to try and help me.

My mother wanted me to talk to someone and I did not try to reject this idea because I was still not at ease with being gay and needed some answers. She suggested my GP but I thought he was ancient and what would he know about someone gay. She then asked about talking to Niamh, my year head in school, and I was okay with this because I had already told her, just in case there was any trouble at school. I was that scared that somebody was going to beat me up or do something terrible.

My mother went to the school and I just managed to get to Niamh before she met my mother so I could tell her not to mention everyone in my year finding out. She later put me in touch with a friend who had three gay brothers. He gave me some good advice but most importantly gave me the number of a psychotherapist. I thought it was dead exciting having my own counsellor and had great pleasure in telling my friends.

Too nervous to ring for an appointment myself, my mother did it for me. I think she hoped I would be cured after a couple of visits. It turned out that Brendan was also a priest and I worried that he was going to tell me I was wrong and these thoughts were not right. I nearly didn't go and see him. I had visions of a seventy-year-old with a white collar around his neck messing with the thoughts in my head.

Meeting psychologist — Brendan (with me aged 17)
I cycled to the Redemptorist building in Rathgar for the first visit one day after school. I walked into an old 1970s style building, but modern on the inside, and asked to see Fr Brendan O'Rourke, saying the 'Father' bit quietly because I'm not religious and I felt uncertain if I was being a hypocrite by addressing him by his full title.

When he walked out he looked younger than I had imagined. He shook my hand and then brought me into a quiet room where we sat in armchairs facing each other. I was always uneasy about saying the word 'gay' to people, let alone in front of a priest. He put my mind to rest by beginning with what my mother had said on the phone and asking me some questions. I soon realised that he wasn't going to try and tell me I'm a hetero.

After only forty minutes with Brendan I left feeling clearer about my sexuality and confident about myself. He was the first person to understand what I was going through and so I quickly realised I wasn't alone in my experience. It was also a relief to finally realise that a lot of myths about gay people were untrue.

On the second visit I asked if there was a charge for my visits. 'A fee only applies to people who need long therapy,' he said. I was surprised, having thought it would probably take years to sort my head out.

Despite feeling great after the first visit, I remained sceptical for a while and worked out what I was going to say before seeing him, thinking that there was no way he would have an answer. It was a defence mechanism for myself — after years of nobody understanding me I was finding it hard to believe that I was finally getting answers.

One time I watched a TV documentary showing a gay guy on the town who ended up sleeping with another man. The two were in bed the following morning and talking about having made love the previous night. They were very camp and unattractive and I was repulsed by it. I went to my next appointment with Brendan, confused about why I should have felt like this. He told me that sometimes within small cultures you are very conscious of what outsiders think and I might see some within the circle as letting the entire group down. In hindsight I have come to realise I was uncomfortable with gay men being effeminate, seeing this as a weakness. Despite Brendan giving varying examples of gay strengths, it took me a year or two to find out for myself. I also found it hard to come to terms with love being involved, seeing this as a weakness also.

Soon appointments with Brendan became further apart, from every week at the beginning to gaps of three and four weeks. I was worried and wondered if I could cope without them. As the questions ran out, the need for Brendan seemed to fade and it came to a natural conclusion.

Family Meeting to Discuss my Sexuality (aged 17)
At the end of the sessions Brendan suggested I invite my family along for a meeting. One Saturday morning we all went along early for a meeting in the Redemptorist building. Everyone said their own bit, my dad talked

about his fears of 'queer bashing'. Brendan suggested I leave gay pubs and clubs in numbers for safety.

When asked who we each felt would have the most trouble with my sexuality, everyone answered my brother, Mark. Brendan asked him awkward questions like names he might have called gays in the past. He said things like 'pillow biter' and 'arse bandit' — terms I had never even heard of before.

It is the only time I can remember the family meeting to discuss anything and it was a comfort that everyone cared enough to be there. Other things like not choosing your sexuality were talked about, but most important to me was that if I had a partner that he should be invited along to occasions just like a girlfriend would.

Going into Gay Pubs and Clubs (still aged 17)

After the meeting I was ready to go to a gay club, and a week later (although I was still only seventeen I had been clubbing since sixteen) I went out. I had read about the Wonderbar, a gay nightclub, in a gay magazine Brendan gave me. To my surprise we walked straight past the bouncers without hassle. On entering, the feeling of joy was so overwhelming I nearly cried. I never knew this many gay people existed — and a couple of hundred under one roof. I had never knowingly met anyone gay before this and I remember thinking I am 'at home'.

We were the first few people there, but my friend Paul, who is straight, did not stay long because he felt uncomfortable. He apologised for leaving but I did not mind. So I sat on my own for a while feeling a bit silly. I noticed one or two people looking at me and one eventually came over.

We talked for a while and then kissed. Most of what was said is a blank but we ended up back at his apartment. I did not particularly fancy him but kissed him anyway. Most gay men seem to go with anyone when they first come out. After all the hurt, it is hard to believe that others find you attractive.

He offered me a cup of tea and I sat down on the sofa. I felt very nervous but wanted to feel grown up and this is what grown ups did, I supposed. He turned on a heterosexual porn film, which I thought was a bit odd and seedy, but sneaked a peak at it. He kissed me but he did not really do anything for me and I soon got up and left.

My first night was adventurous and a bit regrettable. I met up with Mac again the following Saturday for my first Gay Pride parade. I had not even heard of this before but it was really exciting to see even more gay men in large numbers, and some attractive looking ones too. Following the parade we went along to the official Pride party, a one-off club night organised by the parade committee, where he introduced me to some of his friends. He asked me about my intentions for the two of us, but he spoke in a way that gave me the opportunity to say I was not interested.

Later that night, still out with Mac, I met someone else, when I was a bit drunker, called Damian, and I brought him back to a friend's house whose parents were away. I felt a bit more comfortable with Damian, him being around the same age, and we slept together. I know it was very early for sex, and it happened a few more times. It was the years of repression suddenly exploding. A lot of gay men are less inhibited about sex, so certain heterosexual morals did not apply here. It was up to me to later find out what I thought acceptable.

It was frustrating not having a boyfriend, soon discovering that a lot of people just wanted to sleep with me. Although flattering, a lot of 'chickens' (a term used generally to describe gay teenagers) get large amounts of attention and so it was upsetting that some people had no interest in knowing me personally. I got mixed up with the wrong crowds, who seemed to lie frequently and this bothered me. It shattered my illusions that these were my kind of people and that they should be nice to me, considering we all went through the same problems to get where we were at.

When dating someone there would always be someone looking to interfere or tell me that my boyfriend was cheating. I began to resent the gay scene (gay scene being a general term for gay pubs, clubs, cafes, etc.) and distrust most people I encountered, especially the older men — some being old enough to be my dad — who wanted to sleep with me. I felt like I was in a very adult world but too young to be there and this made me grow up very quickly. By the time most people in school were experiencing their first sexual encounters, I had already done this with a man; it was very exciting to have been a bit more grown up than friends. I feel now it is a shame to have lost my innocence so young.

Winning the 'Glorified Cattle Mart' Competition (aged 18)

I eventually met Shane, who was a year younger than me, and it was good to have met him; he was one of the few people I trusted and we talked on the phone sometimes for a long time about our experiences. It gave me a chance to share my feelings and to have someone who did not want to take advantage of me.

Shortly before the Leaving Certificate I went into the Wonderbar and Shane met me at the door and told me there was a competition on; they were short two people, would I enter? Thinking he was taking part I went on stage, but Shane did not follow. I won the heat of the Mr Boilerhouse competition, a sort of gay equivalent to The Rose of Tralee, sponsored by gay sauna the Boilerhouse, and I was delighted. It did wonders for my damaged self-esteem, an effect from years of disliking myself because of my sexuality.

My First Big Crush

Winning the competition was one of the high points of my first year on the gay scene, but I experienced a big low after meeting Brian. From the first time I met him he was gorgeous looking, and he was studying media — an added bonus as I wanted to become a journalist. We had similar interests and so I was crazy about him. A huge crush lasted for months before he told me he was gay and we kissed. He did not want a relationship. Looking at Brian one night from a distance in the Wonderbar, I knew I had to avoid the scene as much as possible for a while; it was breaking my heart to see him and not be his boyfriend. I had to do my Leaving Cert anyway.

Shortly after the exams I met John on one of the few nights I was going out, and we went out for a couple of months but broke up when I realised he was cheating. I wanted to annoy him by being as ambiguous as possible when I broke up. So I never told him why. I realised I still did not want to be with anyone other than Brian, anyway.

Getting Over Brian and Falling in Love (aged 19)

So after a few short-term relationships in my first year and a half on the gay scene, I had had enough. Realising Brian was never going to want to be with me, I was happy to be single for a while. That was until I was talking to a friend who had just started work in a local video shop. He told me about this bloke he worked with 'who was my type', who had just told him he was gay. He suggested we meet.

I went up one day and through the entrance to where all the videos were I saw somebody bending over with a nice bum; it cannot be him, I thought. Then someone came out and we were introduced. I thought he was really good looking and still thought it was not him, but soon found out it was. Something strange inside me knew I was going to end up going out with him and for a long time. Alan, my friend who worked with him, exchanged comments we had said about each other. Each time he would come back I had more questions for him to ask this guy, Colm.

Meanwhile, the Wonderbar was set to close and so I was planning on going along for the closing night with my brother and some friends who I wanted to show the pub to before it shut down because I loved it so much. It turned out Colm was going to go with Alan. When Colm turned up he came upstairs to me, said hello, and put his arm around my shoulder. I'm 'in there,' I thought, and asked him whom he had come in with. He pointed downstairs to his best friend and his boyfriend. I could not believe it, Alan never told me anything about Colm having a boyfriend.

I decided to drop by the video shop a couple of days later to see if he was there and I did this a few more times. My plan of action was to become friends and wait until he was single.

We began to see a bit of each other over the next few weeks and he eventually asked me out. I was really happy. I had not seen Brian for a while at this stage and I was beginning to fall for Colm but worried how I might feel if I was to see Brian again, having felt strongly about him for almost a year.

I began to have very strong feelings for Colm, and when I saw Brian out again after going out with Colm for a couple of months I did not have the same feelings.

After four months, Colm said very quietly in my ear one night that he loved me. I was shocked and I did not respond; it took me a while longer to tell him I loved him. I was still getting over the whole idea of trying to be macho, and saying 'I love you' was for wimps, I thought. When I did eventually say it, it was a huge weight off my shoulders and a leap over a major stumbling block.

Full Acceptance (22 years of age)

We are still together nearly four years later and it is amazing how much a relationship, gay or straight (I presume), can be so fulfilling. Our relationship in so many ways put me at ease with my sexuality. We talk to each other and say things that we would not say to other people. To love and be loved back helped heal a lot of pain.

There are many other facets to the relationship but if I were to mention them it would be straying from telling my story of coming to terms with being gay.

I now fully accept that I am a gay man, and have put to rest any issues I had. Sometimes I feel repressed because, although people say they accept me, there is often an underlying dislike of my sexuality or I get a feeling that some people feel superior as heterosexuals. My fear for the future is of a backlash towards the wave of acceptance of gays — because many have accepted homosexuality unquestioningly, which could easily be manipulated by a person or group with false information much like the way Hitler operated.

priesthood – no place to hide

Martin Taggart

ONE OF THE most memorable phrases I have heard in the last few months consists of five simple words: 'It's nice to meet you.' The greeting didn't come to me from a stranger with whom I had just become acquainted but from a friend of over ten years standing. After perhaps three hours into our meeting for lunch I finally told her: 'I'm gay'. After beating about the bush, my complaining of not living life to the full and a bit of prodding from her about how I could live more fully, the words were uttered. Her reaction in that simple little phrase meant the world to me after years of reluctance to tell people who I am.

She was not the first person I told that I am gay — that happened in 1992. Then I was almost twenty-two, training for the Roman Catholic priesthood, and coming to the end of the first year in a seminary. It happened during one of my regular meetings with the rector/spiritual director and I felt this was something I had to 'confess'. I had to ask him to get me a glass of water before I could get the words out. I think I expected to be told to get my bags packed. That didn't happen and I was eventually considered suitable to carry on with the formation. The rector — to whom I was most grateful at the time — suggested I perhaps wait until my mid-twenties before determining my sexual orientation. I have now come to realise how unhelpful this was.

I continued with the seminary training, living a single existence and attending all the prayer times, masses and classes that were expected of me. I was a most orthodox, conservative Catholic who didn't like the authority of the hierarchy of the church and what it taught. Many would have considered me as certain to be ordained. I never had that certainty, either that I would be ordained or that the church was right. I was continually thinking about my motivation for being there, which takes me back to my life before seminary.

I graduated from the University of Ulster with an arts degree in 1991. A quote from those days that sticks in my mind was not one I found in research but comes from a rather blunt friend who stated: 'You are either gay or you are going to be a priest.' He had noticed the number of female friends I had, none of whom I became romantically involved with. I laughed off his comment but little did he realise how close to the bone it was. It was one I often thought of during my three and a half years in the seminary.

There was no either/or that my university colleague referred to. I was gay and I was going to be a priest. I now have no doubt that my sexual orientation led me to the seminary, even though this may not have been as clear to me when I decided to go there, or I didn't wish to acknowledge it. Celibacy was part of the package, which wasn't so bad as I wasn't going to be able to have a sexual relationship anyway — according to church teaching — as I'm gay. I was also thinking that if I were a priest nobody would wonder why I'm not married or suspect me of being gay. This was not my only motivation for considering the ordained priesthood as a way of life, but I know now that it was a big factor in my decision. It was also the main reason for my decision to leave the seminary, halfway through a theology course in Dublin.

Thankfully the seminary did not remain, nor priesthood become — consciously or unconsciously — the hiding place that I had hoped it would be. I was often in the library of the college, but my attention was not on the books on the reading list for the topics being studied at the time. I was dipping into moral theology books dealing with the issue of sexuality and particularly homosexuality, worried that someone might see what I was reading and that I would be 'found out'. This reading left me with more questions than answers. Although initially I felt I had no choice as a gay man but to be celibate, as more permanent commitment was looming I knew I couldn't base my decision on whether I should be a priest on this earlier assumption. What made my departure more difficult was the fact that I couldn't tell people I was leaving because I was gay. In letters to friends I wrote that I had 'issues' that I needed to look at. The main issue was and is the fact that I'm attracted to men.

I left the seminary in January 1995 and at the time of writing it is almost spring of 2003. For me, that is one of the starkest sentences I have written in this piece. For most of that time I have lived in quiet desperation and I would get very depressed if I allowed myself to dwell on that.

After leaving the seminary in 1995, I returned to live at home, which is a rural part of Northern Ireland. With hindsight, this was probably not a good idea but it has happened and there is no point expending energy on the 'what ifs'. I put considerable energy into training for the workplace and getting a job. I bought a house, which I subsequently sold with a view to taking off on my travels around the world. The travel didn't happen, but I think that was for the best. I know I would have been running away and my discontent, loneliness and indeed desperation may still have been there on my return.

Thankfully, I had a couple of friends to whom I could talk. Despite my disillusionment at times with things Catholic, there is a part of me that seeks help from and trusts those living out a very obvious Christian commitment. The two friends with whom I talked about my struggles with being gay are both religious sisters. They were understanding and encouraged me to do something about it. One of them put me in touch with a gay man she knows who had also been training for the priesthood but was not ordained. My meeting with him in early 2002 was the first time I spoke to a person whom I knew to be gay. It was he who introduced me to the magazine catering for gay people, *Gay Community News*, a resource that was very helpful.

Other tentative steps along the way included buying my first copy of the English magazine *Gay Times*. It was while on holiday in Cork that I plucked up the courage to buy this after checking if there was anyone in the shop who knew me. I also rang a helpline I found in *Gay Times* for an organisation in England that suggested I get in touch with a group in Belfast. I decided not to, crippled by fear that someone I know might find out I was gay if I contacted this organisation.

Eventually I decided to act. I had read about a Belfast-based organisation called the Rainbow Project several years ago. Being an organisation that offers support to people who are gay, I committed its name to memory, in the same way one might spot a contact number for a group offering support, cut it out or write it down and hold onto it. The courage might eventually come, or one would become so exhausted by what seems to be a meaningless existence, the number would be used and the group contacted.

I find the address of 'Rainbow' in the phonebook so I'm off on my journey to Belfast. I walk one way up the street past the office door but don't stop in case I might be seen. I walk back again but still I can't push the buzzer. What if someone sees me going in? What if there is someone in the centre who will recognise me? What sort of people am I going to meet there? The fear wins again. After walking several times past the door I decide to go home, annoyed and disappointed with myself. I eventually resolve to telephone the office and make an appointment, which I did and I was back the following week. This was July 2002. I was offered the services of a counsellor whom I decided to contact.

This process helped me move from the rut I had been stuck in, but which I knew I wanted to move out of. I moved out by getting in touch with two organisations in Dublin — one spiritual, the other social — through which I have been able to meet other gay men. Here I pay tribute to *Gay Community News* for its Directory page. Through this I was able to get in touch by email with the groups and particular people involved in them, easing my attendance at the first meeting/outing. It was in November that I started what I would describe as this exciting and wonderful journey.

I have always regarded with scepticism 'born-again' Christians who could cite a date and place where they accepted Jesus Christ as their saviour. However, in the few months that I have been in touch with groups for gay people in Dublin, and when I have started to be happy about living for the first time in years, there have been significant dates.

One such occasion was Saturday, 7 December 2002, when I attended the Reach Christmas Carol Service in the Unitarian Church on St Stephen's Green in Dublin. During the service, those assembled were invited to come forward and light a candle. As I queued up to light the candle the thought going through my head was 'I am here'. This was a statement about my presence — which for me was significant — but it was also much more than that. 'I am here — I exist, I'm gay, I'm happy, I'm nervous, I'm excited and it's great.' Oh yes, somewhere in all of this was the affirmation from my friend: 'It's nice to meet you.'

the saturday night lad

Paul Crowe

'H E'S GORGEOUS! I thought, glaring at the cute blond across the kiosk from myself. 'Shouldn't I be thinking that about his pretty girlfriend standing next to him? Nah, she gets to go home with this stud, what more attention could she need?' I laughed to myself, yet felt the seriousness of what I was laughing at hit me like whiplash. I was different, and no one could ever know because, this being such a small, close-knit village, I was at great risk of being victimised, ostracised, ignored, or even tortured. If anyone ever knew that I was gay the repercussions could be very damaging, I remember thinking.

Sweet seventeen, still a child, and trying to take on the world. I had lived in the same village all my life — everybody knew everybody. 'People talk,' is how my mum puts it. It was the sort of village that few inhabitants drifted out of. Life didn't exist beyond it; that was uncharted territory. Everyone was most content to absorb themselves in *Coronation Street* and *Changing Rooms* at night, while discussing the latest adventures of the Smiths at number 86, or the 'musical beds' that occurred opposite the post office. There was no escaping it, or so it seemed…

Working weekend nights at the local convenience store may not have been the most obvious choice of work for a young lad trying to come to terms with his sexuality, but what was? Is there really a 'set agenda' for someone in this position? I, like everyone else, had to find my own way — nobody else could have (or would have) done it for me. It really wasn't difficult for me to realise my inclination, and to accept it. I have always just gotten on with things – there's no point in trying to argue with your feelings: you are what you are. I'm not denying that it was difficult, but you should never oppose what you believe, simply in order to please others. It would have been so easy for me to just start dating girls. I could have been the 'normal' son, one of the 'lads', got married and had children and grandchildren. However, if I had, then I wouldn't have been me. I would have lived a lie and ruined my wife's life, not to mention that of my children. It would have been an easy escape route, but even heterosexual people have problems, so I would only have been exchanging one set of problems for another.

I suppose that every mother expects her child to give her grandchildren — tradition expects it — but it is selfish for a mother to force her child into a marriage without love simply to bear children. Unity is possible within the gay community, but children are a very difficult subject matter. Of the whole 'gay' thing, coming to terms with never being a proper father or part of a typical family has been the most difficult aspect to deal with. Knowing that there would never be a 'little me' running around the house to feed, watch grow, show off, and love, came as a blow to me when I was young. But when you considered things from another point of view, there were always going to be alternatives: improvements in medical technology, adoption. Many heterosexual people never have children anyhow. There was no danger of me getting tied down to the needs of a little baby as a young adult, which was something less to worry about. It meant for me the opportunity to go out into the world and do what I wanted to do, to try and find success without being forced into settling down unnecessarily. I always try to turn a negative into a positive.

High school days are supposed to be the best days of your life, but that's a rather personal opinion. My high school days were spent either dodging crowds to avoid being taunted, or skipping classes so as to avoid those confrontations that could potentially humiliate you. How could they know? I thought to myself, I never told anyone, why are they treating me like this? I don't wish them any harm. I didn't ask to be like this. Teachers aren't interested, and you can't discuss it with parents. What do you do? It would be so easy to just…

As for my parents, they were aware of my sexuality after coming across some letters of mine from a pen-pal in England. These letters 'outed' me at a stage when I was only establishing in my own mind what I was. I was dabbling with various ideas, finding school and my inclination difficult to deal with; the last thing I needed was the added pressure from parents. Nevertheless, I had been exposed, perhaps that wasn't a bad thing, as it saved me from having to choose to tell them. But the reception was less than welcoming. My mother cried in her bed, which had a knock-on effect with my father, who became angry with the upset. They incessantly asked me if I was gay, to the reply 'I don't know', which is unacceptable since, at seventeen, you must be clear about your sexuality, through the eyes of my parents. If not for your sake, for theirs.

Time helped to heal. There were no more aggressive outbursts, and the issue was swept under the carpet, so to speak. It suited everyone; I wanted more time to deal with it on my own, and my parents probably wanted to hear nothing about it.

Embarrassing situations arose in the living room, however, when anything gay-orientated appeared on the television screen. I cringed and appeared uninterested as my mum looked concernedly at my father. I often wondered if they spoke about it to each other when I wasn't around. However they did it, they coped and got through it: they had no choice. I had heard plenty of stories about teenagers being evicted from their family homes for their sexuality, so I was lucky to have parents who loved me unconditionally. They may not have been the most understanding or approachable couple, but they loved me and they were there. It must be difficult for parents too, for having a son who is disapproved of by many in society makes them vulnerable, even more so in the little village I came from. Nevertheless, home life continued and tension was evident.

High school drained me of any confidence I ever had. Meanwhile, work in the store continued. Fewer people knew me there. I had the chance to start afresh. They may not have been the most broad-minded lot, but if I could just prove to myself there that I could be popular, interesting, enjoyable company, and less shy, maybe I could feel better about myself. It took a while for me to actually believe that I too could make good friends and feel loved. My work colleagues were fantastic; they weren't from my school so they had no previous knowledge of me, or prejudice of any sort.

This was all great, but still I felt alone. I was eighteen, and I had never been in a relationship. I had never experienced the closeness of anyone.

The girls at school never took a liking to me, at least not the ones I had been interested in, at one time. I had lost all of that from my teenage years also. I may have gained more of a voice, but confidence in my looks was low. Nevertheless, I needed to talk with others the same as me, whether there was attraction or not. It had become a necessity. I knew what I had to do. The only way to go about it seemed to be to venture into a gay bar.

For a teenager who, up until this point, had led a very sheltered life and was now venturing into the 'big city', this was quite a daunting feat. I recall being moderately anxious about the reception in the bar, yet not overwhelmingly so. I was sure of my sexuality and, never having led a straight life, I was a 'blank slate', so it was only nerves about entering my first bar that shook my comfort. This was the first nightclub I had visited and I was more than ready for it.

In comparison to what I am now, I was still remarkably shy and naïve, although I had come a long way from early high school days. Who would have thought it? My marks at school began to improve because I was enjoying life, and I felt more confident when I was there because I could see a future and a life…with possible happiness. Also, I had the added boost that I knew I had done it all myself by taking control.

After a couple of weeks of going out 'on the scene' I met and fell in love with a guy. He was one year my senior but a lot more mature and experienced. In retrospect, this wasn't the best move I could have made as it hindered me later on. I had lacked a loved one up until this point so it was easy to fall in love, but I relied on him too much when what I really needed to do was develop my own strength and find my own style. We had some great times, though. Some of my wildest nights were back then. Finishing my Saturday job at ten, I can recall the apprehension of a country boy not knowing where he was going to be taken to that night, thinking about the masses of strangers he would be introduced to, and wondering where he would finally rest his head at the end of the night. It was an adrenalin rush, like being on a rollercoaster, not knowing what the next night would bring. Because I was from the country I had never lived such a life — it was exhilarating and exciting, adventurous but nerve-wracking. Nerve-wracking because, following years of low self-esteem and being far from 'streetwise', I had no control over my weekend life, and that was scary.

The affair lasted about six months, which was about how long it took me to realise that I needed to be on my own for a while, to learn to do things for myself and make my own friends — independence. I couldn't do this with an over-protective boyfriend following me around the club. I had to be my own person and not live in someone else's shadow, yet I wouldn't change any of it. That relationship shaped me — it was an experience, but one that was kept well hidden from others.

The very fact that when we are born there is so much expected of us is frightening. It's a sad state of affairs when everyone is presumed to be heterosexual, white, male and able-bodied. These characteristics certainly put some individuals to an advantage over other unfortunates. Society presumes these trends, and Northern Ireland/Ireland is a lot more conservative than the remainder of the British Isles.

Ignorant and narrow-minded people, both those in positions of power and simple citizens of this country, see homosexuality as a 'spectacle' or something you are judged upon. It is not an abnormality but simply less common. Belfast lags behind other British cities in various ways — fashion, food, variety — so it's not surprising that weekend pubbers and clubbers frown when they see two guys walking through Shaftesbury Square holding hands. It doesn't happen. You would be very lucky to escape unscathed by the imminent attack of drunk men. This is why so many choose to leave the country, or to live alternatively. But this doesn't solve the problem.

My village had accepted me for who I am, I began to realise over the course of a few years. That was a big hurdle. But, if I could be accepted and valued there, why not everywhere else? It was too late to change the opinion of classmates at school; their minds had already been decided, but there was hope for the future. I wanted to feel respect for being me. Doesn't everyone? Why shouldn't I? I'm no different, no matter what I might be told. The next big step was the switch to university.

Everyone told me that this would be great for me. University was a place where people had the opportunity to be themselves and get away with being more individual. It was very true indeed. I could start from the beginning there, and I could be honest about myself, for I knew more about who I was by then. I was beginning to feel so alive; I just wanted to keep improving myself because my body told me I had the ability to do so. I had broken free of that school, and this was my new chance to be me. I had always been so preoccupied with trying to please others and behave in a way that they would approve of, now I was looking at things from another perspective. I really didn't care what others thought of me, I can't be what I'm not. If they don't like me they don't have to bother with me, was my new attitude. It worked a treat. I made every attempt to engage with my new friends, hiding nothing, and it all came so naturally. I had nothing to lose. I was being honest with others, and if they are worth anything at all they will return that favour.

I began to gain more and more friends, straight and gay. Before I came out I was never really very close to anyone so there wasn't anyone to tell who was going to already have an opinion of me, except for my family. I began socialising quite heavily during the week and at weekends with a few girls from high school and new friends at university. My Saturday night job in the shop had helped my conversational skills to develop wonderfully. So, at university and in bars I found it very simple to talk to others and to 'hold my own', which was a very useful skill to have. It was also a very special gift and beneficial talent for someone my age coming from such an unknown place. I wasn't socialising with farmers and car mechanics any longer. It surprised me how educated and impressive the people I was now talking with and listening to were. A lot of the time, I felt like I was rather out of my depth, but I stuck with it. After all, if these people were so clever and successful and they were devoting time to me, then gay men can't be as bad as what my family had previously made them out to be. I was a lot younger and a lot more vulnerable but I came to no harm. Visiting nightclubs helped me to be more 'streetwise', but I doubt you are in any more danger in a gay club than you would be in a straight one.

I made a lot of friends there and learnt how to party all night, and I became proud of myself for having achieved it myself. After having sunk so low I was now rising to the top. My personality carried me through, it seems, or maybe I was being watched over. Frequenting the big city of Belfast helped me to lose my fears of the outside world, and was responsible for taking me out of the little village life to somewhere with a great deal more opportunity and vitality. I had been given a future.

My early teenage years were lost, to say the least. I was weak due to numerous factors. Other kids my age were out actively doing things and making small successes while I sat up in my room pondering what would become of me because I was low in confidence, self-esteem, faith, friends, and every other imaginable aspect.

Most of all, I had no respect for myself, and without that you are nothing. If you cannot love and respect yourself you can hardly expect anyone else to. But, the tables can turn. Now, I am the one capable of a relationship, strong enough to get involved and aware of the hurt that may result, but it's a mistake that's worth making. I have dabbled with various clubs and societies and am currently founder and president of a society at university, not to mention involvement with the students' union and other ventures. A lot of people I have met have been very encouraging and very influential. Many of them I see no longer, yet I'll never forget the effect they had on me. Others are important but there must be personal faith. Very cliched, but anything is possible if you believe in yourself. Success may not be guaranteed, but the point is to try, and not to give up. The worst thing I could have done is to have done nothing. The only way I could really have failed is to have reached the end of my life and realised I hadn't done what I wanted.

As for the state of Northern Ireland, not all of today's youth, but some of it, are intolerant of homosexual behaviour because of stereotyping and the heavy influence of past generations and their opinion. It's a country where people are at war because of religion and different beliefs, so it's not surprising that they are so intolerant of homosexual activity. However, looking at it in a positive light, it is improving.

Prejudice exists but laws have changed considerably, attitudes of many have altered, and it is a lot different to what it was like fifty years ago. Improvements should not stop as there is plenty more to be done, but there is reason to be optimistic. Would it have been acceptable to 'come out' in society at all fifty years ago? I think not. Another encouraging point to make is the arrival of several gay clubs and outlets for people of this sexuality to meet. The number of clubs in existence, and the attendance, is proof that homosexuality is more common than some would believe, and it is not about to go away! Conditions will keep getting better, equality will be achieved (some day), and prejudice will be erased somewhere in the future.

galway wedding

Rachel Armstrong (GCN)

O N 28 SEPTEMBER, the press had a field day: 'Unholy Row Erupts over Gay Blessing' screamed one. 'Here Comes the Bride and the Bride!' yelled another. It was a story that ran and ran and was tabloid heaven for some weeks. After their required time of contemplation, the more respected press had their say, to the extent that there have been letters in the blessed *Irish Times* expressing people's support (mainly) for the couple who got married. So who are the people who inspired these provocative headlines?

I travelled down to Galway to meet with the couple and their friends Anne and Greta (who run Strano's bar) and was greeted by four of the nicest women you could meet. Kevina and Maggie are a couple who have been together for some time, are very much in love and last year decided to get married. If they were man and woman, this would hardly be enough to raise an eyebrow. But, being two women, it raises a storm let alone an eyebrow. So why do it at all? Without a note of romance in her voice Maggie explains, 'I went sailing for Multiple Sclerosis last year and for the first time in my life I missed someone. So when I came back I asked Kevina to marry me.' Simple. However, the next step was more difficult — finding a location.

Nuptial Knockbacks
'We were originally going to do it in a friend's conservatory but changed our minds,' Kevina begins, with Maggie adding, 'I think the gay community in Galway deserved to be there, to be with us because they

235

made us so welcome when we moved here. They were as happy as we were on the day; when we cried, they cried. It was for everybody.' To celebrate with the community in Galway (gay and straight) the girls needed a bigger venue. Their friends Anne and Greta offered the use of their bar, Strano's, and the venue was sorted.

The girls, though, had more in mind. They wanted to be blessed in a church. Maggie explains what turned out to be a controversial decision: 'I wanted to have a church blessing because my mother, who is dead, was quite a church woman and we thought it would be nice.' Just like any other couple who wish to be blessed in church, they called around to the churches in the area. 'We tried a few places,' begins Kevina, 'and got a few nasty knockbacks from a few of the "Christian" churches around the town. Maggie was actually told, "Don't be so stupid, we wouldn't deal with something like that." They were quite nasty. Then a friend of ours mentioned St Nicholas.'

Kevina and Maggie had been hurt and messed around so much by the churches in Galway that when they met with the rector of St Nicholas, Maggie blurted out, 'I'm a lesbian and this is my partner. I'm not here for you to judge me but I'd like to have your church for a blessing.' He replied, 'If you're going to be as straight with me as that we'll go and talk about it.' 'Then he went and spoke to whoever it was he needed to speak to and got back to us and that was that.'

St Nicholas

Kevina and Maggie have absolutely nothing but great things to say about the rector of St Nicholas. 'He was very, very supportive of us,' says Kevina. 'His response took the sting out of the others. It relaxed us because it was a very nerve-wracking thing to have to ask.' Maggie adds: 'He is a very, very brave man. And is such a respectful man.' The couple's friend Anne continues: 'He wants all of God's children to be included. He's a real Christian. Unfortunately, his words about the actual truth of the ceremony were lost in the small print in the papers. He knew and made it clear from the beginning that he couldn't do a marriage ceremony. The papers ran with that and said that it was a gay wedding, which wasn't fair to him. Obviously the girls would have liked a gay wedding, but what he was able to do was to bless their friendship and their commitment to each other and that's what the whole ceremony was about.' Kevina agrees: 'We knew from day one that it was not a wedding and we want that made clear. We were quite happy with that.' She oozes happiness when she goes on to add, 'It was a day I never thought I'd get unless I married a man. I never thought I'd have that day that I saw my sisters have and my brother have, but I outclassed them!'

So, what would Maggie's mother have thought? 'She would have loved it,' smiles Maggie, 'I told the rector this and he actually suggested that we bring in some photographs of those who couldn't be with us. It helped the families to understand what being gay is about.'

Media Response

On the morning the couple were to go on honeymoon to America, they arrived in Strano's to say goodbye to Anne and Greta and were greeted by applause from the clientèle. Then they looked at the tabloids. 'My first concern was for the rector. We were also concerned for my parents. They're in their seventies and have just gotten used to the idea; they don't need to get grief going down the town doing their thing. That was a great worry for me,' states Kevina, with Anne adding, 'We were also concerned for the community here because everyone isn't out, for their own reasons. Then one of the papers put this silly picture of two women, one dressed as the bride and the other as the groom, which is what the stereotype is and that wasn't fair.' Ever the joker, Kevina goes on to say, 'As for us, I felt like a bit of a film star!' When I ask if all of the hassle they received from the tabloids took the shine off the wedding, Maggie replies in a truly selfless fashion: 'It didn't take the shine off for us,' she says. 'We were just worried about our friends and the rector.'

The ever-optimistic quartet is philosophical about the press coverage. Maggie explains: 'We have made a step forward. Gay marriage happens already but now straight people have realised it.' Anne commented that: 'The papers will go into many homes and there will be debate around the dinner table. It will go into a straight house, people who have no access to what's going on in the gay community, and they will see that this goes on.'

On the surface Maggie and Kevina may seem to be two ordinary, everyday lesbians. Meeting them on the street (or, if you're me, at the train station) you would never know that they are pioneers breaking new ground in that most entrenched of institutions, and they are doing it for all the right reasons.

my gay dad

David

L AST WEDNESDAY I finished my third year in college and because I live away from home my dad arrived yesterday to collect all my stuff and bring it home for the summer. Although I often don't see my family for weeks at a time, I had been at home only a week earlier. Even though it had been just a week since I'd seen my dad I was really looking forward to spending the day with him. Dad arrived with his partner and my girlfriend and I joined them for dinner. After loading all my stuff into the car, my dad headed home and I remained at college for another week 'til my results come out. When I return home for the summer I'll be living with my mum, not my dad, but I know that I'll see him regularly, I'll ring him and I generally have a great relationship with him.

My family have gone through some very tough times over the last eight or nine years, which is roughly when my dad first came out to my mum and told her he was gay. I don't know how soon after I realised myself that my dad was a gay man but I know that I had worked it out ever before I was told officially. This was a very confusing time for me as I had some very wrong ideas about what it meant to be gay. Many of the dates now seem vague but I knew my dad was gay by the time I sat my Junior Cert in 1996. I remember that the atmosphere hd changed dramatically at home and there was always tension between my parents as they began to argue over the smallest of things. I don't have clear memories of them having big rows but I do know that they regularly stayed up talking very late at night.

There was no real change in this situation until my dad told my sister and I that he was a gay man. Once he had confirmed this, I was able to ask many of the questions that had been going through my head for some time. We talked at length about his life and specifically about the decisions he had made during his life which had resulted in him ending up married witth two children. I dont believe I ever hated or stopped loving my dad at any time but I was often very angry with him. I understood what a huge step he had taken in coming-out to his wife, children and family including his brother and sisters and parents but that this action which freed my dad also sentenced my mum, my sister and myself.

After talking to my dad over and over about his choices to get married and to have children, I began to accept and understand the choices he had made. My mum, on the other hand, has always found it much harder to accept that the decisions my dad made were in good faith at the time. My dad is also guilty of not always being understanding of the pain he has caused my mum. I think he finds it too hard to understand that she is still in love with him and that the way she has dealt with her life changing in uncontrolable ways is due to the position he put her in. I know that my mum believed that she was married for life and that when the marriage collapsed she realised she had been part of a lie.

I began going for counselling towards the end of 1999. I didnt believe I needed to go, but rather that if I went it would convince my sister who was clearly not dealing with the problem of my parents' separation and my dad being gay. I was very slow to open up and talk to the counsellor but after a number of weeks it got easier and during the seven months I went to counselling I dealt with a lot of major issues surrounding my parents' separation and my dad being gay.

At 22, I have a fantastic relationship with both my parents. I'm very proud of my mum because her life changed for the worst around 1994 in ways she could never have imagined and although she hit rock bottom, with the help of family and friends she is getting her life back together. I know she is still very resentful of the hurt my dad caused her but she is at a place now which was only a dream five years ago and I know with more time she will continue to cope better. I'm also very proud of my dad. He has always tried to make it as painless as possible for everyone and in many ways he prepared me all my life for the fact that he was gay. He raised two children that were open minded and unbiased and most importantly because he has always tried to be the best father he could be, it was ultimately so much easier to accept him as a gay man.

I offered to write my story because I want people in the gay community to know that there are success stories to maritial breakdown due to a spouse being gay. You just need to be very understanding to the feelings of those you love, especially in the case of a spouse. It is going to be a very big shock and if you are not accepted by your loved ones straight away, I'm sure it will happen with time. For anyone who has just realised that their father or husband is gay, try to see that this has not been a sudden change in their personality and although this fact may have been hidden from you, that you have always loved a gay man and that they haven't suddenly changed, rather just your opinion of them.

to a.

Julia

'OH MY GOD she looks beautiful.' I turn to my friend, speaking in awe of the woman standing in front of me. A woman I have seen over the last eight months every day, five days a week, she looks at me with those big brown eyes. My heart is thumping and my head racing. The girl sitting beside me looks confused not understanding why I am saying what I am! More to the point neither do I. I am thirteen years of age; the woman standing in front of me is my teacher. I have never really heard of gays or lesbians. Yet I am having the most influential moment of my life.

Four years later, still in awe of this woman who has now become a close friend and mentor, I meet a young girl a few years younger than me. She knew and admitted that she is gay. What's that? Why do you feel this way? I ask denying or not understanding everything I was feeling. I have a boyfriend. I am happy!

At nineteen years of age my friend and I head to Holland and get a summer job picking tulips. There I have a similar experience to the one I had six years previous. She was so beautiful, but I am speechless. Every time I try to speak to her the words don't come out and I'm standing there bright red. Had to get my friend to ask her for pegs to hang my clothes, her blue eyes, blonde hair, her face, her body, all of it makes me nervous. Why? Must be that gay thing popping its little head up again! But why? I date men!

I arrive home more confused than when I left! Still dating men. Why? Too scared perhaps? What would my friend say? What would people think? Especially my parents. I brought them enough heartache, how would they cope? More men, that's the way. Deny all – it will go away.

Then I meet her so silent sitting in the corner, but with that look and some sort of connection, what is it? Why do I feel this way? We talk, it's good. She puts her hand on mine. I jump. Run and quick run my head tells me, yet I stay. 'Have you ever kissed a woman,' she asks. I wanted to say no but don't think the words came out. Too late the strange tingle from my lips all the way down my spine. Is this what being gay is? Is this what I have been yearning for? This is it, I have feelings, I have sexual tingles through my whole body. Then it strikes me, no man no matter how many I try will ever make my body tremble and feel this amazing world I am about to enter. I'm gay, I'm proud, I'm in love!

For most people your first love never lasts but the feelings remain. To have a relationship with someone love is good, but even better if they love you back This was not the case in this relationship, so needless to say it didn't last long. I cried like never before. What do you mean? Why can't we be together? But I love you! The hurt, is it worth all the fun and happiness you've had? Not when it's raw but yes when you can look back and see the enjoyment, the laugh and the intimacy, it's worth it. So my first relationship, my real feelings, the real pain I felt when we were finished. Maybe men are the better option no pain, no hurt but no love or no tingles, Yes it's better to have loved than never love at all.

In our local nightclub I see her. There it is again: the connection the look, the eye contact. Is she? I wonder. How will I know? How do you find out? Stand there staring for the night and go home still wondering? Go and talk to her. She might look at you strange, walk away or worse give you a slap! Or maybe just maybe she is like me! 'Hi,' I say. She smiles, she is, she has to be, please let her be. She is. Yippee, first hurdle over with. Second one to go, 'Can I buy you a drink?' Can't ask her to dance it's a 'straight' bar. 'No, I'm fine,' she replies. Fuck, what next? So we talk 'til near the end of the disco It's very comfortable, maybe she is attracted to me like I am to her, but it's different to the norm of boy meet girl in a nightclub. No slow dancing, no holding hands, no kissing, all only for the privacy of your own home.

So how do you know if the woman in front of you is interested. You ask her back to your place for tea or coffee. So I do and she does. I thought all my birthdays had come at once. The start of another wonderful relationship. But she has a baby 'ok', but how do I deal with this? You do your best a friend said and I did and we became a family. Like his mother, I fell in love with him too. We spent every spare moment together, hold hands, smile in our own special way. We became friends and lovers at the same time. Lying in bed not wanting to be anywhere else and even better she loves me back.

Then why, several months later did it all go wrong? Was it going too fast or not fast enough. What's the next stage, move in together? Not ready for that: too young! Time to move on again but this time I lose not only my partner but also her son.

The town I live in is small but every couple of months we have a disco for gays and lesbians in a small function room at the back of a hotel. So time to go and see what this is all about. A bit daunting at first but at least it's a place to go to meet new people in similar circumstances. There I met some interesting woman and had my fair share of one-night stands. Some would say I had their fair share too. At least we have somewhere to go. A place were we can openly hold hands and kiss but the biggest novelty for me was being able to dance with your partner. The main thing is being in a situation where there is no judgement, no one looking strangely at you or making crude comments about your sexuality, just everyone accepting everyone else. Why can't this be like this everywhere?

At my job some new girls start and we all eventually become good friends. One girl in particular caught my attention but she started dating one of the lads. We spend most weekends out together. They are all aware that I am a lesbian, which makes no difference to them. On one occasion at a house party in the early hours of the morning, a little the worse for wear, we all pile into beds, somewhere, anywhere. I end up in bed beside the girl who first caught my attention and she had just recently split from the guy she was dating. But sure she is straight, I thought! Then it all changed. We kissed, it's good, real good and once again I find myself in a relationship. This time it develops, it's so different than the previous ones. It's what I've been looking for. We become a partnership! I'm sure our friends found it strange that two of their female friends have become a couple, but once again they accept us. After a good and happy year we take the big step to move in together. Who knows what the future will bring or what will happen but for me it feels like the best decision I have made to date.

****

This is a basic story of growing up and trying to understand what you're feeling knowing that you are and will be living a difficult life that not everyone will comprehend.

But one of the hardest things to do is to accept yourself for who you are. Some assume sexuality is a choice, I believe if it is, it's a choice between being happy or not and when you choose the happy road it can sometimes be the hardest. You're limited in meeting people and you also have the added extra pressure from society having no real recognition of who you are, of a partnership you have, and realise that having children is not an easy task. A lot can do with how you feel inside. You know that what you're doing may not be right in the eyes of others but to accept it for yourself is harder.

My friends have been a great support and that is one of the most important things for me. Without that who knows how I would have survived. When I told one of my best friends on that trip to Holland in a two man tent with no one else, her response was 'Do you fancy me?' 'I don't,' I responded. 'Why not?' she replies. She didn't judge and nothing changed.

Once I told my close friends I still had to tell my parents! With them there is more emotion involved. When I told mine, my mother walked out and my father gave me a hug with a look that told me he already knew. After several unanswered calls from my mother she eventually got me and told me she loved me. That was all I needed to hear.

PART TWO

the bible and christian living:
homosexuality as a test case

Sean Freyne

T HE PROBLEM OF discussing the Bible's relevance to any issue of
contemporary living is that it raises so many questions of a more
fundamental nature that call for resolution before one even
begins to tackle the specific topic to be addressed, be it homosexuality,
divorce, or any other one cares to think about. In the space of this short
essay I cannot hope to lay out fully an adequate approach to the use of the
bible today, especially in the area of ethical conduct. Within the Christian
family in the broadest sense it is best described as the Word of God, to be
heard gratefully and without question, and by which all our human
actions and endeavours are judged, especially for those of an evangelical
persuasion, For those of a more fundamentalist mind-set it provides a
code of iron-cast rules by which we are to live our lives. For others of a
more liberal bent it is deemed to be one source of wisdom among others,
in the on-going search for a life-style and values that we would deem
adequate to the human and Christian calling with which we have been
graced through the fact of our existence and our particular histories.

For reasons that will hopefully emerge more clearly, it is this last
point of view that I feel constrained to adopt the more I consider the vast
gulf(s) – cultural, social and religious – that separate our own time from
that of the biblical authors. Already the notion of one book, the bible,
having multiple authors covering a time-span of almost 1000 years
severely challenges our notions of a single, unchanging message being
somehow dictated from on high. The Christian Bible is increasingly
recognised today as a collection of writings from different contexts and

with very different points of view, reflecting the experiences, assumptions, prejudices and concerns of Israelites, Jews and Christians living in quite different historical, social and political circumstances. The presupposition of all contemporary critical study of the bible is that this diversity of voices needs to be recognised and allowed its full play before any attempt is made to reduce this potential cacophony to a harmony[1]. In the light of such considerations one has to be suspicious of generalised statements about 'the bible and ....' – statements which on closer examination can often be seen to be based on considerations other than biblical, but which draw on the bible's authority in an uncritical way to bolster the particular point of view being proposed. In this case the bible is being treated as a timeless collection of proof texts that can be drawn on as the occasion demands.

The Biblical Witness to Same-Sex Relations.

These introductory remarks provide a starting point for our consideration of the bible's contribution to a consideration of same-sex relations – male or female – from a Christian perspective. If one were to take the proof-text approach the matter could be deemed closed from the outset. Two texts, one from, each testament, seem to be definitive on the question of homosexual practices:

> You shall not give any of your offspring to sacrifice them to Moloch, and to profane the name of your God: I am the Lord. You shall not lie with a male as with a woman; it is an abomination.
>
> (Lev 18, 21-22; cf. 20, 13).

> Ever since the creation of the world his eternal power and divine nature, invisible though they are, have been understood through the things he has made. So they are without excuse; for though they knew God, they did not honour him as God or give thanks to him, but they became futile in their thinking, and their senseless minds were darkened. Claiming to be wise, they became fools; and they exchanged the glory of the immortal God for images resembling a mortal human being or birds or four-footed animals or reptiles.

---

1. See Seán Freyne and Ellen van Wolde eds. *The Many Voices of the Bible, Concilium 2002/1*, London: SCM Press.

Therefore, God gave them up to the lusts of their hearts to impurity, to the degrading of their bodies among themselves, because they exchanged the truth about God for a lie and worshiped and served the creature rather than the Creator, who is blessed forever, Amen. For this reason God gave them up to degrading passions. Their women exchanged natural intercourse for unnatural, and in the same way also, the men, giving up natural intercourse with women, were consumed with passion for one another. Men commited shameless acts with men and received in their own person the due penalty for this error.'

(Rm 1, 20-27).

Both texts are unequivocal in their condemnation. It is an abomination 'for a man to lie with another' and Paul speaks of homo-eroticism, male or female, as unnatural and shameful, meriting God' s wrath. Both texts, but especially the Pauline one, have determined Christian theological attitudes to homosexuality, down to the present day. Thus, e.g. the Roman Catholic Church's position, restated as late as 1986, is that sexual acts between people of the same sex are 'intrinsically disordered and cannot in any instance be approved.' This notion of 'intrinsic disorder' is based on Thomas Aquinas' articulation of the tradition in the twelfth century when he wrote that genital expression which did not conform to the procreative ordering of the sexual act was 'a sin against nature in which the natural order itself is violated, and a sin against God who is the Creator of that order.' (*Summa Theologica* I-II, Q 154). Paul's use of the word 'unnatural' (*para physin*) in the passage just cited here becomes enshrined in Thomas' account of Christian morality based on the natural law, itself an idea derived from the ancient Stoic philosophy, which claimed that human nature was determined by unchanging laws which governed the whole universe. Human sexuality was thereby directly connected with the continued procreation of life and with that alone, so that any other intention associated with the sexual act was inherently sinful and based on human concupiscence, thus violating the perceived divine order in the world. It is this understanding of sexuality that has continued to inform Roman Catholic resistance to the use of contraceptives in heterosexual marriages, as stated most recently in the encyclical letter *Humanae Vitae* of Pope Paul VI in 1969. While other Christian churches have been more lenient in this matter, the profound influence of Aquinas on official Catholic teaching has ensured that a more rigid line has been maintained officially despite the questioning of a whole generation of Catholic moral theologians. This attitude has also precluded any reconsideration of the questions associated with homosexuality, despite advances in modern understanding of the psychological aspect of sexuality as an integral part of human development and self-expression.

Attempts at a Re-evaluation.

Despite this negative impact of the Pauline condemnation there have been several attempts to re-interpret the various biblical texts in which homosexual activity is condemned in the light of modern views of human sexuality. Central to such efforts from the side of biblical scholars has been the insight, drawn from cultural anthropology, that the writers of the bible were operating with very different social and cultural assumptions to ours, and that these must be taken into account in interpreting passages which on the surface appear to close the door to any reconsideration of these issues today. Values are culturally created, symbolising, as they do, different perceptions of what different societies deem important and to be safeguarded in human social interactions. In particular, the understanding of the differing roles of males and females in the area of sexual relations is fundamental. In ancient societies generally sexual activity is directly related to that most pivotal of values, honor, which was a public, not as in our societies a private value dealing with one's own self-esteem. A male's honor is at stake in the performance of his social duty, which is to ensure the continuation of the line by the propagation of male heirs. This was achieved by implanting the seed in the female's womb that will generate new human life, just as it is his responsibility to sow the seed in the earth in order to produce the food to nourish that life. The female is seen as the passive receptacle, just like the earth itself. For a male to 'lie with another male' therefore was to incur shame in adopting a passive role, like that of a woman, thereby not fulfilling his public duty that was defined for him by the cultural script within which life was determined and honor ascribed. On the other hand for a woman to refuse her passive role in this interchange was to bring shame on her husband, whose property she was deemed to be, thereby making herself the subject of public opprobrium[2].

When one reads many of the biblical stories of the Old Testament against that backdrop they are cast in a very different light. Clearly, modernity's emphasis on personal development of the individual, and our understanding of how sexuality is an integral part of our overall maturing process do not belong to the biblical perspective. The classic case is Gn 19, the sin of the Sodomites, which has been traditionally interpreted as a sin of homosexual rape. However, recent reading of the story with the honor/shame script in mind sees the matter differently. What is really at stake is the violation of the law of hospitality through rape of the visitors to whom Lot has pledged his word. The Sodomites therefore challenge Lot's honor, who is the only one among them prepared to offer the traditional hospitality to visitors, even though they were strangers. The author of the story is not concerned about the fact that Lot was willing to offer his own virgin daughters in order to avert the disgrace on his city, an aspect that clearly offends modern sensibilities. The real point from the author's perspective is that violation of the honor/shame code brings with it the most severe penalties, and in the end God visits his retribution on the Sodomites, but Lot who is of the lineage of the faithful Abraham is saved[3].

Two general points with regard to the texts cited above are worth making at the outset. Firstly, there is no mention of women engaging in homosexual acts in the Old Testament – the emphasis is on the male only: 'if a man ('*ish*) should lie with another' (Lv 18, 22; 20, 13). On the other hand Paul does mention females quite separately from males (Rm 1, 26), even though as Bernadette Brooten remarks, his comments on female homo-eroticism have often been subsumed under the rubric of male sexuality to the point where it is assumed that when Paul speaks of women abandoning their roles, he is referring, not to lesbian relations, but to unnatural heterosexual intercourse[4]. This absence of any reflection on lesbianism in the Hebrew Scriptures is a particular example of the androcentric perspective of the Hebrew Scriptures in which women remain largely invisible. The role of the male in Israelite society, especially

---

2. Leland J. White, 'Does the Bible Speak about Gays or Same-Sex Orientation? A Test Case in Biblical Ethics,' *Biblical Theology Bulletin* 25(1995) 14- 23.

3. Ibid. 20f.

4. Bernadette J. Brooten, ' Patristic Interpretations of Romans 1, 26,' in *Studia Patristica* XVIII, Oxford, 1984, 287-291.

in maintaining purity is a particular concern of the holiness code of Leviticus (chs. 16-26), centred as it is on the temple and the rules that apply to its holiness. There in particular the invisibility and subordination of women was most clearly underlined in terms of their lack of access to the holy place and the threat they were perceived to pose to the pollution of the sanctuary because of the menstrual cycle. In this regard at least, Paul's explicit mention of women as well as men, if only to develop his argument about the sinfulness of the whole human race is more inclusive, probably influenced by his reading of the Genesis story of the Fall. If men and women share equally in the depraved condition of the human race they will also share in the new life in Christ that has been achieved in which 'there is neither male and female' (Galatians 3, 28) – a formulation which seems to suggest the androgynous state of an end of gender distinction, rather than an equality of males and females in Christ. Thus, despite the apparent 'breakthrough' in terms of recognition of women's independent position in the drama of the fall and redemption, it is quite remarkable how quickly the Church Fathers revert to the Old Testament attitudes. Clement of Alexandria e.g. ignores Paul's mention of females, commenting on male homoeroticism by claiming that the practice was unnatural 'in that they passively play the role of women.'

The second point to note about the texts cited is that they both occur in the context of the condemnation of idolatry. The ordinance in Leviticus is one of a series of prohibitions with regard to sexual behaviour that will differentiate the Israelites from their predecessors in the land, who, because of the abominations which they had committed were driven out. (Lev 18, 25-29). Paul's argument in Romans is that immoral behaviour of various kinds, among which homoeroticism is listed, is the result of God's 'giving them (humans) up' (reiterated three times in this passage vv.24; 26; 28) to depravity, because of their failure to recognise the true God from the things which he had made. Here Paul is drawing heavily on an argument developed among Hellenistic Jews which claimed that the Creator God, as the true God of Israel, should have been recognised by pagans from the things that he had created, were it not for their depravity (Wisdom of Solomon 13). Thus in neither text is the author dealing with homosexuality in isolation, but both are concerned to draw a distinction between what they perceive to be true and false religion, and in the process associate moral conduct with the acknowledgement of the true God.

For the author of Leviticus it is participation in the pagan practices of the Canaanites, which may have had sexual implications, thus blurring the distinction between Israelite and non-Israelite peoples, that is being condemned. Paul instances homosexuality – male and female – as examples of the depravity to which humankind has fallen prey in Rm 1, 26-28. However, this catalogue of sinfulness is further developed in the succeeding verses where a list of vices includes sexual as well as other human failings. This bleak picture of the human condition is rounded off with a ringing statement: 'For we have already made the charge that all, both Jew and Greek are under the power of Sin' (Rm 3, 9). This is merely a prelude, however, to the announcement of the redemption achieved in Christ, whom Paul describes as the New Adam, thereby suggesting a restoration of right relationships between God, humans, and the earth, which had been destroyed by the first parents according to the Genesis story of origins on which Paul is drawing heavily in the letter (Rm 5, 1-11; 8, 18-25). The important point for this discussion is that Paul's argument is to establish the universal human need for salvation, which, he believes, has now been accomplished in Christ. In painting his picture of evil in the world he draws on Jewish views of the depravity of the gentile world as well as on various lists of vices current among Greco-Roman philosophers as a means of explaining how humanity had declined from the former Golden Age. Paramount is the view that idolatry is the 'exchanging of truth of the living God for a lie' (Rm 1, 25), since it 'opens up the floodgates for vices which destroy social relations and turn creation back into terrible chaos.'[5]

It is not difficult to see why some scholars such as John Boswell have argued that these two most explicit condemnations of homosexual practices, once they are read in their immediate literary and historical contexts, do not address the issues surrounding homosexuality today, and therefore do not provide the necessary biblical warrant for its blanket condemnation as intrinsically evil, as has been claimed in later Christian theology[6]. On the one hand, it is argued, Leviticus is concerned with the

---

5. Ernst Käsemann, *Commentary on Romans*, London:SCM Press, 1980, 46f.
6. John Boswell, *Christianity, Social Tolerance and Homosexuality: Gay People in Western*

purity of Israel as being totally separate from the nations, and a stereotype of pagan misdemeanours is developed. Paul, on the other hand, has picked up on, but has not endorsed in any detail, similar contemporary views of pagan/barbarian behaviour. He thus paints a 'worst case scenario' of human depravity in order to prepare for the exposition of the good news, which, he believed, had been revealed in the life, death and resurrection of Jesus.

This approach to the problems posed by the biblical texts to modern gay and lesbian consciousness in a Christian context poses particular difficulties, however. Thus Lynn C. Boughton for example has shown that Boswell's attempt to restrict the Levitical condemnation to a concern for the purity laws with no ethical implications is not well grounded exegetically[7]. He points to the fact that the condemnation of homosexual actions is not included in the list of prohibited foods which constitute the heart of the purity regulations. The condemnation occurs instead in a list of sexual misdemeanours which includes incest, adultery, infanticide and bestiality (Lev 18, 20-23). Boughton also claims that Boswell's treatment of the New Testament evidence amounts to special pleading, in that the texts and the terminology do not support Boswell's distinctions between homosexually-oriented males on the one hand and those who are 'naturally attracted' to the other sex, but who engage in homoerotic behaviour on the other.

These finer points of exegesis can be debated endlessly, but a more telling argument for not basing the case for a positive understanding of homosexual actions on diminishing the apparent rigidity of such texts has been made by Ken Stone[8]. It is his contention that the Leviticus text must be viewed against the background of the ideological issues that were at stake for the author. What Stone describes as 'the hermeneutics of abomination' is not based on any empirical information about sexual mores of various 'outsiders,' but rather on the need for strong self-definition of the in-group, who may or may not be in danger of adopting their neighbours practices. In

---

Europe from the Beginning of the Christian Era to the Fourteenth Century, Chicago: University of Chicago Press, 1980.

7. Lynne C. Boughton, 'Biblical Texts and Homosexuality. A Response to John Boswell,' *ITQ* 58(1992) 141-152.

8. Ken Stone, 'The Hermeneutics of Abomination: On Gay Men, Canaanites, and Biblical Interpretation,' *Biblical Theology Bulletin* 27(1997) 36-41.

Stone's words, 'Homophobia is the paradigm of border anxiety.' It would scarcely advance the cause of a more tolerant attitude to gay people to base the argument on a concentration on texts which are themselves ideologically biased against the perceived threat of outsiders, giving rise to exaggerated and distorted accounts of their behavioural patterns, especially in the area of alleged 'sexual deviance,' which is the mirror image of the experience of gays and lesbians themselves today.

While Stone does not deal with the New Testament texts, his strictures are equally valid in dealing with Paul's case. Like the author of Leviticus, Paul is concerned also with maintaining boundaries by presenting the early Christian community as counter-cultural in terms of the larger environment. He repeatedly has recourse to the language of holiness in order to create a sense of 'otherness' from the profane world for Christian communities. Paul's indices of difference are not the same as those of Leviticus, since he rejects the Jewish dietary and other regulations, on the basis that his gospel is for both Jews and Gentiles alike. It is on their differing ethical standards that Paul bases his case, especially at Corinth where sexual promiscuity was a byword for that city in antiquity (1 Cor 6, 6-10). In writing to the Romans, a community which Paul had not himself founded, he is also anxious to adopt a conciliatory approach, advising Christians to live peaceable lives and to be obedient to the authorities (Rm 13). His condemnation of homosexuality – both male and female – resonates with official state policy in Rome from the early imperial period, which encouraged a return to the old ways in regard to conventional marriages. Thus the Roman orator Horace in his famous paen celebrating the Augustan Age and the return to the old ways, the *Carmen Saeculare*, appeals to the goddess Lucina, patroness of pregnant women, as follows: 'Whether you prefer to be addressed as Lucina or Genitalis, rear up our youth, O goddess, and bless the Fathers' edicts concerning wedlock and the marriage-law, destined, we pray to be prolific in new offspring.' This edict of the Fathers refers to the *Lex Julia de Adulteris* which was intended to outlaw sexual promiscuity and sought to foster conventional marriage in order to maintain the birth-rate which had been in serious decline.

Towards a Pardigm for Christian Gay Relations.

Thus far the results of our enquiry have been somewhat negative. Despite our best efforts it seems to be both debatable and in any case, a dubious long-term strategy to seek to build a case for a greater tolerance towards gay and lesbian relations on the basis of a re-consideration of the key texts which have shaped western moralistic attitudes towards the issue. These texts share the cultural assumptions of their time and place, both in terms of what is deemed 'natural' and the stereotyping of outsiders, be they Canaanites or Pagans, as examples of depravity, especially in sexual matters. It does little to change overall perspectives to say that the inclusion of homosexual activity in this stereotyping is part of the rhetoric of vilification. The fact is that whether the ensuing picture is fictional or real, homosexual activity is judged as depraved and to be avoided.

However, the matter need not nor should not end there. Mention has already been made of the different understanding of what is involved in the homosexual orientation, due to modern psychological and biological investigation of human sexuality. It comes as a shock to learn that it was a late as 1975 before homosexuality was declassified as a mental illness by the American Psychological Society. This was at least a step in the right direction, even if it has not been definitively decided whether one's sexual orientation is genetically or environmentally determined. At the same time there has been a slow recognition in church circles at least that sexual intimacy can play a crucial role in establishing and maintaining long-lasting, stable and loving relations, quite independently of the generative potential of such expressions of intimacy[9]. These developments in the understanding of the relational aspect of sexual expression in terms of what constitutes a full and meaningful human life have posed new questions for theologians, biblical scholars and others who feel called on to pronounce matters to do with both heterosexual and same-sex relationships.

In addition to developments which challenge the traditional position that all homosexual activity is inherently evil, new ways of appropriating the biblical tradition provide a different interpretative strategy in dealing

---

9. See Ailin A. Doyle, *A Case to be Made for the Revising of the Traditional Evaluation of Homosexuality,* M.Litt. Dissertation, School of Hebrew, Biblical and Theological Studies, Trinity College, Dublin, 1993.

with the biblical evidence on the matter, already discussed. In particular feminist interpretation theory has pointed the way for other minorities in dealing with what have been described as 'texts of terror' within the biblical Canon. Thus, Sandra Schneiders for example asks the pertinent question as to whether particular texts and readings offer transformative possibilities for women seeking recognition as full and equal members of God's family, or whether in fact they maintain a patriarchal order of control and subordination of women, an order that is often buttressed by an appeal to the Bible[10]. For Schneiders, the challenge for Christian women is to enter into a fresh dialogue with the text on the understanding that an essential aspect of describing these texts as the Word of God must be the recognition that they express the promise of God's Shalom (in the sense of both wholeness and peace) for all God's creation, but especially for the marginalised. Instead of the hermeneutics of abomination of which Stone speaks, therefore, Schneiders calls for one of blessing, that will encourage women not to abandon these texts but to continue to struggle with them in order to release their potential to convey a message of hope and wholeness for those who feel alienated and suppressed within patriarchal structures.

Schneiders' interpretative move is carried a step farther by feminist ethician, Margaret Farley, who formulates a fundamental criterion for any authentic interpretation of the Scriptures on the basis of what she describes as a 'feminist consciousness.'[11] By this she means 'those convictions that are so basic that to contradict them would be to experience violence done to the integrity of the self'. Farley is only too well aware that such an approach is all too prone to the temptation to read into the scriptures one's own prejudices, thereby claiming the authority of the Word of God for them. For her the notion of a fundamental conviction provides only 'the negative limits' of the interpretation process, in that it refuses to recognise as authoritative for human and Christian living those readings or texts which deny or destroy the deepest levels of our own self-understanding as human beings. Yet the very fact that one can, after due

---

10. Sandra M. Schneiders, *Beyond Patching: Faith and Feminism in the Catholic Church*, New York: Paulist Press, 1991, especially 36-71.
11. Margaret A. Farley, 'Feminist Consciousness and the Interpretation of Scripture,' in Letty M. Russell ed. *Feminist Interpretation of the Bible*, Philadelphia, Westminster Press, 1985, 41-51.

reflection, apply this principle, merely raises the further question as to how the bible does in fact shed light on human experience, so that it can 'offer positive clues for the on-going task of finding meaning and making decisions in our concrete lives.' New questions are stimuli for new understandings, so that probing the scriptures from the perspective of a feminist consciousness leaves one open to discovering the truth of God's Word in new and transformative ways.

How might these interpretative moves of feminist theologians assist gay men and women in appropriating the scriptures in a more positive way than that of mere 'damage limitation' by relativising such apparently blanket condemnations of their lifestyle as Lv 18 or Rm 1? A number of possibilities come to mind, once one begins to operate with the insights for reading that Schneiders and Farley offer. To begin with, the texts in question, negative though they undoubtedly are for gay men and women, especially because of the history of their later reception in the Christian churches, include other forms of sexual misdemeanour also, but these are rarely highlighted in the way that the condemnation of homosexual activity is, whether this be based on bias, ignorance or the homophobia of 'border anxiety.' These lists of human failings are, as was previously noted, all related to idolatry, that is the worship of false gods. In biblical terms 'the living and true God' is the one who shares life with the whole of creation, including humans, but who thereby also expects a God-like generosity from humans, as the self-conscious part of God's creation, in all our living and acting. Idolatry is in essence the placing of creatures, be they mere possessions, other humans, or ourselves, above the Creator, who is the one source of life and love in the world. Failure to acknowledge this fundamental reality of human life leads to distortions in both our human relations and our relations with the earth, giving rise to various forms of exploitation, selfishness and destructiveness. It is this theological grounding of the ethical imperative that is at the heart of biblical moral thinking, and the message is the same for gays, lesbians or heterosexuals, whether they are engaged in special relationships or not. From the biblical perspective, the 'texts of terror,' no matter how culturally conditioned and mythologically inspired they may be, are reminders of how easily we can become exploitative of others. Yet, equally when they are read in the context of the whole biblical story, they are reminders that evil and destructiveness is never the last word when confronted with the God who is recognised as the Creator of all life.

On a more positive note Ken Stone has suggested that gay and lesbian readings of the Bible should be seen as one example among many in contemporary approaches, where 'social location' of the reader/interpreter becomes a determinative factor in deciding the meaning of the biblical text.[12] While Stone recognises that there are many different locations for gay and lesbian readers, they all share a common experience of stigmatisation, marginalisation, and in many cases victimisation in western society which sees one's sexuality as most determinative of one's true nature and identity, something that becomes most apparent through the biological sex of one's chosen partner. This 'essentialist' view of the relationship between human nature and sexual preference is now being challenged through cross-cultural studies which stress that even among gays, sexual identity and practice are, like all aspects of gender, socially constructed and can vary from place to place. When this insight is brought to one's reading strategy of biblical stories they stand out in a very different light, especially now that we are becoming increasingly aware that the social script of the Bible is Mediterranean, not western.

As a Jewish male within a Mediterranean context Jesus' choice of life-style was deviant, if not subversive by the gender stereotypes of his own culture. Instead of establishing a family unit through which the generational succession of his own people could be enhanced, he chose to break with the kinship patterns of the traditional family in order to establish an alternative fictive family-like group that included males and females (Mk 3, 33-35), without any concern for the purity and other regulations that the Jewish male householder was expected to maintain and support.[13] From this perspective Jesus was a deviant male in his own culture. Nor did this itinerant life-style inhibit him from developing special friendships with both women (Mary and Martha) and men (the beloved disciple). What is especially important for gays and lesbians, but also for heterosexual readers of the bible, is not to seek for stories, situations and

---

12. Ken Stone, 'What happens when Gays read the Bible,' in Freyne and van Wolde, eds. *The Many Voices of the Bible*, 77-85.
13. For a fuller account of Jesus' ministry in its social and cultural context see several articles in my collection *Texts, Contexts and Cultures: Essays on Biblical Themes*, Dublin: Veritas Publications, 2002.

characters that seem to translate easily into our world, but rather to recognise how Jesus as well as other biblical characters, real and fictional, repeatedly transgress the boundaries of what is deemed normal in the Mediterranean and near Eastern worlds. Jesus in particular dared to violate the insider/outsider social scripts of his own time and place. He did not observe the established norms with regard to gender or class, race or territory, and could never be accused of the homophobia that 'border anxiety' generated in his culture and in ours. His 'transgressions' are beacons of hope for all who feel marginalised by such exclusions today, even in the churches which claim to celebrate his memory, but fail all too often to follow his example.

love's endeavour love's expense

Bernard Lynch

HERE COMES A time in all of our lives when the need for truth is so great, when the lies and distortions have made ourselves and the selves of those we love – our mothers and our fathers, our sisters and our brothers, our lovers and our friends – and when the things we believe in are so unrecognisable, that at any cost we must go in search of our truth so that we can be free, no matter how long and how hard and how lonely the road.

There comes a time of spiritual awakening, a time when we realise we are like people who continue to live together, but who have long since lost the ability to look at one another in the eye. There comes a time when our need to regain the power to love is so great that, at any risk and at any price, we must regain that power. Meeting Billy, my life partner, in 1993 was such a time.

Although indeed Irish, I grew up in New York spiritually and sexually in the fabulous gay '70s. When Aids hit us like a nuclear holocaust in the early '80s, I witnessed first hand the decimation on an entire generation of young gay men my own age. As priest and theological consultant to Dignity New York, the largest then known homophile group in the United States, I saw person after person fall prey to this unknown ignominious disease. Six hundred of our membership had passed on in less than ten years, amongst whom was my greatest priest friend and mentor Father Jeremy.

People with the virus known as GRID (gay related immune deficiency) were both feared and ostracised in ways that are inconceivable and unimaginable today. There was no HIV test. People got sick and died. Everyone who was gay, haemophilic, or an IV drug user thought they had it, as there was no way of knowing how it was contracted. People's lives ran wild with fear and paranoia. Those of us working with those with Aids spent more time changing bed sheets and makeshift diapers for our friends, that we did trying to understand and make sense of what was happening.

There was no time! People were diagnosed on a Wednesday and dead on a Sunday. Hospital orderlies and nurses refused to do their job, even refusing to take food to patients in their sick rooms. They were afraid that they would 'get it'. Churches, synagogues and funeral homes closed their doors for the same reasons. Camus' *Plague* was reality. I flew to Ireland in the summer of 1982 to tell my parents that I would be dead by the end of the year. By the end of the year three of my closest priest friends had already died. We took bodies in body bags from hospitals to crematoriums. More ashes of more people went into the Hudson River at Christopher Street, Greenwich Village than I care to remember. We drank from our own wells, and the water was blood.

HIV/Aids is a disease often contracted in people's attempts to be in touch with another human being. In my experience, particularly in the gay community, people contracted HIV/Aids in trying to experience some kind of affirmation and acceptance, to know even for a moment some kind of love. This was my Pauline conversion to the goodness and beauty of love and justice for lesbian, gay, transgendered, and bisexual people. There was no going back. If those whose lives were lost to this plague were to have any meaning, then the love for which they lived and died in their courage and in their conscience had to be testified to and given witness to in a homophobic and hostile church and society. 'The truth shall set you free' Jesus said. What he forgot to add to this is, 'sometimes it kills you first.'

The Lacota Sioux Indians tell us that when life gives us a heavy burden, then it also gives us a gift. Over the past twenty years of my involvement with HIV/Aids, I like so many others have, amidst the most horrific suffering I have ever seen before or afterwards, received many, many great gifts. It is only in recent times, since we have been able to withdraw from the front lines as it were, that we have had the opportunity to reflect on, name and 'celebrate' with gratitude some of the many gifts received. In the words of T.S. Eliot: 'We have had the experience; let us now not miss the meaning.' My life love with Billy is one such gift.

Because HIV-Aids was first named in the Western Hemisphere amongst gay men, I count sexual integrity and spiritual enlightenment as being possibly one of the most profound freedoms achieved by many in this darkest of winters. This gift for all people – straight, gay, lesbian, transgendered and bisexual – that has come to and from so many in the HIV/Aids communities, is one that both the infected and affected have bought often with their very lives.

Many people like me, grew up believing with Simon and Garfunkel that 'God laid his hands on us all' …"and our backs were to the wall'. We swallowed whole the belief, that if we were ever to get close to God, and by extension our own happiness, then our sexuality had to be oppressed, repressed and suppressed at any and every cost.

Surely the question for all of us is, how to be human? To be born is to be human, but it is also to become human. Becoming ourselves in all the fullness of our personhood, psychologically, emotionally, sexually, intellectually and spiritually, is the mark of personal existentialist meaning. Therefore, the first paradigm I want to present is this: Either our sexuality is a way of enabling and enobling our humanity or it is not. Another way of saying this is either our sexuality takes us closer to God, Our True Self, or it alienates us from God. Any self-alienation is God-alienation. Anyone or anything that would hurt or destroy that self which we and others are created to be –Image of God – is not of God. Anyone or anything on the other hand that enables and empowers the true self to come into being must be of God. For the human authenticity and the religious authenticity are always one. It is not what we say about God that matters, but rather who we are as a result of our belief in Him or Her. To try to give to God that which we are not (lesbian, gay, transgendered, or bisexual people pretending to be straight) is to my mind blasphemy. What we are doing in such situations is basically saying to God: 'Your gay image that you created me in, is not good enough. Take it back and make me straight.' This kind of pathological behaviour is encouraged and endorsed of course by the official line of the Vatican on homosexuality and has destroyed the life in the souls of so many people.

On one level, life to me seems to be about finding our ego (who we are) and letting it go (who we can become). Death – Resurrection if you will. I have discovered this to be particularly true in the journeys I have made with those living with HIV/Aids. For the mind wants a God that the heart understands, but if the heart understood God, the mind would reject it. God is for the heart. If the heart is right, God is right. If the heart is wrong, God is wrong. For sexual minorities, the order of the heart is usually reversed. Everyone and everything from the most formative years of life, tell them either they should not exist, or if they do exist then at best they are second class. In fact non-heterosexuals are the only minority born into families that do not know how to love them. No parents pray to have a baby boy who is gay, or a baby girl who is lesbian. Parents assume their offspring are going to be 'normal', meaning straight. By birth lesbian and gay children are robbed of their birth right. In a white world for example, black children are usually taught by their parents how to survive in the face of racism, as are Jewish children in a Gentile world. But no such preparation, education or enculturation is provided in a patriarchal heterosexist world for LGTB children. On the contrary, such children are taught either by omission or commission to hate and fear their most divine human relational longings. The church more than any institution I know is conduit to this dehumanisation. Hence the reason that we who are part of this hatred must love the church into God who is love and co-equality for all His creation. As the Book of Genesis tells us, all human beings are coequally made in His/Her image and likeness. Spinoza tells us: 'She/he who loves God becomes god.' Love alone is the absolute. Ultimately, there is nothing else in the entire human eschalon that we can judge ourselves by. Either we who are sexually different in our loving are equal or we are not. There are no two ways about it. Like everyone else we are created equal in the image of the creator for love or we are not. It is time for the church to put up or shut up.

Becoming who we are created to be then is to my mind our most noble human and divine endeavour. Simply put, for the gay man to be the gay image of God is an essential and necessary part of his vocation. The second paradigm I wish to make is, to be human is to be in relationship. Tangential to this is the psychosexual fact that our sexuality is the seat of our relationality. Our sexuality is that apotheosis of power where we are instinctively attracted and attractive to life, to love and to God. To find someone to love – if one does not have the gift of celibacy – is to embrace in all its mystery of joy and pain the human face of God. We learn to love, not simply by being told to love, but by being loved and by loving. There is of course a loneliness in the heart of all of us, that nothing or no one can overcome. This is God-space. The fascination and bitterness of sexual experience lies precisely there. Sexual orgasm (ecstasy) points to a total sharing that cannot be realised, at least in this time called life. That is why I think the French like to call orgasm, 'le petit mort,' the little death. Sexuality being the second most powerful instinct in our humanity has as much to do with how one celebrates Mass, appreciates a piece of music as indeed the person one chooses to make love to. I reiterate, sexuality is the seat of all our relationality. It can never be reduced, or ought it to be reduced to mere genitality. Even healthy masturbatory sexuality always includes the relational fantasy of another.

Spirituality is the essence or soul of all living things and at the very heart of all human intimacy and relationship. Therefore, I believe that in their genesis sexuality and spirituality are one. They are the alpha point from which we live and move and have our being. The same source of the one river that is split and divides at birth or very soon afterwards. To my knowledge this is a socio-cultural phenomenon, particularly encouraged and endorsed by organised religion. Hence the experience of most people that they cannot be sexual and spiritual.

Thomas Merton says, we are already one in our spirituality and sexuality. Their separateness is an illusion. If HIV/Aids is teaching us anything it is teaching us this, that it is better to be whole than good. Being good is the stuff of religion, which is about control. Being whole is the work of spirituality, which is about wholiness, integrity, freedom and joy. John of the Cross says, 'Here on the mountain top there are no laws, no trodden paths.' We find the path by walking it. This we know. For we live in a world that is not only erotophobic and homophobic, but godphobic. A world where sexuality and spirituality are seen as not only split, but in continuous and consistent conflict. I believe through my work with people with the virus, that sexuality and spirituality are the one energy, the same pure water of the uncreated life of God. This is HIV/Aids greatest gift – as I see it – to our broken society and culture.

That is the gift of an integrated sexuality and spirituality as experienced by many people with the virus. We are discovering again that there is one source, one energy, one desire. Sexuality is not a distraction from the spiritual. It is total, ecstatic self-transcendence. The sacredness of sexuality, the holiness of sexuality, the mystery of sexuality speak to the fact that we are one body and one spiritual experience.

Here God is found beyond God. The deeper we go in our spirituality, the more we understand our sexuality. The first conversion is our release through knowing that it is ok to be sexual. The second is realising that our sexuality is a way into God. The third is 'coming out' wherein the personal becomes political. Here we need supportive communities and not gay ghettos. These 'conversions' may involve an exodus as personal and political as Moses and the people of Israel from Egypt. 'Leave your family, your country and your father's house, for the land that I will show you.' This 'coming out' with or without a partner forces the soul to grow by a process of subtraction, for all spirituality is based on truth. The truth of our experience. As Voltaire put it so well, 'Humankind cannot bear very much truth.' There is no more hiding or pretending. To my mind being in the church as an openly gay person (with or without a partner) is the most profound act of faith any woman or man will ever be asked to make at this side of God. This for a LGTB person may indeed involve leaving all to follow Him/Her who is at the very heart of all their searching and seeking. To be true to who they are and to be expressive of that divinity in whose image they are created in love, their living and loving may indeed involve a poverty, chastity and obedience to the Holy Spirit that is as radical as that of Christ. Too, too many LGTB people in my experience have had to leave family, country, church in order to simply be who they are in love. Yet I would say that there is no price too high or cost too dear to gain one's own soul. Jesus got it perfect when he said: 'It profits us nothing to gain the approval of the whole world and suffer the loss of ourselves.' Yes indeed, it is far better to be hated for who we are, than loved for who we are not.

With Piaget and Kohlberg we have models of educational and moral development. In the very important pursuit of sexual maturity we have as yet not been able to work out any authentic pedagogy in response to the sexual revolution of the sixties. Yet very often, particularly within church circles, one is expected to go from sexual kindergarten to postdoctoral chastity without anything in between. We have witnessed some of the tragic consequences of this in recent church scandals.

To be open to God's love in this we must be ready to go into the desert, whereas with HIV/Aids the dark reveals God as mystery, as nothingness, as emptiness. The desert is the place of encounter with death, freedom, despair, Mystery. Here with Meister Eckhart, we may pray God to rid us of God. Atheism may be necessary. Agnosticism is a must. This is the holy road of purification. As structures fall apart, God is the very darkness itself. Authentic faith takes us beyond security, casting our anchor deep down into God our only Love. Lovers of God have no religion but God.

The true self is like a shy wild animal. It only comes out in the stillness when we have given up all pretences of being in control. OUR TRUE SELF IS GOD.

Therefore we come into our sexuality-relationality still in pain, still struggling, into the light. The touchstone of who we are, a point of nothingness, a point without return, a point without illusion, the pure glory of God in us. A point of poverty in exile! The one who is in exile come home. We discover that we do indeed belong to the universe. Sexuality and spirituality become one. Joy and sorrow become one. Free of fear we are one with the river. This is a place of deep deep surrender. God comes into us as it were. With the ancient monks of Mount Athos we can say, the one being kissed by God becomes the kisser. This is THE MOMENT of conversion. We become God's lover. Our heart becomes Her/His heart We, who were not worthy of love, now become Love's lover…

And lovers of God we are, for as long and as often as we love one another. This was and is for Christ the denominator of belongingness to God:

By this you shall know you are mine
By your love one for the other

When this love of God in Christ is concretised in the sexual love of one person for another then to my mind such love is a sacrament of the presence of divine love in the world. This the church recognises in the covenanted relationship of a man and woman. But those of us who are not so gifted with heterosexual love have a duty and responsibility to sacramentalise our different way of loving as witness to the divinity's true catholicity of love. Is there, I wonder, so much love in this world that we can afford to label any of it disordered? Such diversity of loving causes more gladness in the godhead than all the dogma and all the doctrine taught in the name of all religion.

Love, like all human community worthy of the name is a work of justice. A work within which we seek co-equality for all: black, white, women, men, straight, gay, rich, poor, Jewish and Palestinian.

Choosing to live and love with my partner Billy is to my mind part of my baptismal covenant. I could do no other, without flying in the face of Him/Her in whose image I am made. As gay, lesbian, transgendered, bisexual people we remain part of the church in order to give witness to the gay face of God in Christ. As Celie in *The Colour Purple* has it: 'We do not find God in church, we take him to church, or we do not find him.' This is another way of saying as Christ said: 'Let your light shine before people" This to my mind is the mission and message of every queer person, to be who they are for the sake of Love. 'What I am is me, for that I came' (Yeats). We are in the most authentic sense of the Word missionaries to a homophobic church and world. Only the truth of our lives and loves will enable and empower the entire church to be free to love as coequals in Christ all of her people without prejudice or preference. This is the Gospel in action. This is the justice that God's kingdom demands. This is why I thank God daily for the gift of his body and blood in my partner. It is a holy human communion.

the garda gay liaison officer

Finbarr Murphy

I HAD FINISHED EARLY in court and I was not due to start work until 2pm. It was now only 12 o'clock so there was time for a read of the newspaper and a cup of tea in the station kitchen. With the tea made and the newspaper at the ready I was just about to relax when the superintendent popped his head around the door and with eyebrows raised and a look of expectation asked 'are you doing anything for the next twenty minutes?' Not wishing to disappoint the good superintendent, I found myself walking down the corridor to sit in on a meeting 'with some journalist from a gay magazine who wants to talk about attacks on the gay community'. As a beat sergeant I was familiar with the attacks and the particular area in question namely Dame Street and South Great Georges Street and it was hoped that as such, I would be able to assist the superintendent with the interview.

We entered the small interview room, a room that I was intimately familiar with and it was strange on this occasion to be on the receiving end of the questions. Never before had I noticed how small the room was or the lack of natural light not to mention the lack of air and how hot it could get.

The introductions were formal and nervous.

'Cathal Kelly from *Gay Community News*, very pleased to meet you. Thank you for your time superintendent, I can only imagine how busy you are in such a central station as Pearse Streeet.'

'You're very welcome Cathal. I'm Superintendent Eugene O'Shea and this is Sergeant Finbarr Murphy.'

We shook hands and it was hard to tell who was the most uneasy of this unusual trilogy. Eugene O'Shea was a seasoned officer in the gardaí. From Limerick, a man's man, who knew lots about hurling and a little about golf, who had served from Cork to Donegal, who had recovered provo guns at Five Finger Strand and who had supervised the policing of EU summits. He knew all there was to know about policing and was comfortable with his knowledge. He was generally soft spoken and had a relaxing manner about him but for some reason on this occasion his chair was not as comfortable as normal.

His uneasiness seemed infectious and I too was a little edgy. Having been hijacked from my mid-day siesta I was unsure of my role at the interview. I was a newly promoted sergeant and keen to impress the boss but I was acutely aware that I was now presented with an unrivalled opportunity to really make a mess of things. Not only did I not know what to say but I didn't even know what the boss wanted me to say. I sat with my elbows defensively placed on the table, hands wringing at chin level waiting for the sport to begin.

Cathal Kelly was also struggling to be easy. He was a fresh faced young journalist with reddish cheeks. This couldn't have been easy for him, facing two policemen on their home ground and what must have been really difficult for him was that he knew the questions he was going to ask and he knew they were awkward questions.

'Superintendent, what do you propose to do about the spate of attacks on gay men in the Dame Street area?'

'Superintendent, how many men do you have on the beat on a weekend night?'

'Superintendent …' and on and on it went and the answers kept coming from the superintendent and the more he answered the more the questions came and all the while I sat like a spectator at a tennis match my eyes flashing from left to right, from right to left and back again. There was no let up, the skill of the answers matched the craft of the questions and still no one could break the others serve.

'Stop, stop, stop,' said the super. 'Stop for a minute young man. It appears that we could joust for the remainder of the day. You have all the questions and I have all the answers but we're going nowhere. Let me ask the next question.'

'Fair enough superintendent, you ask the next question.'

Was this the serve breaker, an ace, would this leave the young journalist floundering across the base line, swishing at fresh air as the ball spun low and left away?

Then came the question.

'What do you want me to do to solve the problem, you tell me what you want me to do?'

What a serve, surely an ace! My eyes shot from left to right. But just as the ball spun away the journalist stretched long and slicing down with the racquet replied

'Appoint a gay liaison officer.'

What a return. Eyes right to left.

'OK. I will.'

Eyes left to right, back to the journalist. He closes in on the net.

'When?'

Eyes right to left back to Super. Runs to net.

"Now"

Eyes left to right. Journalist volleys.

'Who?'

Eyes right to left. Super volleys.

'Him.'

Eyes left to right.

'Who?'

Eyes right to left.

'Him.'

All eyes on me.

'ME?'

Simultaneous from super and journalist

'Yes Finbarr, YOU, congratulations.'

The super and the journalist shook hands and chatted like old friends as they walked to the door of the station. 'Sure we'll see you again Cathal if there's ever anything I can do for you don't hesitate to give me a shout.'

I had just witnessed the first ever tennis match where both players had won at the expense of the lone spectator who had remained silent throughout the whole match.

Superintendent O'Shea walked back into the increasingly small room, took one look at my bewildered face and said in a soft Limerick accent 'Sure we can always keep this between ourselves. You can go to a few meetings with them from time to time, and no one will be any the wiser.'

One week later *Gay Community News* hit the newsstand.

'GAY LIAISON SERGEANT APPOINTED'

One week and one day later, Pearse Street Garda Station received its first calls from the *Evening Herald*, RTÉ's *Live at Three*, Gerry Ryan and a plethora of local radio stations all looking to have an interview with the 'Gay Sergeant'.

And so it was in October 1998, Ireland's gay community got their first garda liaison officer. That was me, but the only problem was, I had no idea what the job was, I had no idea what was expected of me and I had no idea what to do.

At first the calls were few. I attended a few meetings where I listened to gay men and women telling their stories about how they were assaulted, jeered, set upon and humiliated simply because they were gay. In most cases the victims did not report the assault for a variety of reasons.

'If I report it I will have to go to court and it will come out that I was in a gay bar.'

'I don't want my name on a computer as being a victim of a gay attack because my uncle's a guard and I'm not out.'

'I wouldn't report it because the gardaí wouldn't take me serious.'

The reasons were many and varied and all made sense.

'Did any of you report your cases?' I asked.

'Yes I did,' replied a very feminine young man camping things up for the crowd

'I did and I must say that the guard was great but I think I must have met an angel from Templemore.'

The room burst into laughter and I knew I was making progress. A few more volunteered the fact that they too had good experiences but each one felt that they were the lucky ones, who each happened to find their own angel from Templemore.

I was pleased because what I was hearing was that the perception that gardaí would not be sympathetic to gays or would not take them seriously was being proved to be an incorrect perception. In reality, those that went to the gardaí were treated with kindness and respect. But the problem remained, if assaults were not reported, then statistically they did not happen and therefore, there was no problem. I now needed to change the perception if any progress was to be made in the real world. I set about this by writing articles in the *Gay Community News*, placing a contact number there and helping in organising the policing for the Gay Pride parade. It seemed to work and the calls began to come in and the more the calls came in the more the word spread.

'I got your number from I friend, I believe you deal with attacks on gays.'

'I'm living in a midland town and I had a gay encounter with a bloke and now he's blackmailing me.'

'I'm being stalked by my former lover and he keeps turning up at my work. I'm a teacher in a Catholic secondary school and no one there knows I'm gay. I think my job is on the line.'

Gay Switchboard then began sending me referrals as did the Samaritans.

'I was caught by the gardaí with a male prostitute and the garda said he would be sending me a summons. I'm suicidal because if he summons goes to my house my wife will find out that I'm gay.'

'My boyfriend beats me up and I can't go to the gardaí because they won't take me seriously.'

'My neighbour's kids torment me and my partner calling us queers and faggots and the latest thing now is they got hold of my mobile phone number and they're constantly sending me obscene text messages.'

These weren't statistics or people in need of angels. These were real people with real problems, with lives of their own and rights the same as everyone else and somehow, somewhere along the line, someone else had stolen those rights. Someone else without any authority was now exercising control over their lives and they felt that they were helpless

The first thing I would do is speak with the caller and try to put some degree of control back into their lives. I would tell them that they now decided if they did not want to go to court that they decided that if the offending behaviour ceased then there would be no need for further action. I would tell them that they decided not to give their name but just to report an incident so that it might prevent a similar event occurring to someone else or to give a description of an offender.

The next thing was to agree a plan and in most cases that was simple enough. Since most cases were at a fairly advanced stage by the time they got to me it usually meant that the only real option involved direct contact with the offender and as is the case when dealing with all bullies, the best contact was head on and right between the eyes.

'My name is Finbarr Murphy and I'm the Gay Liaison Officer. I believe that you know Joe Bloggs and he has made a complaint to me about your behaviour. I would prefer not to deal with this over the phone so do you want me to call to your place of work or out to your house or maybe you would like to call to see me at Pearse Street Garda Station?' The attendance rate was spectacular and the more information that you had about the person before you made the call the healthier the response. Likewise the results were most satisfying. Although very few cases went to court almost all resulted in the victim getting back in control of their own lives and being able to move on from there and in the end of the day, that's what it's all about, being allowed to get on with your life as you see fit.

In November 2001 the Garda Commissioner appointed thirteen new gay liaison officers in various garda stations throughout the country.

In August 2002 I was promoted to inspector and handed over the mantle of the 'Gay Sergeant' to Detective Sergeant Mark Kavanagh in Pearse Street Garda Station.

I was no longer the gay sergeant. Free at last.

One week later Garda Community Relations, Harcourt Square, Dublin 2 received their first phone call from a member of the gay community looking to speak to the gay inspector who was now in charge of the thirteen gay liaison officers.

And life goes on.

implementing equality for lesbian, gay and bisexual people

Niall Crowley

I T IS A time for optimism - a time to believe that change is not only necessary but possible. It is a time for ambition – a time to believe our society can further reinvent itself.

This is a reinvention that must involve a rejection of the experiences of minority communities of hostility, harassment or invisibility. It is a reinvention that requires a commitment of solidarity from the majority community – a solidarity that, above all, demands change by the majority community in terms of attitudes, practices and values.

This concept of reinvention also has a relevance within minority communities. This is a reinvention that looks to the diversity within those communities of gender, ages, disabilities, ethnicities, religions and sexual orientations. It is a reinvention involving the minority community reflecting on its own culture and inclusiveness.

The Report

The Equality Authority sought to seize this moment with its recent report on *Implementing Equality for Lesbians, Gays and Bisexuals*. This is a report that seeks change and establishes a wide-ranging strategy to shape and drive forward that change.

The report sought to give a voice to lesbian and gay organisations to define their difference as a community. This difference was named in the report in terms of family formation, loving relationships and sexual values. It was also named in terms of experiences and situations shaped by a context of homophobia.

Central to the theme of change in the report was the experience of difference in Irish society. Change must be about moving from situations where difference is denied and hidden to situations where difference is acknowledged and celebrated. It must be about moving from difference being seen in terms of deviance or defiance to a context where difference is valued as an asset and is seen as vital to the well being of society. It must be about moving from an understanding of difference as something exotic or romantic to an understanding that difference has practical implications for society and its institutions and how they operate.

Significant store was placed on the word 'implementing' in the title of the report. This came from a concern that it must stimulate and support practical action and initiative. This report was not to be another piece of research. Rather it was about gathering the knowledge that was available and shaping it into a coherent and holistic strategy for change.

Where from?

The origins of the report lie in the new equality legislation – the Employment Equality Act, 1988 and the Equal Status Act, 2000 – and the institution established to implement it – the Equality Authority. This legislation covers nine different grounds including that of sexual orientation.

For the first time gay, lesbian and bisexual people were protected from discrimination in the workplace, in the provision of goods, services, accommodation and education and in the operation of registered clubs. For the first time there was a clear affirmation in legislation of the diversity of our society – a diversity that includes and celebrates the presence of lesbian, gay and bisexual people. This had to be and has been an important motor for change.

The Equality Authority was given a broad mandate to combat discrimination and to promote equality across the nine grounds. In seeking to develop integrated approaches to promoting equality that brought forward all nine grounds simultaneously we were concerned to ensure a visibility for all nine grounds. The sexual orientation ground had up to this point been characterised by an invisibility. Hence the idea for the report was born.

We were also concerned to respond positively to the suggestion of many lesbian and gay organisations for a task force to establish a strategy for change in their situation and experience. This was to mirror approaches already well developed on other grounds in such as the Commission on the Status of Women, the Task Force on the Travelling Community and the Commission on the Status of People with Disabilities.

Big Themes

The big themes that emerge in the report reflect a vision for equality that involves:

- Redistribution in terms of access to employment, and income and economic development and in terms of access to accommodation, health and education.
- Representation in terms of access to a participation in decision making and to a capacity to organise and articulate shared interests in this decision making.
- Recognition in terms of according a status to difference and to a diversity of identities and taking account of these in policy and practice.
- Respect in terms of access to relationships of trust, respect and solidarity in place of experiences of hostility, harassment or abuse.

It is no surprise then that the recommendations include a focus on partnership rights, on participation and organisation building and on institutional change in the public and private sectors.

Institutional change is framed in terms of organisations:

- Presenting and communicating a gay, lesbian and bisexual friendly profile for the organisation.
- Establishing planned approaches to equality, putting in place equality policies and naming lesbian, gay and bisexual people within equality objectives.
- Creating a capacity to combat homophobia, to prevent discrimination and to develop an organisational culture that is welcoming to lesbian, bisexual and gay people with equality training playing a big role in this.
- Accommodating difference as defined and experienced by

bisexual, gay and lesbian people in employment practices, policy making and the design and delivery of services.

Where to?

An ambitious agenda is established in the report across a wide range of areas. Would it now live up to its title and turn strategy into new situations and experiences for lesbian, gay and bisexual people? The response to date holds some promise.

The social partners took on, in the Programme for Prosperity and Fairness, to support a response to the recommendations in the report. This valuable commitment was turned into practical initiative by the National Economic and Social Forum (NESF).

The NESF convened a work group to explore the recommendations, to examine the potential for their implementation within the current policy and practice context and to dialogue with key public sector bodies about their response. This unique and innovative exercise focused attention on the report and has been a key stimulus for implementation. The NESF will report on the exercise once it is completed.

Conclusion

This of course is a story that remains unfinished. Optimism suggests that there must be many further chapters to come. Equality can be difficult, slow and controversial in the making and yet progress is evident.

The Equality Authority looks forward to continuing as a significant actor in these further chapters. Each new achievement opens up new possibilities and new challenges to be addressed and met. The report is one such achievement.

welcoming church

Christopher Hudson

T HE UNITARIAN CHURCH in St Stephen's Green Dublin has been there since 1863. Many people who pass by consider it just another Protestant Church. Most Dubliners would not be aware that it is the only church in the city of Dublin, which gives witness to the concept of religious liberalism.

The Unitarian Church does not have a set creed nor does it demand that its members or people wishing to worship in the church subscribe to a fixed or orthodox theology. People are welcomed into the church according to their own consciences. The only thing that is expected is that they believe in tolerance with regard to other religions and other individual beliefs.

For many years in the church newsletter the following statement is carried 'Love is the doctrine of this church the quest of truth is its sacrament and service is its prayer. To delve together in peace, to seek knowledge and freedom, to serve mankind and fellowship to the end that all souls shall grow in harmony with the divine, this do we convenant with each other and with God.'

Of late the attendance at church service has increased quite dramatically at Sunday Service and now at the Saturday evening service (which is held on the first Saturday of every month). Sometimes members say that it is the church of exiles, the exiles from other more orthodox religions. Obviously with the falloff in church attendance at the major churches many people are seeking a new alternative to worship. The Unitarian Church does not claim to have all the answers, indeed if anything the church claims to have no answers. Only that we welcome others to come and worship with us in the knowledge that they are worshipping in freedom and according to their own conscience. Part of the history of the Unitarian Church has been its contribution to rationalism that science and religion should not necessarily be in conflict but should operate in harmony.

The church is considered a welcoming space for many in the gay and lesbian community. Here they can give witness to their religious and spiritual needs. It is not always understood that members of the gay and lesbian community have the same religious needs as many in other communities. The need for spiritual wellbeing and to be in communion with others. The important thing about the Unitarian Church is that members of the gay community can worship without feeling marginalised. It is not a case of loving the sinner but not the sin because sexual orientation in the Unitarian Church of any persuasion is not regarded as sinful. Therefore members of the gay and lesbian community can worship in the wholeness of their person and their being.

Over the years Reach (a gay and lesbian Christian society) has held their Christmas carol service in the Unitarian Church. It has developed into one of the most joyful and wonderful occasions in the calendar of events in the church. This event is full of hope, Christmas spirit and comradeship.

At one of these carol services two young men met, let's call them Bill and John and they fell in love as people do. Eventually they set up home together and have been together for a number of years. However, recently they came to the church to see if they could receive its blessing. It was an absolute pleasure for me to be able to bless their union and acknowledge their love for each other. Their wedding service was a wonderful occasion. The family of one of the boys, a simple rural Irish Catholic family, was very moved by the celebration and the validation of their union. As one of the parents said to me, I now understand my son's choice now that his choice has been blessed.

It is imperative that gay people feel that when they come to church, they do not come in a passive way but can participate at all levels. Not only in worship but also up to and including the ministry. That is the nature of the Unitarian Church. We are delighted that within our congregations in England a number of the ministers are openly gay and living with their partners. If we are asking society to acknowledge the rights of the gay and lesbian community and to acknowledge their presence then we have obligations too. Those obligations are to clearly manifest that we accept people from the gay and lesbian community in the fullness of their being.

APPENDIX

support groups

Belfast

Aids Helpline Northern Ireland
The Centre, Warehouse, Third Floor, 7 James Street South, Belfast BT2 8DN
Support services for people living with HIV and a range of complimentary therapies.
Mon-Fri 9am-5pm and 7-10pm; Sat 2-5pm
Tel: 0800 137 437 and 028 9024 9268
Email: info@aidshelpline.org.uk
Web: www.aidshelpline.org.uk

Cara Friend Belfast Helpline
PO Box 44, Belfast BT1 1SH
Mon-Wed 7.30-10pm
Tel: 028 9032 2023

Lesbian Line Belfast
PO Box 44, Belfast BT1 1SH
Thurs 7.30-10pm
Tel: 028 9023 8668

NIGRA – Northern Ireland Gay Rights Association
PO Box 44, Belfast BT1 1SH
Meets first Thursday of the month at 8pm in Cathedral Buildings, ring bell CF, Lower Donegall Street:
Tel: 028 9066 4111
Email: jeffreydudgeon@hotmail.com

Rainbow Project
Unit 2, 6 Union Street, Belfast
Provides sexual health support and counselling for gay men.
Tel: 028 9031 9030
Email: info@rainbow-project.com
Web: www.rainbow-project.com

Clare

Clare Lesbian Line
Tues 7pm-9pm
Tel: 065 6866820
Email: callnow@eircom.net

Cork

Aids Helpline
The Alliance, Centre for Sexual Health, 16 Peter Street
Mon-Fri 10am-5pm, Tues 7-9pm
Helpline: Tel: 021 427 6676
Young persons' helpline: 021 427 5615
The Alliance Tel: 021 427 5837   Fax: 021 427 4370

Cork Lesbian Line (CLL)
Thurs 8-10pm
Tel: 021 431 8318

Garda Liaison Officer for Gay Community
Ban Garda Eleanor O'Kelly, Bridewell Station, Cornmarket Street, Cork
Tel: 021 427 0681

Gay Information Cork
Tues & Wed 7-9pm
Tel: 021 427 1087
Email: gayswitchcork@hotmail.com

HIV/Aids Family Support and Help
22 MacCurtain Street, Cork
Hospital/home visits and counselling including pastoral care/spiritual needs
Tel: 021 455 1331

L.inc (Lesbians In Cork)
11A White Street, Cork
Drop-in centre for lesbian and bi-sexual women. Cork's lesbian space. .
Tel: 021 480 8600
Email: info@linc.ie
Web: www.linc.ie

Live & Let Live L & G-friendly AA group.
Literary discussion group
First and third Tues of the month at The Other Place café at 8pm
Tel: GIC, L Line

Married/Separated Men's Group and Helpline
Last Mon of month, 7-9pm, at The Other Place café
Tel: 021 427 8470

Reach Gay Christian Group
Tues 7.30-9pm
Tel: 021 431 9008

Southern Gay Health Project
8 South Main Street Cork
Info and health support services to the gay & bi community
Tel: 021 427 8470

STD Clinic Victoria Hospital
Outpatients Mon, Tues, Thurs 9.30-11.45 / Wed 2.30-4.30pm
Tel: 021 496 6844

UCC LGB Society
Email: ucclgb@hotmail.com
Web: www.ucc.ie/lgbsoc

Derry

Foyle Friend Community Resource Centre with drop-in coffee bar
32 Great James Street, Derry
Mon-Fri 12-5pm and Sat 2-4pm
Tel: 028 7126 3120
Email: info@foylefriend.org
Helpline Mon-Fri, 12 noon-5pm
Email: helpline@foylefriend.org

Foyle Friend Youth Project for under 25s
Tel: 028 7126 3120
Email: youth@foylefriend.org

GUM Clinic
Altnagelvin Hospital, Anderson House, Derry
Mon, Wed, Fri 9.30-11am, Wed 1.30-3pm
Women only Thurs 9.30-11am
Tel: 028 7161 1269

Live & Let Live
For people with a desire to recover from alcohol and/or drug addiction at
Foyle Friend
Tues 8.30pm
Tel: 028 7126 3120
Email: sean@foylefriend.org

North West Butterfly Club
Support for TV, TS & TG, meets third Mon of the month at 8pm
Tel: Foyle Friend or 078 8543 0408

Rainbow Project
37 Clarendon Street, Derry BT48 7ER
Provides sexual health support and counselling for gay men
Tel 028 7128 3030
Email: david@rainbow-project.com

Spiritual Group
Last Wed of the month at 8pm
Tel: Foyle Friend

Dublin

AA Group
Aids care education & training
Meets at OUThouse Fri 8pm

A Christian response to HIV & Aids
PO Box 3400, Dublin 14
Tel: 01 878 7700

Amnesty International LGBT group
Meets first Thurs of the month at 6:30pm in Amnesty Office, 48 Fleet
Street, Dublin 2
Tel: Jim on 01 677 6361
Email: jloughra@amnesty.iol.ie

Bi-Irish Group
Meetsat OUThouse first Tues of the month at 8.00pm
Email: bi.irish@bi.org or bi-irish@yahoogroups.com
Web: www.geocities.org/bi_irish2002

Cáirde
19 Belvedere Place, Dublin 1
Free and confidential support services for people affected by HIV/Aids
Tel: 01 855 2111
Web: www.cairde.org

Club 20th
Gay naturist group
Email: club20th@hotmail.com

Dining Out
Evening dinners for gay men
Tel: 087 286 3349
Email: diningout@hotmail.com

Drugs/HIV Helpline
Seven days a week, 10am-5pm
Tel: Helpline 1800 459 459

Dublin AIDS Alliance
Eri Centre, 53 Parnell Square, Dublin 1
Tel: 01 873 3799

Dun Laoghaire Institute of Art, Design & Technology LGB Society
Email: lgbt_dliadt@hotmail.com

EVE – Equality and Visibility Everywhere
Dublin's lesbian and bi women's group c/o OUThouse
Email: contactevenow@hotmail.com

First Out
Confidential support group for women exploring their sexuality meets at
OUThouse first Wed and third Sat of the month 7.30-9.30pm

Friends
Meeting House (Live & Let Live, L&G AA/NA) Eustace Street, Dublin 2

Garda Liaison Officer for lesbian & gay community
Mark Kavanagh, Pearse Street, Dublin 2
Tel: 01 666 3804
Email: agecard@iol.ie

Gay Men's Health Project
19 Haddington Road, Dublin4
Drop-in and sexual health clinic Tues and Wed 6.30-8pm also Outreach
Team Drop-in at OUThouse Tue & Thurs
Tel: 01 660 2189 and 873 4952
Email: gmhp@eircom.net

Gay Switchboard Dublin (GSD)
Carmichael House, North Brunswick Street, Dublin7
Sun-Fri 8-10pm, Sat 3.30-6pm
Tel: 01 872 1055
Email: gsd@iol.ie
Web: www.iol.ie/~gsd

Gay Trekkies
Meet second Tues of the month at OUThouse 8pm
Email:gaytrekdublin@hotmail.com
Web: www.gaire.com/trek

Glória
Lesbian and gay choir
Tel: Ian 087 206 3309 or Karin 01 862 0420/087 259 5268
Email: gloriadublin@hotmail.com

Greenbow LGB Deaf Group
Email: greenbowLGB@hotmail.com

Holistic Health Project
C/o Dublin AIDS Alliance
Tel: 01 873 3799

Icebreakers
Informal social group for gay men and women coming out or looking to
make friends, first Sat of the month, 8pm
Tel: GSD

IRIS GLBTT Mutual Mental Health Support Group
Meets Sat, if interested
Tel: OUThouse or Gay Men's Health Project

Johnny
Gay peer action group meets second Tues at 6.30pm in OUThouse
Tel: 01 672 6164
Email: johnny_info@yahoo.co.uk
Web: www.johnny.ie

Julian Fellowship
PO Box 5155, Churchtown, Dublin 14
Safe, supportive, confidential space, for lesbian woman exploring
spirituality/sexuality/personal development issues. Monthly meetings,
occasional social outings.
Email: julianfellowship@hotmail.com

Lesbian Line
C/o Carmichael House, North Brunswick Street, Dublin 7
Thurs 7-9pm
Tel: 01 872 9911

LUBE (Leather Uniform Bears Encounter)
Group for gay men meets second Wed of the month at OUThouse
Email: info@lube.ie
Web: www.lube.ie

Marriage and Relationship Counselling Services (MRCS)
38 Fitzwilliam Street, Dublin 2
Straight spouses support group
Tel: 01 678 5256

Married Gay Men's Group
Support group meets monthly in Dublin
Tel: GSD

National Transvestite Line TV & TS
Thurs 6.30-9.30pm
Tel: 087 996 9977

Open Heart House
Challenging isolation through peer support. Support for people living
with HIV & Aids
Tel: 01 830 5000

Out & About Cycling Group
Meets first & third Sun of the month at National Concert Hall, Earlsfort
Terrace, Dublin 2 at 10.00am. (Bring lunch and rain gear.)

Out & About Hiking Group
Meets second and last Sun of the month at National Concert Hall,
Earlsfort Terrace, Dublin 2 at 10.00am. (Bring lunch and rain gear)
Web: www.esatclear.ie/~gay-hiking/

OUThouse
105 Capel Street, Dublin 1
Queer community resource centre. Café, drop-in, library, advice and
info. Mon-Fri 12 noon-6pm
Tel: 01 873 4932
Fax 01 873 4933
Email: info@outhouse.ie
Web: www.outhouse.ie

OutYouth
Support and social group for LGBT guys and gals under 23. Call GSD
for details.
Email: outyouthdublin@hotmail.com

Parents' Support
Support & info for and by parents of L & G. Info at GSD.
Email: parentssupport@ireland.com

Reach
Gay Christian group, c/o OUThouse. Meets second and last Sat of the
month at Marianella, 75 Orwell Road, Rathgar, Dublin 6 at 7.30pm.
Tel: GSD
Email: reach_ie@hotmail.com
Web: http://homepage.eircom.net/~reach

Sí Help
C/o 37 Claremont Court, Dublin 11
Support and social group for TVs, TSs & in-betweenies.
Mon, Tues and Fri 12-6pm. Wed 12-10pm. Thurs 12pm-12am. Social last Thurs of the month.
Tel: 01 878 3621
Email: si@transgender.org

St James' Hospital GUIDE Clinics Hospital 5
STD clinic preferably by appointment.: Mon and Fri 9.30-11am, Tues and Thurs 1.30-3pm. HIV clinic: Mon 1.30-3.30pm, Wed 9.30-11.30am
Tel: 01 416 2315 or 416 2316

Swimmin, Wimmin
Sunday 7pm
Tel: Noeleen 087 773 1557

Singles Dining Club for Women
Are you over 38 and looking for an alternative to the scene?
Tel: Sharon 087 666 3539
Email: shargrave@hotmail.com

WERRC (Women's Education, Research & Resource Centre)
2nd Floor, Arts Annex, UCD, Belfield, Dublin 4
Tel 01 706 8571
Email: werrc@ucd.ie
Web: www.ucd.ie/~werrc/

Women's Aid
Tel: 1800 341 900

Galway

AIDS West
Ozanam House, St Augustine Street, Galway
Support, education & prevention
Tel: 091 566 266 and helpline: 091 562 213
Email: aidswest@iol.ie

Blue Diamonds Women's Football Team
Tel: Galway Lesbian Line

Galway Gay Helpline
PO Box 45, Eglinton Street, Galway
Tues and Thurs 8-10pm
Tel 091 566 134

Galway Lesbian Line (GLL)
Wed 8-10pm
Tel: 091 564 611

Jellybean Society
Weekly Galway-Mayo IT LBG society
Email: stu2@aran.gmit.ie

LGB Drop-ins
Films, workshops, chat, coffee Sun 4pm
Tel: Lines for info

Stranos gay bar
William Street West, Galway
Tel: 091 588 219

Women Out West
Support group for women coming out. GLL for info.

Kerry

Kerry Gay Men's Group
Support and friendship group for gay men in Kerry area. Meets second
Tues in Tralee from 7.30-10.30pm
Tel: 086 324 1862
Email: kerrygaygroup@hotmail.com

Women in Touch
Outreach group for women in Kerry area. Wed 8-10pm
Tel: Kay at 086 330 6237 or Mar at 087 770 3287
Email: womblestwo@yahoo.com

Kildare

Maynooth LGB Society
Meets every Monday at 6pm in CS1 in the Callan Building opposite the
students' bar
Email: maynoothglb@hotmail.com
Web: www.nuimsu.com/socs/glb

Limerick

Dining Club
Meets fortnightly.
Tel: GSL

Gay Switchboard Limerick (GSL)
PO Box 151, GPO, Limerick
Mon, Tues 7.30-9.30pm
Tel: 061 310 101

Heaven
University of Limerick LGB Society
Email: student1_ul@yahoo.com
Web: http://ul-heaven.tripod.com

Limerick AIDS Helpline
Mon-Fri 9.30am-5.30pm
Tel: 061 316 661

Lesbian Line Limerick (LLL)
Thurs 7.30-9.30pm
Tel: 061 310 101

OutFun
LGBT social group pursuing alternatives to scene
Email: outfun@hotmail.com
Queer na nÓg
LGBT youth group for 17-25 year old men and women
Tel: Rainbow House 061 468 611

Rainbow Support Services
Rainbow House, 29 Mallow Street, Limerick
Support project for LGBT people in the mid-west region.
Tel: 061 468 611
Email: rainbowlmk@eircom.net

Red Ribbon Project
9 Cecil Street, Limerick
Library, support, info, chat. Mon-Fri 9.30am-5.30pm
Tel: 061 314 354

Transvestite Line Limerick
Fri 7.30-9.30pm
Tel: 061 310 101

University of Limerick LGB Society
Meets Thurs in meeting room of Arena Sports Bar at 9pm
Email: 706321@student.ul.ie
Web: www.cn.ul.ie/~lgb/

Louth

Dundalk Outcomers
PO Box 76, Dundalk, Co Louth
Tel: 24 hr infoline 042 935 2915
Email: outcomers@hotmail.com
Web: www.clubi.ie/club2000/outcomers

Drop-in Centre
8 Roden Place, Dundalk, Co Louth

Outlouth LGB group
Tel: 086 324 1579
Email: info@outlouth.com
Web: www.outlouth.com

Mayo and Roscommon

OutWest
PO Box 58, Castlebar, Co Mayo
Mayo/Roscommon gay social group.
Tel: 087) 972 5586/268 6717
Email: info@outwestireland.ie
Web: www.outwestireland.ie

Midlands

Alcoholics Anonymous for the Midlands and West of Ireland
Tel: 087 912 2685 or 087 679 8495

GLAM (gay lesbian action midlands)
Bi-sexuals welcome. Meets second Thurs of the month in Co Longford
Tel: 087 652 4608 or 086 269 7679
Email: kevinddardis@eircom.net

Portlaoise

Over The Rainbow
Youth group
Tel: 086 303 5597
Email: overtherainbowoffice@eircom.net

Sligo

Sligo IT/Freedom
Contact Students' Union

Sligo Gay Group
Email: sligout@hotmail.com

Women Out and About
C/o The Family Centre, 49 The Mall, Sligo
Lesbian meetings, social group. Meets first Thurs of each month.
Confidentiality assured.
Email: womenoutandabout@hotmail.com

Northwest Lesbian Line
Confidential info and support. Tues 8-10pm
Tel: 071 47905

Waterford

Gay Line South East (GLSE)
PO Box 24, GPO, Waterford
Gay Men's phoneline. Wed 7.30-9.30 pm
Tel: 051 879 907
Web: www.gaywaterford.com/switchboard

GLAM Society (WIT LGB Soc.)
Clubs and Societies Office, WIT, Cork Road, Waterford
Email: glamwit@angelfire.com
Web: www:angelfire.com/wa/glamwit

Parents' Support
Support and info for and by parents of gays & lesbians
Tel: GLSE

Prism
LGBT Community Centre, Luke Wadding House, Lady Lane,
Waterford
Tel: 087 207 3838
Web: www.gaywaterford.com/prism

STD Clinic
Waterford Regional Hospital, Ardkeen, Waterford
Mon 2-4pm and Thurs 10am-12pm. Clinic in Clonmel, each Wed, by
appointment.
Tel: 051 854 149

Waterford Lesbian and Gay Resource Group
C/o Youth Resource Centre, St John's Park, Waterford
Community development group
Tel: 087 638 7931
Email: resourceworker@gaywaterford.com

Women's Basketball
At Waterford Crystal Sports Centre, Cork Road, Waterford. Fri 5-6pm

Wexford

GLOW (Gays & Lesbians Of Wexford)
Meetings third Sun
Tel: GLSE
Email: glow@iol.ie

Westmeath

Athlone LGB Society
Bringing info and people together locally to provide an understanding of
their sexual identity.
Tel: 087 665 5711
Email: athloneglb@yahoo.com

Wicklow

Amach
Wicklow LGB group open to all in Co Wicklow and surrounding area.
Meets second Wed of month in the bar of Ashford House.
Email: amach_wicklow@yahoo.com
Web: www.geocities.com/amach_wicklow

National services

Coalition on Sexual Orientation
2 -6 Union Street, Belfast BT1 2JF
Working towards equality for LGBT in Northern Ireland
Tel: 7788 570007
Fax: 028 9031 90031
Email: admin@coso.org.uk
Web: www.coso.org.uk

Equality Authority
2 Clonmel Street, Dublin 2
Tel: 01 417 3333 or 1890 245545
Email: info@equality.ie
Web: www.equality.ie

FTM Network
C/o BM Network, London WC1N 3XX, England
Support group for female to male transsexuals. Contact: Stephen Whittle
Email: stwhittle@ntlworld.com

GLEN
C/o OUThouse. Email: ghs@nexus.ie

GLYNI
16-25 years Mon 6.30pm at Cathedral Buildings, 64 Donegall St, Belfast
Tel: 028 9027 8636
Web: www.glyni.org.uk

Gay Health Network
C/o 33 Church Lane, Belfast and PO Box 4792, Dublin 2.

Gay HIV Strategies
Fumbally Court, Dublin 8
Tel: 01 473 0599
Email: ghs@nexus.ie

GayNI
Gay website for Northern Ireland
Web: http://communities.msn.com.gayni

Irish Names Quilt DAA
53 Parnell Square, Dublin 1
Workshop Tues 7-9.30pm
Tel: 01 873 3799

Poz Ireland
PO Box 5187, Dublin 6
HIV diagnosis/treatment info. Email: gpi@poz.iol.ie

Press for Change
Political lobbying and education for transsexuals
Tel: 00 44 777 991 6519
Web: www.pfc.org.uk
Irish contacts: andrearobertabrown@eircom.net and Diane Hughes
canygwynt@eircom.net or 086 344 0131

Survivors for male survivors of abuse or rape
e: survivors@ireland.com

select bibliography

Alexander, Christopher J.
Growth and Intimacy for Gay Men: A Workbook
The Harrington Park Press, 1997
ISBN 1-56023-901-8
A workbook that offers help with intimacy, emotional and spiritual growth. Looks at shame, codependency, friendship and relationships, recovery from childhood abuse, and dealing with aging.

Alison, James
Faith Beyond Resentrment: Fragments Catholic and Gay
Darton, Longman & Todd, 2001
ISBN 0-232-52411-4
An English Catholic theologian writes with an appreciation of the best in Catholic tradition and presents a fresh, daring, catholic theology, from a gay perspective. Solid and radical!

Bayer, Richard
Homosexuality and American Psychiatry: The Politics of Diagnosis
Basic Books, New York, 1981
Intriguing account of the struggle to have homosexuality removed from the psychiatric classification of illnesses in the US.

Birkett, Stephen
Ulster Alien
Gay Men's Press, 1999
A gay novel. A coming out story in a troubled Northern Ireland.

Boswell, John; Maguire, Daniel R; & Ruether Rosemary R.
Homosexuality in the Priesthood and Religious Life
Crossroad, New York, 1989
An important acknowledgement of the reality of gay and lesbian priests
and religious and the issues they face.

Brash, Alan A.
Facing Our Differences: The Churches and their Gay and Lesbian Members
Risk Book Series, WCC Publications, Geneva 1995
ISBN 2-8254-1165-5
75 solid pages encouraging realistic and fair dialogue in and between the
churches on the issue of homosexuality. Excellent!

Carson, Michael
Sucking Sherbert Lemons
Black Swan, 1994
ISBN 0-552-99348-4
A humourous novel about Catholicism, homosexuality and coming out.

Cherry, Kittredge and Sherwood, Zalmon(editors)
Equal Rites: Lesbian and Gay Worship, Ceremonies and Celebrations
Westminster John Knox Press, Louisville Kentucky 1995
ISBN 0-664-25535-3
Contains a range of prayers and ceremonies to mark beginnings, healing,
blessings, funerals, covenanted unions, gay pride and other life events. A
valuable resource and inspiration.

Comstock, Gary David
Unrepentant, Self-Affirming, Practicing: Lesbian/Bisexual/Gay People
within Organized Religion
Continuum, New York 1996
ISBN 0-8264-0881-8
Based on 27 studies of gay people in organized religion this book succeeds
in presenting gay people's view of the churches and different faiths.

Crawford, David
Easing the Ache: Gay Men Recovering from Compulsive Behaviors
Dutton, New York 1990
ISBN 0-525-24871-4
An earthy and true description of the struggles, defeats and triumphs of
gay men overcoming addictions. Strongly endorses AA, NA, and other
12-Step groups.

Coleman, Eli, editor
Integrated Identity for Gay Men and Lesbians: Psychotherapeutic
Approaches for Emotional Well-Being
Harrington Park Press, New York, London, 1988
Worthwhile for psychotherapists and others interested in varying
approaches to understanding and assisting normal development of gays
and lesbians.

Coleman, Gerard D., SS
Homosexuality: Catholic Teaching and Pastoral Practice
Paulist Press, New York/Mawah 1995
ISBN 0-8091-3605-8
A more traditional Roman Catholic position but a book that does engage
seriously in the religious debate about homosexuality. Not for beginners!

Clark, Don
Loving Someone Gay
Celestial Arts, Millbrae, California, 1977 (third edition, 2000)
ISBN: 0-89087-837-4 [2000 revision]
A seminal, life-changing work, one of the earlier books on coming to
terms with homosexuality and learning to accept it and embrace it.

Doe, Michael
Seeking the Truth in Love: The Church and Homosexuality
Darton Longman and Todd, 2000.
ISBN 0-232-52399-1
With a foreword by Archbishop Rowan Williams, it discusses the gay
issue from an Anglican perspective.

Dohaghe, Ronald L.
Common Sons: Two Young Men Search for the Courage to Face Their
Feelings
Commonwealth Publications, Canada, 1997
A gay novel. Social bigotry clashes with courage and parental love.

Ford, Michael
Father Mychal Judge: An Authentic American Hero
Paulist Press, Mahwah, N.J., 2002
ISBN 0-8091-0552-7
A biography of an impressive big-hearted compassionate man who was
gay, a Franciscan priest, and chaplain to the firefighters in NYC and was
the first registered death of September 11th.

Fortunato, John E.
Embracing the Exile: Healing Journeys of Gay Christians
The Seabury Press, 1982
ISBN 0-8164-2637-6
Very readable. Strikes a note of encouragement and hope. Good for gays, families and friends.

Gonsiorek, John C.
A Guide to Psychiatry with Gay and Lesbian Clients
Harrington Press, New York, Binghamton, 1985
Some very worthwhile contributions.

Gramick, Jeannine and Furey, Pat
The Vatican and Homosexuality: Reactions to the 'Letter to the Bishops of the Catholic Church on the Pastoral Care of Homosexual Persons'
Crossroad, New York 1988
ISBN 0-8245-0864-5
25 scholars, including bishops, engage in a compelling, heated analysis and critique of a letter about homosexuality written in the Vatican in 1986.

Graham, Larry Kent
Discovering Images of God: Narratives of Care among Lesbians and Gays
Westminster John Knox Press, Louisville, Kentucky 1997
ISBN 0-664-25626-0
An important book that finds in the stories of lesbians and gay men powerful, fresh, images and revelations of God.

Gantz, Joe
Whose Child Cries
Jalmar Press, California, 1983
ISBN: 0-915190-39-7
From the days when children of gay parents were almost always from those parent's heterosexual marriages rather than the very diverse ways children nowadays find themselves with gay parents.

Hanigan, James P.
Homosexuality: The Test Case for Christian Sexual Ethics
Paulist Press, New York, Mahwah, 1988
While Hanigan may not come to conclusions that would be accepted by many gay people this work is worthy of serious consideration as it is both scholarly and also evidences a careful and respectful listening to gay/lesbian experience.

Hollinghurst, Alan
The Swimming Pool Library
Pengiun, 1989
ISBN 0-14-011610-9
A gay novel described as 'darkly erotic', it gives an insight into
relationships and promiscuity.

Isay, Richard A.
Being Homosexual: Gay men and their Development
Farrar, Straus, Giroux, New York 1989
One commentator described this as 'a thoughtful, psychologically
unorthodox view of male homosexuality.' A worthwhile fresh attempt to
understand in a positive way.

Isensee, Rik
Love Between Men: Enhancing Intimacy and Keeping your Relationship
Alive
Alyson Publications, Los Angeles, 1990
ISBN 1-55583-362-4
A wide-ranging book for gay couples and of much use for other couples
too!

Jarman, Derek
Modern Nature: The Journals of Derek Jarman
Vintage Books, 1992
ISBN 0-09-911631-6
At once a volume of autobiography, a lament for a lost generation and a
celebration of gay sexuality.

Jones, Anderson and Fields, David
Men Together: Portraits of Love Commitment and Life
Running Press, 1997.
ISBN 0-7624-0062-5
This is a book with the stories of 29 men in essay form and
photographs… lasting relationships are possible.

Lennon, Tom
When Love Comes to Town
Dublin, 1993
A gay novel set in contemporary Dublin. Playful and touching.

Marcus, Eric
Is it a Choice?
HarperSanFrancisco, 1993
ISBN 0-06-250664-1
Contains what the author says are 300 of the most frequently asked
questions about gays and lesbians. Lots of solid information.

McDougall, Bryce, editor
My Child is Gay: How Parents React When they Hear the News
Allen & Unwin, 1998
ISBN 1 86448 658 9
Contains lots of letters from parents expressing their struggle to deal with
the revelation that their son/daughter is gay/lesbian.

McNaught, Brian
A Disturbed Peace: Selected Writings of an Irish Catholic Homosexual
Dignity, Inc. Washington, D.C., 1981
On Being Gay: Thoughts on Family, Faith and Love
St. Martin's Press, New York, 1988
Now that I'm Out What Do I Do?
First Stonewall Inn Edition, 1998

All of McNaught's books are worthwhile reading. American with Irish
Catholic background Brian speaks a language that particularly many Irish
Catholics would readily understand.

McNeill, John J.
The Church and the Homosexual
Pocket Books, New York, 1978
A classic and radical investigation of the Catholic Church's teaching on
homosexuality. It was written 25 years ago but is still fresh in its outlook.

Nelson, James B.
Between Two Gardens: Reflections on Sexuality and Religious Experience
Pilgrim Press, New York, 1983
A profound book. Not focused on gay experience as such but includes it
and is gay friendly.

Nelson, James B.
The Intimate Connection: Male Sexuality, Masculine Spirituality
Westminster Press, Philadelphia, 1988
Explores deeply male sexuality and finds there a male spirituality. Is
inclusive of all male sexuality.

Nimmons, David
The Soul Beneath the Skin: The Unseen Hearts and Habits of Gay Men
St Martin's Press, New York, 2002
ISBN 0-312-26919-6
A truly great book. It identifies the positive track record and virtues of
lesbians and gay men. Also shows how gays and lesbians can sell
themselves short as a community and as individuals.

Nugent, Robert and Gramick, Jeannine
Building Bridges: Gay and Lesbian Reality and the Catholic Church
Twenty-Third Publications, Mystic, CT, 1992
Nugent and Gramick have been silenced by the Vatican. In this book we
see their attempts to bridge the gulf between official church teaching and
the lives of lesbian and gay people.

O'Brien, Glen
Praying from the Margins: Gospel Reflections of a Gay Man
The Columba Press, Dublin, 2001
ISBN 1-85607-324-6
23 short reflections on the meaning of the Gospels as seen through the
eyes and mind and heart of a gay man. Excellent!

O'Carroll, Ide, editor
Lesbian and Gay Visions of Ireland
Cassell, 1995
ISBN 0-304-33229-1
20 essays by gay men and women about gay Ireland

O'Hare, Andrew
Green Eyes
Gay Men's Press, 2001
Gay novel by an Irish author set in the troubles of Northern Ireland.

O'Neill, Craig and Ritter, Kathleen
Coming Out Within: Stages of Spiritual Awakening for Lesbians and
Gay Men; the Journey from Love to Transformation
HarperSanFrancisco, 1992
ISBN 0-06-250706-0
A truly great book that identifies stages of growth for lesbians and gay
men. A work that invites deep liberation and full living!

Philpott, Ger
Deep End
Poolbeg, 1995
ISBN 1-85371-442-9
Novel, first gay Irish death from Aids, 1980s

Rose, Kieran
Diverse Communities
Evolution of gay and lesbian politics in Ireland

Sanderson, Terry
A Stranger in the Family: How to Cope if your Child is Gay
The Other Way Press, 1996
ISBN 0-948982-08-X
Very down-to-earth, compassionate, and hopeful with lots of realistic
examples.

Shinnick, Maurice
This Remarkable Gift: Being Gay and Catholic
Allen & Unwin, 1997
ISBN 1-86448-462-4
An Australian Roman Catholic priest presents an overview of issues
surrounding homosexuality and sees homosexuality as God's gift not
God's curse.

Siegel, Stanley and Lowe, Ed, Jr.
Uncharted Lives: Understanding the Life Passages of Gay Men
A Dutton Book, 1994
ISBN 0-525-93813-3
A remarkable book which would intrigue many gay men and maybe
disturb some. A very honest presentation of the reality of the gay journey.

Shyer, Marlene and Shyer, Christopher
Not Like Other Boys
US mother and son look back at son growing up gay

Sullivan, Andrew
Love Undetectable: Reflections on Friendship, Sex and Survival
Vintage, 1999
ISBN 0-09-927532-5
An exceptionally moving book, rich in philosophical and psychological
insight, great on friendship.

Sullivan, Andrew
Virtually Normal
An argument about homosexuality and same-sex marriage. Pro and con.

Warren, Patricia Nell
The Front Runner
Bantam Books, New York, 1974
The Fancy Dancer
Bantam Books, New York, 1976
Though almost 30 years old, two good gay novels. Good story-lines.

Whitehead, Sally Lowe
The Truth Shall Set You Free
Westminster John Knox Press, Louisville, Kentucky, 1997
ISBN: 0-664-25818-2
One of the many recent contributions in the area of the straight spouses
of gay partners, this one yet another with a fundamentalist religious
upbringing as one of its foundations

Williams, Rowan, Archbishop of Canterbury
The Body's Grace
LGCM 1989
ISSN 0140-5993
'The best lecture about sexuality in the 20th century. Williams aims to
show how committed same-sex relationships fit well with what Christians
have said about the purpose of marriage, celibacy and the Christian life.'

the irish hospice foundation

The Irish Hospice Foundation is a not-for-profit organisation that promotes the hospice philosophy and supports the development of hospice and palliative care. Our vision is that no one should have to face death without appropriate care and support. This includes support for the family, extending into bereavement.

Since 1986 we have promoted this philosophy all over Ireland. Among the work we have carried out is:

- funding the building of an Education Centre at Our Lady's Hospice, Harold's Cross and a 19-bed hospice (St Francis) in Raheny;
- financing the set-up of the Children's Oncology Nursing Liaison Service at Our Lady's Hospital for Sick Children in Crumlin;
- pioneering the introduction of palliative care services in general hospitals: St. James', St. Vincent's and Beaumont hospitals in Dublin and the Regional Hospital in Cork;
- introducing two hospice fundraising events (Sunflower Days and Ireland's Biggest Coffee Morning) which have since become well established on a national basis.

At present we are further developing our newly launched Education and Bereavement Centre, whose facilities include a specialist reference library housing books, journals and training materials; undertaking various new initiatives in education in association with a Dublin University. Plans are being finalised for a post-graduate Higher Diploma in Bereavement Studies, to commence by 2004; funding a new post at Our Lady's Hospital for Sick Children – this person is Ireland's first specialist palliative care nurse for children; funding, together with the Department of Health, a nationwide assessment of the palliative care needs of children.

The Irish Hospice Foundation
4th Floor, Morrison Chambers, 32 Nassau Street, Dublin 2.
Tel: 01 679 3188
Fax: 01 673 0040
E-mail: info@hospice-foundation.ie
Web: www.hospice-foundation.ie

iqa: the irish lesbian and queer archive

The IQA is the valuable collection of newspapers, letters, journals, films, posters and administrative records of the National Lesbian and Gay Federation, now lodged at OUThouse, the Dublin lesbian and gay centre in Capel Street.

The IQA is run entirely by voluntary committee, headed by the curator, Tonie Walsh, dependant on the generosity of its many friends and supporters. Much of the unique material is in safe storage, waiting cataloguing by a team of volunteers. However numerous lectures and touring exhibitions from the IQA keeps this material to the forefront and attracts many new supporters each year.

This is the living history of Ireland's lesbian and gay community, recording the political and social struggle for equality, which led to decriminalisation in 1993. Much of the material in this wonderful collection comes from the 1970s, 1980s and the early 1990s, a time of great social change and excitement. Within the archive, there is a wealth of posters, t-shirts, videos, pamphlets, and various other memorabilia as well as personal histories, testament to the diverse lives lived within Ireland's lesbian and gay community up to the present. This is a most valuable and worthwhile collection, surviving only on goodwill and personal commitment and gives us a mirror into the history of one of Ireland's most vibrant and diverse communities.

Irish Queer Archive
Unit 2 Scarlet Row, West Essex Street, Temple Bar, Dublin 8
Email: irishqueerarchive@ireland.com
Web: www.anthologystore.com/IQA/about.html

also by glen o'brien

Praying from the Margins
Gospel Reflections of a Gay Man

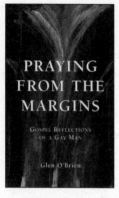

Glen O'Brien recounts some spiritual experiences of gay men, and then reflects on these experiences in the light of stories and events in the gospels. In the presence of Jesus to the 'sinners and outcasts' of his time he sees a clear statement of God's love and compassion for all people, and a context for dealing with the pain that many gay people suffer in their sense of exclusion from the Christian community.

These reflections will be read with joy by some, with concern by others. Hopefully they will make every reader stop and think.

1-85607-324-6 • 96pp • €7.99

'To read such positive discussion of homosexuality in the context of Christian religious doctrine is refreshing… It is heartening to know that despite the Chuch's continuing bashing of gays, Irish people like O'Brien are still experiencing their religion through deep spiritual awareness with themselves and other gay men. – *Gay Community News*

'This really is worth calling a *vade mecum*. Its handy size makes it a real pocket book that could be dipped into on a bus or train journey, to be kept by your bedside or used as a basis for a group meeting – or even of value to a chaplain at a house Mass' – *Quest Review*

'The insights are more than just intellectually enlightening, they are deeply spiritual, echoing the wisdom and love of the Holy Spirit. To read this text with an open mind is to be touched by that same Spirit.
– *Spirituality*

the columba press   www.columba.ie